Atlas of World History

For Ashley, Aaron, Kyle, Alisa, Maggie, and Drake:
Explore as much of the world as you can, but also take time
to fathom the depth of the human experience.

Picture credits

p. 6 MS.Pococke 375 folio 3v–4r, The Bodleian Library, Oxford

p. 14 © Copyright The British Museum

p. 46 MS.1474, Biblioteca Apostolica Vaticana, Rome

p. 70 Bildarchiv Preussischer Kulturbesitz, Berlin

p. 141 From *The State of the World Atlas* 5th edition, by Michael Kidron and Ronald Segal, New York
and London: Penguin Books, 1995, copyright © Myriad Editions Limited

Published in 2002 by Grange Books
an imprint of Grange Books Plc
The Grange
Kingsnorth Industrial Estate
Hoo, nr Rochester
Kent ME3 9ND
www.Grangebooks.co.uk

A catalogue record for this book is available from the British Library

ISBN 1-84013-492-5

 This book was designed and produced by
LAURENCE KING PUBLISHING LTD, London
www.laurenceking.co.uk

Designed by Karen Stafford

Development work by Melanie White

Picture research by Sue Bolsom-Morris

Maps by Ailsa Heritage and Andrea Fairbrass/Advanced Illustration

Printed in China

Atlas of World History

Gerald A. Danzer
University of Illinois at Chicago

Contents

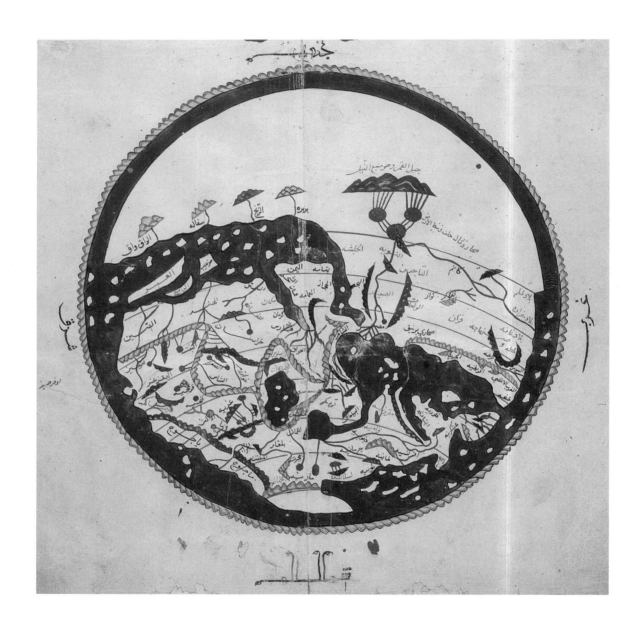

A 1553 copy of an Islamic map of the World first prepared
in 1154 by the writer and traveler Ash-Sharif al-Idrisi for
Roger II of Sicily. Islamic cartographers did not divide the
earth into continents, preferring to envision the land mass
as a whole with Mecca at its center. Primary source maps
such as this one can provide evidence about the prevailing
thought and conditions at the time they were made.

Introduction

If we engage maps in active conversation, they have a way of leading us down exciting paths of discovery. This atlas is designed to help readers interested in world history engage over a hundred maps in a stimulating dialogue. The maps serve as active guides to be used alongside books and other media as the reader explores the progress of world history. Thus the major thrust of the atlas is to trace the history of the world in a sequence of historical maps, that is maps drawn today to illustrate conditions at specific points in the past.

The historical maps are placed in chronological order and grouped within the four major eras of world history. Each of these periods forms a discrete unit of study and the introduction to each era summarizes its major themes, pointing out how the historical maps connect with the topics at hand.

Each historical map is then accompanied by a commentary on the history presented on the map, often explaining how geographic conditions affected the course of events. The caption accompanying the map seeks to actively engage the reader with the map. Sometimes this interactive feature advises readers to seek out certain details on the map. At other times it offers suggestions, observations, reflections, or questions, encouraging us to take up the map in a cartographic conversation.

Historical Maps

What features make an image a "historical map?" Maps become "historical" when they show change over time. The problem is that maps, as two dimensional objects, have difficulty enough showing the added third dimension of space, but get really pressed when called upon to show a temporal aspect as well. The limitations of any single map must be overcome by using one's imagination and developing a historical eye. "History," someone once wisely remarked, "is the fourth dimension of geography. It gives it both time and meaning."

The student of history is thus commissioned to bring an awareness of time and a quest for meaning to any particular map. Historical maps are designed to show what things were like in the past, usually at one particular date but often covering an entire period. As the time is stretched beyond a particular date, problems begin to appear because the earth itself and the societies that occupy it are constantly changing.

To deal with the problem of showing the passage of time in a single map, some cartographers put dates next to the items labeled on their maps, others use a color code or special symbols to represent different times. Arrows may be employed to show the date, direction, and intensity of movement. As a last resort, a series of maps, each one showing the same area, but at different times, can be used.

Maps as Primary Sources

Historians use maps in two distinct ways, as primary and as secondary sources. In the first instance, the maps become documents providing evidence about the conditions when they were made – the state of geographic knowledge, for example. In the second case, maps function as secondary sources when they become instruments to help readers understand something about the earth's surface, its present state or past conditions.

All maps were originally drawn to function as secondary sources. But as time moved on and changes occurred, the old maps became out of date and fell out of active use. Then their value to historians as original documents became more and more apparent. All maps are really primary sources from their creation. They provide windows for viewing the cultures of their makers and users at the same time that they describe the earth.

It should come as no surprise that historians several hundred years hence might use our maps, even our reference maps, as primary sources. Maybe they will comment on how interesting it is that in 2000 CE people thought it was so important to divide up the world into separate nations. Or perhaps they will remark on the fact that we omitted any warning on our maps of ecological crisis zones. In any event, we, like all peoples, reveal some things about ourselves as we make our maps. Therefore all maps become primary sources when we use them as historical documents.

Each section of this book opens with an image of a primary source map from the era to be covered in that part. Comparing these primary source maps and going on to explore the thousands and thousands of similar examples will soon convince one that there is more to the story than a single line of development that shows maps of greater and greater scientific accuracy emerging over the centuries. Instead, students of world history will be struck by the many ways people have pictured their world, each with its own logic and purpose.

Using Maps For Reference

This atlas will be used by today's readers primarily as a secondary source, to help them with specific questions or to grasp the general flow of the history of the human community. They will use the book as a handy reference or a ready guide.

The book begins with a world map presenting current political entities. The maps which follow often combine physical and political features, providing a more detailed look at the earth's land surface over the course of time. When searching for a particular place in world history use the index. Then it is a good idea to locate it both on a regional map and on the world map, the latter to remind ourselves of the global context for any particular location.

This atlas also provides readers with more than specific answers to particular questions. The brief captions and the more extensive commentaries should tempt readers to pause after finding explanations for individual queries. Taking an extra minute to review some of the points can open up ways to expand the initial proposition, placing specific concerns into a broader context of geographical and historical understanding.

Taken as a whole, the maps and their commentaries provide a very abbreviated introduction to world history and geography. In a sense, however we are misusing this phrase because "geography," in its original meaning, meant to consider something in its global context. To describe or map a portion of the earth, like a region or continent, was known as the science of chorography in classical times. Topography was the word used to portray a particular spot on the earth, where the scale would permit depicting its hills and valleys, its streams and ponds. World history, however, as much as it may rely on chorography and topography to develop particular understandings, encourages us to think geographically, considering the earth as a whole.

In the final analysis, the study of world history demands that students think of the earth as a whole. It also suggests that the historical approach has special ways of encouraging a global outlook.

Using maps as windows to the past is an appropriate activity for those interested in learning more about history. This process also provides a key ingredient in cartographic literacy, namely the ability to see every map, even the reference maps in this atlas, as purposeful human creations. All maps are shaped by the intentions of the cartographers and the culture of their readers. As such, maps become informative historical documents in their own right.

But, again, we must not be simply passive admirers as we look via the medium of maps at times past and places far away. Instead, we must present questions to ask of these maps. Then, as we engage them in conversation, they will open up new worlds to our view. And as we begin to see our earth in different ways we will become more at home in our global surroundings, treasuring our world and its history. In the end, we will know ourselves better, cherishing the future all the more, passing on to posterity an abiding respect for our common earth and its history.

Gerald A. Danzer
Chicago, 2000

CHINA AND EAST ASIA	SOUTH AND CENTRAL ASIA	THE NEAR EAST
3000 BCE Rice cultivated in China and Southeast Asia	**3000 BCE** Cotton cultivated since c.5500 BCE in the Indus Valley	**3000 BCE** Agricultural settlements extend back to c.6,500 BCE, wheels and plows in use
	2500 BCE Harappan civilization in northern India reaches peak	**2370 BCE** Sargon of Agade
		1750 BCE Hammurabi
2000 BCE Wheat and barley cultivated in China		
1600–1100 BCE Shang dynasty	**1500 BCE** Indus cities destroyed	**1200 BCE** Moses and the Exodus
1100–256 BCE Zhou dynasty	**1300–1000 BCE** Aryan migration into Ganges Valley	**900–612 BCE** Assyrian Empire
		520 BCE Persian Empire under Darius
500 BCE Confucius teaches	**500 BCE** The Buddha teaches	**323 BCE** Alexander the Great dies
221 bce–220 CE Qin and Han dynasties	**325–184 BCE** Mauryan Empire	
		1 BCE Jesus born
220–581 CE Wei and Chin dynasties		
	320 CE Gupta Empire begins	
581–906 CE Sui and Tang dynasties	**520 CE** Indian scholars invent decimal system	**622 CE** Muhammad's hejira
960–1279 CE Song dynasty	**751 CE** Battle of Talas River	**750 CE** Abbasid Caliphate established
1279–1368 Yuan dynasty	**1201 CE** Genghis Khan	
1368–1644 Ming dynasty	**1341 CE** Black Death spreads across the silk route	
		1501 Safavids rule Persia
1644–1912 Qing dynasty		
	1764 British East India Company controls Bengal and Pakistan	**1869** Suez Canal opens
1868 Meiji Restoration in Japan		**1948** Israel established
1949 Mao Zedong and Communists control China	**1947** India and Pakistan gain independence	**1980–1988** Iran-Iraq war

3,000 BCE
2,500
2,000
1,500
1,000
500
1
500 CE
1,000
1,500
2,000

AFRICA	EUROPE	THE AMERICAS AND THE PACIFIC WORLD	
3000 BCE Saharan rock painting about 1000 years old, continues until c.1000 BCE		**3000 BCE** Corn cultivated since c.6000 BCE in Mexico	— 3,000 BCE
3000 BCE Egypt unified			
2590 BCE First pyramid in Egypt			
		2500 BCE Beginnings of Mayan civilization	— 2,500
2000 BCE Irrigation projects along Nile	**2000 BCE** Early Minoan civilization, Crete	**2000 BCE** Metalworking in Peru	— 2,000
	1900 BCE Stonehenge erected		
	1600 BCE Early Mycenean civilization, Greece		— 1,500
1100 BCE Decline of Ancient Egyptian society begins		**1150 BCE** Olmec civilization begins	— 1,000
814 BCE Carthage founded	**750 BCE** Homer's poetry		
		600 BCE Chavín civilization in Andes	— 500
332 BCE Alexander the Great founds Alexandria	**450–404 BCE** Golden Age of Athens	**325 BCE** Mayan civilization enters classic period	
	14 BCE Augustus establishes Roman Empire		— 1
325 CE Axum destroys Meroe	**324 CE** Constantinople becomes a Roman capital	**100–500 CE** Teotihuacan civilization in Mexico	
400 CE Rise of Niger River trading cities	**476** Roman Empire ends in the West	**500 CE** Polynesians reach Hawaii	— 500 CE
700 CE Empire of Ghana	**732** Arab expansion stopped at Poitiers		
969 CE Fatimids found Cairo		**1000 CE** Cahokia a large city on Mississippi river	— 1,000
1260 CE Great Zimbabwe built	**1095** First crusade		
1450 CE Songhay and Benin empires flourish	**1493** Columbus returns after voyage of discovery	**1519–1533** Spanish conquest of Aztec and Inca empires	— 1,500
1520s Atlantic slave trade begins	**1517** Protestant Reformation begins		
1652 Dutch colony in South Africa	**1776** Watt's steam engine	**1776** Declaration of American Independence	
	1789–1815 French Revolution and Napoleon	**1804–1838** Liberation movements in Latin America	
1884 Berlin Conference advances New Imperialism	**1848** Year of Revolutions	**1863, 1888** Emancipation of slaves in US and Brazil	
1960 Sixteen nations gain independence	**1914** World War I begins		
	1939 Outbreak of World War II		
1992 New constitution in South Africa grants majority rule	**1990** Breakup of Soviet Union	**1992** Earth Summit at Rio de Janeiro	
			— 2,000

World Political Map. The concept of the nation-state, plus the rush by European powers to claim land for colonies in the late nineteenth century, has brought most of the earth's land surface into one political division or another. The one exception is Antarctica, parts of which have been claimed by several nations, but no political division of the ice-covered continent has ever been recognized by the international community.

World Political Map: An Introduction

North America is divided into three major nations: the United States across the middle latitudes with Canada to the north and Mexico to the south. Greenland, although physically close to North America, is associated with Denmark. France controls several small islands near the entrance to the Gulf of St. Lawrence.

Mexico and the other seven political divisions in Central America, the island-states in the Caribbean, and the nations of South America are often grouped together as Latin America because almost all of these use the Spanish or Portuguese languages, derived from ancient Latin. People in some areas, however, speak native American languages and a few political divisions use English or French as their official languages.

Europe is often divided into subregions. Northern Europe includes eight Scandinavian and Baltic nations. Western Europe, extending from Ireland to Austria, embraces nine nations. Eastern Europe, from Poland to Romania, now has over a dozen political divisions due to the breakup of the former Yugoslavia.

Africa is also often treated in a regional way like Europe. North Africa refers to the five nations on the Mediterranean. West Africa includes 17 nations from Cape Verde to Chad. East Africa, from the Sudan south to Madagascar, embraces 18 political divisions, including several island nations. Central Africa, from Cameroon to Angola, is divided into nine nation states while Southern Africa has five independent political units.

In Asia, there is no political grouping of "North Asia" because Siberia belongs to Russia. East Asia includes China, Japan, and their neighbors. South Asia centers on India and takes in the nations between Iran and Bangladesh. Southeast Asia extends from Myanmar (Burma) to Indonesia.

Southwest Asia, often called the Middle East, stretches from Turkey to the Arabian Sea. Central Asia is made up of the eight independent nations that once formed the southern tier of republics in the Soviet Union.

Australia is both a continent and a nation-state. It is often grouped with New Zealand and a dozen small island states in the Pacific Ocean, collectively referred to as Oceania.

The World Before
the Common Era

THE DEVELOPMENT OF CIVILIZATION occurred as Neolithic villages banded together to form larger societies. This growth led to more complex ways of living and eventually to the use of writing to send messages, to keep records, to preserve rites and stories, and to express points of view. The rise of civilization, one of the fundamental movements in world history, is not easy to fully grasp or entirely understand. It is a complex process involving institutional development probably even more than population growth or technological advances, although these later factors are more easily read in the archaeological record.

THE RISE OF CIVILIZATIONS

At one time historians were so impressed by the complexity of the process by which civilization emerged that they were tempted to say that a great breakthrough occurred in one favored spot (Mesopotamia) and then spread to other places in Afro-Eurasia where similar geographic conditions existed. Such a momentous achievement, they reasoned, could happen only once but would soon be imitated by other groups of people. There is some truth to this diffusionist hypothesis, especially on a regional scale, but most of the evidence points in another direction, to multiple points of origin.

Major civilizations seem to have risen independently in various parts of the world where an agricultural surplus of sufficient size could be produced. Moreover, archaeologists are continually unearthing smaller societies in other locations which were well on the way to civilization at the same time that the classic river valley communities featured on the maps in this section were flourishing.

Therefore, blank spaces on these maps should not be viewed as places where not much was happening. Many smaller societies which could certainly claim civilized status are often left off the map to simplify the story. In some cases scholars are just beginning to appreciate the role that some of these "newly discovered" peoples played in world history. Furthermore, one of the major achievements of human beings during this period was the evolution of herding groups in the grassland areas into pastoral societies with enough numbers and power to challenge the great river valley civilizations. Because herding societies did not build large cities, their presence is often hard to trace in the archaeological record and on subsequent maps.

THE EARLY WORLD VIEW

The mobility of pastoral societies may have encouraged their people to think of the earth in broad terms. The earliest cartographic records that exist, and these are almost entirely from settled, agricultural societies, focus on a single place, or, if they expand their coverage, are concerned with what is above and beneath the earth's surface, rather than what lies beyond the horizon. Gradually some scholars in the Greek-speaking Mediterranean world, perhaps influenced by contacts with pastoral peoples, began thinking about how to construct a map of the world as a whole.

THE BABYLONIAN WORLD

The oldest surviving world map, however, comes from another tradition, one that looks backward to about 500 BCE rather than forward to modern day maps. The cuneiform tablet pictured opposite provides a fascinating glimpse of a lost society. The small tablet, now in the British Museum in London, may have been part of an elementary textbook used by schoolboys twenty-five centuries ago, providing a world view in the Mesopotamian tradition.

The tablet shows a cosmos divided into four regions. The first region is the circle of land with Babylon in the center, representing the inhabited regions. Beyond the land was an encircling ocean of bitter (salty) water. At great distances across this bitter river a number of mysterious islands were situated as transitional regions between the earth and the heavens. These islands, beyond the reach of ordinary mortals, were the abode of strange phenomena such as the continual darkness in the far north. The fourth region or realm, that of the starry heavens, not visible in this image, was set over the whole earth like a dome.

The great city of Babylon dominates the circle of inhabited lands, the ecumene. A river flows through it, running from the mountains in the north to the salty Persian Gulf in the south. Some of the waters, however are detained in the waterstream marsh which provided the reeds which were used in the Mesopotamian world for everything from building materials to the stylus which drew this map.

The Paleolithic World: The Beginnings of Human Society

TRACING THE BEGINNINGS of human society presents an especially challenging task to both cartographers and map readers because the extent of the time span is so vast. Map 1, The Paleolithic World, for example, needs about five million years in order to locate the major sites where fossil remains of the earliest human ancestors have been found. Each new archaeological discovery might call for a revision of this map because the evidence is so fragmentary.

Map 2 (see p. 18) similarly covers a vast reach of time, but it must extend its coverage to the whole world to show the sites where human remains have been found during the last advance of the great ice sheets. Land bridges appeared when so much water was locked up in the glaciers and the world ocean subsided. This encouraged the further distribution of people to new lands and places. A migratory habit kept humanity in motion until virtually every habitable place was occupied, even the more remote islands in Oceania. This heroic tale of adventure in the Pacific Ocean – a process which took perhaps 50,000 years – is the subject of the third map. Human society changed as peoples began to leave the Afro-Eurasian land mass and travel from island to island across the vast sea. This transformation in lifestyle, which is often called the Neolithic Revolution, introduced agriculture as a way to help sustain groups of people. Maps 4 and 5 (see p. 20) show several regions where agriculture appeared at an early date to usher in Neolithic times: the Fertile Crescent in the Near East, the Nile Valley in Africa, and the Huang He Valley in China. When Polynesians started island hopping across the Pacific Ocean, they brought agriculture with them: both plants and animals were included in their baggage.

The development of plant and animal husbandry might be called the supreme achievement of the Paleolithic Age. The production and storage of a food surplus provided time for other activities and eventually led to specialized occupations and permanent settlements in the Neolithic Age.

To look at any historical map with discerning eyes is to view it as one stage in a sequence of maps that show change over time. It is also helpful to bring concepts to the maps to help engage them in serious conversation. For starters, we might employ the following handful of basic ideas:

Map 1 tells several stories. One is the great length of time needed to trace the emergence of modern people in the context of other hominid types. Sites where specimens of early hominids have been found are represented by color coded circles on the map. Note, however, that *Australopithecus* and *Homo habilis* have been found only in Africa, adding support to the thesis that Africa was the birthplace of human beings.

Another story is the far-flung dispersal of hominids across the Afro-Eurasian land mass in Paleolithic times. As more sites are found, the dispersal will probably be even more extensive. Australia could be approached by a land bridge to Asia during the Glacial Age when the freezing over of the ice sheets took up water and thus lowered the level of the oceans. Borneo and Java in the East Indies were parts of this passageway. But a voyage across the sea was necessary to reach the southern continent (see map 3, p. 19).

A third tale is one of ecological impact. Traditionally it was thought that humans in Paleolithic times blended in with the natural environment, acting as part of the ecosystem, although occupying the top level in the food chain due to their ability to communicate, remember, cooperate, use tools, and adapt to new situations. Perhaps this concept of "people blending in with nature" was true of the early Stone Age but modern archaeologists are finding many examples of how these groups improved their ability to manipulate their environments so that, over time, they came to master them and dramatically change them.

The advanced hunter-gatherer societies, often called Mesolithic, or middle stone-age peoples, usually had small populations. The coming of agriculture to the North European Plain, ushering in the Neolithic Period, for example, brought population increases of 20 or 30 times the original inhabitants. In terms of extinctions of plants and animals, however, the Mesolithic impact on the North European Plain was probably even greater than that of the Neolithic Revolution.

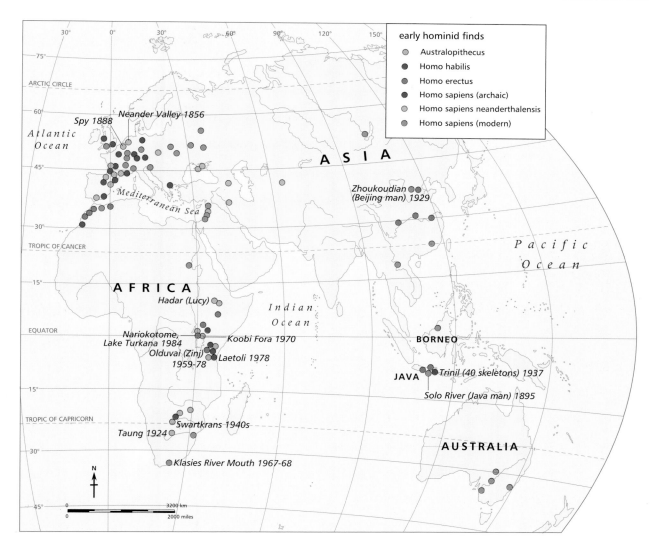

early hominid finds
- ◯ Australopithecus
- ◯ Homo habilis
- ◯ Homo erectus
- ◯ Homo sapiens (archaic)
- ◯ Homo sapiens neanderthalensis
- ◯ Homo sapiens (modern)

Spy 1888
Neander Valley 1856
Atlantic Ocean
ARCTIC CIRCLE
Mediterranean Sea
TROPIC OF CANCER
AFRICA
Hadar (Lucy)
EQUATOR
Nariokotome, Lake Turkana 1984
Koobi Fora 1970
Olduvai (Zinj) 1959-78
Laetoli 1978
Swartkrans 1940s
Taung 1924
Klasies River Mouth 1967-68

ASIA
Zhoukoudian (Beijing man) 1929
Pacific Ocean
Indian Ocean
BORNEO
JAVA
Trinil (40 skeletons) 1937
Solo River (Java man) 1895
AUSTRALIA

N
3200 km
2000 miles

Map 1 The Paleolithic World If some early hominid skeletons were to be found in the Americas, how might this change the current interpretation of human origins? In fact, some evidence of very early human occupation has been found in the Amazon basin in South America (see map 7, p. 22), but these sites only reach back eleven millennia and we can be sure that they were occupied by modern Homo sapiens groups. In contrast, earlier *Homo sapiens* finds date back three or four hundred times earlier in the Old World. The information on a map like this will surely change in the future. But it is much more likely that evidence will be modified in the future by additional discoveries of ancient hominid traces in the Old World rather than in the New World.

A fourth story, a modern one, recalls the adventure of discovery as anthropologists have extended our knowledge about prehistoric peoples. An account of a discovery in Ethiopia has been provided by D. C. Johnson and M. R. Edey, in *Lucy: The Beginnings of Mankind* (1981). Upon examination of her remains, scientists concluded that "Lucy" probably lived about three million years ago, walked upright, stood between 3½ to 4 ft tall (106 to 122cm), and weighed only about 60lbs (27kg).

The Last Ice Age and the Colonization of the Pacific

MAP 2 HELPS us to picture the face of the earth about 20,000 years ago at the height of the Wisconsin stage of the Ice Age. This was the last advance of the ice sheets before the current warm period. The millennia of recorded human history will perhaps represent only a brief interval before the ice starts to advance again. Or maybe the thaw has not yet ended and the ice packs on Greenland, the Arctic Islands, and Antarctica will continue to melt, sending ocean levels to heights well above current levels. It is possible that the extensive human burning of fossil fuels will have accelerated this melting cycle.

At any rate, this map forcefully reminds us that the earth is a dynamic planet, constantly changing its surface, albeit on a geological time scale that is difficult to grasp within the scale one human lifetime. Two great changes are shown. First, extensive areas were covered with great ice sheets several miles thick. The influence of these frozen areas extended far beyond their edges, causing harsh climatic conditions and enormous floods when they melted. Plant and animal life was devastated by these changes, forcing living things to move away from the glaciated areas. Human beings were part of these migrations. The second major change on the earth's surface was the enlargement of the continents and the exposure of islands as water was drawn away from the seas when the ice sheets formed.

Map 2 The Last Ice Age, 20,000 BP. The early human sites in North America seem to suggest a pattern of north to south movement, but the story is probably much more complex because some sites recently found in South America may be older than those discovered so far in North America. Worldwide, the major human achievement was surviving the glacial challenge by adapting to harsh conditions and moving to advantageous locations.

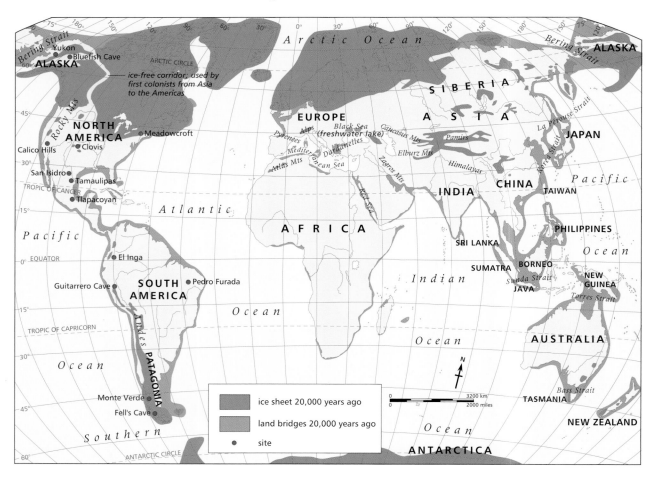

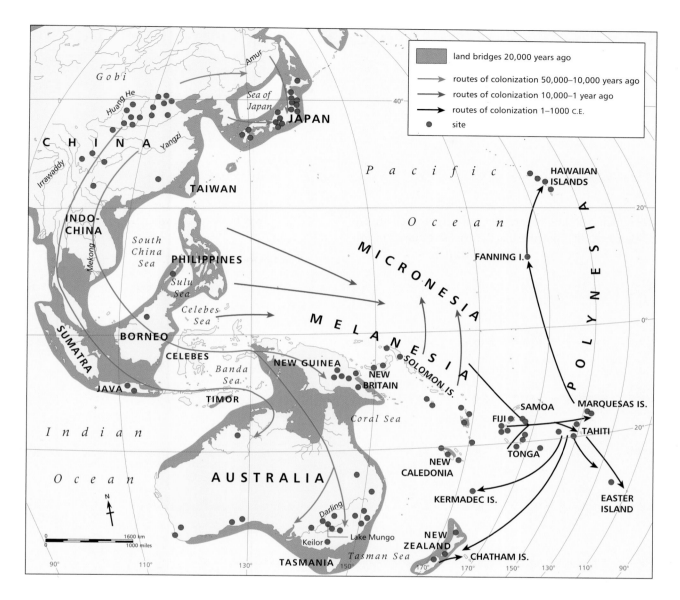

Map 3 starts with the earth as it was at the height of the last stage of the Glacial Age, about 20,000 years ago. At the beginning of the period human beings were already widely dispersed in East Asia and Australia. The red arrows show the supposed general direction of movement from central China to peripheral locations in Japan, the East Indies, and Australia. Land bridges aided much of this dispersal, but seafaring skills were needed to cross the Banda Sea to reach New Guinea and Australia from the Asian mainland.

The colonization of distant Pacific islands began about 10,000 years ago when venturesome people found their way to various places in Melanesia and Micronesia. This advance is shown by the blue arrows on the map.

Map 3 Colonization of the Pacific. This map is distorted so that all of the islands can be conveniently placed on one page. Note the meridians which mark off degrees of longitude and how the map gradually reduces these spaces as one goes from left to right. Trace the Polynesian dispersal on a globe to appreciate the full impact of this achievement.

The final dispersal of peoples occupied the first millennium of our era, establishing settlements on the far flung islands of Polynesia and New Zealand. The diaspora began in the Tonga and Samoa area which had been colonized as early as 1000 BCE. The outposts of Easter Island and the Hawaiian Islands were reached by 500 CE. The last phase brought settlers to New Zealand about 800 CE.

The Rise of Agriculture and The Spread of Civilizations, 10,000 BCE–500 CE

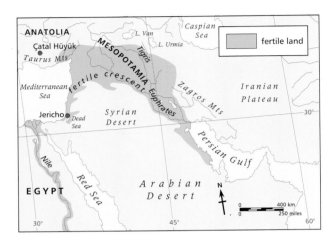

Map 4 The Fertile Crescent, 10,000–5000 BCE. At the time shown on Map 4 the Tigris and Euphrates Rivers each reached the Persian Gulf in their own deltas which created a vast sea of reeds (or Waterstream Marsh). This geographic feature appears prominently on the ancient Babylonian map featured on page 14.

A lively account of one of these early Neolithic settlements is given in the fascinating *Çatal Hüyük* (1967) by James Mellart, the archaeologist who supervised the excavation of the settlement.

THE RISE of civilization depended on agriculture. Maps 4 and 5 center on the rise of agricultural communities in the great river valleys of the Near East and China. The sites in the former are much earlier and, according to our present knowledge, predate farming communities anywhere on the earth. There may be some connection between the development of agriculture in China and the Near East, but it is just as likely that farming started independently in both places. The emergence of agricultural settlements in Southeast Asia, sub-Saharan Africa, and the Americas also seems to have little connection with earlier farming regions. In every case, the crops and techniques are very different and vast distances separated the original centers.

The human adaptation to the settled life of an agricultural society was a very gradual process spread over thousands of years and hundreds of generations. Gathering plants and seeds for food by its very nature encouraged the selection of the largest and finest examples. As some of these seeds were dropped at the edge of a camp site, or were purposefully returned to the Mother Earth as a sign of thankful devotion, the next generation of plants reproduced those qualities that the gatherers had selected. A sort of plant breeding thus seems to have accompanied gathering societies.

Although it seems like a short step from this early form of plant selection to the purposeful planting of fields of crops, this was a step not quickly taken.

As communities developed increasing dependence on field crops for their food supply, they developed permanent settlements which led to new ways of living. The Neolithic Revolution ushered in a new age characterized by agricultural villages. Several of these are identified on the maps. Jericho in the middle East is probably the oldest community, but Çatal Hüyük in Turkey is especially well preserved. Ban Po in China is now in an arid region, but the rich alluvial soil was once easy to work and the principal crop, millet, was drought resistant.

Map 5 Early Agriculture in China, 9,000–6,000 BCE. The marking of the ancient coastline on the China map shows that geographic conditions were quite different when farming villages arose along the Huang He (Yellow River). Neolithic Societies in Anatolia, Mesopotamia, the Fertile Crescent, and Egypt were once thought to be much older than those in China, but evidence now suggests that they may date from roughly the same time.

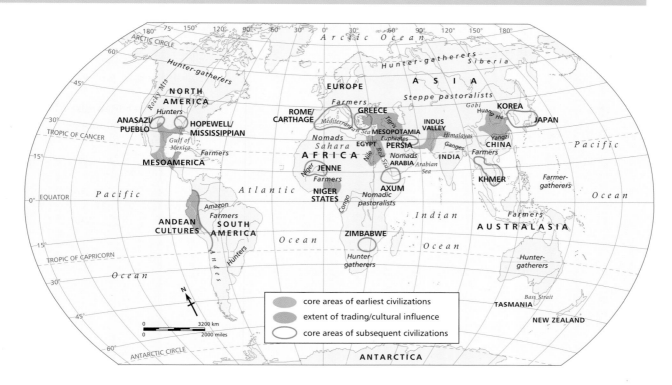

Map 6 The Spread of Early Civilizations. Note that the four primary civilizations in the middle latitudes of the Old World – in Asia and Africa – were set in riverine environments. The presence of a great river is often considered a major factor in the rise and development of these civilizations. The Tigris-Euphrates, the Nile, the Indus, and the Huang He are all key geographic elements in understanding the rise and spread of these earliest civilizations.

The geographic concept of diffusion from a core area to a peripheral region is one factor that animates map 6. Another factor is the historical dynamic of change over time. The world map sets both diffusion and change in a global context.

The purple areas on the map designate seven major core areas where civilization emerged about 10,000 BCE from a dense base of agricultural settlements. The surplus food produced by the villages freed some individuals for more specialized tasks in governing, performing rites, keeping records, providing education, building storehouses, erecting monumental buildings, establishing networks of trade, manufacturing goods, providing defense, and exploring areas beyond the community. All of these factors played a hand in developing civilized societies, largely independently, in the purple areas.

From these primary cores, the pattern of civilization that had developed in each one spread to neighboring areas, colored in green, reaching beyond the geographic conditions – the favorable climate and soil conditions – which first gave rise to the emergence of civilization. In almost every case the expansion to areas of a different geographical character permitted the inclusion in new empires of diverse peoples and products. These added to the sophistication of the imperial society.

The passage of time witnessed great changes as powerful states declined and fell into ruins. Imitation also led to the development of subsequent empires, often in similar regions located nearby.

Ancient Mesopotamia

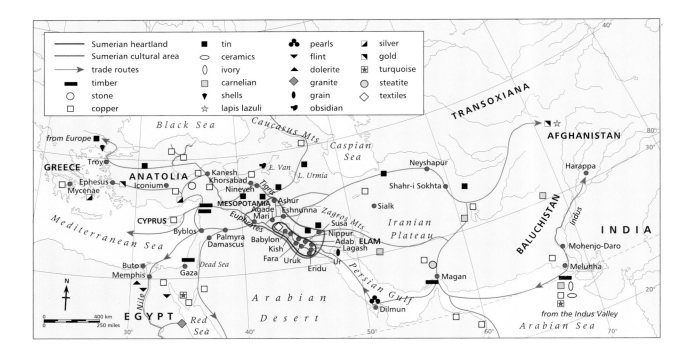

Map 7 The Sumerian Trading Network, 3500–2000 BCE. The trading activities on this map can be divided into two major groups: those goods that could be easily transported and those that required technology or extra manpower to move. Gold and gemstones would fall into the first group, while timber, stone, grain, ceramics, and metals would usually fall into the second. Copper and tin could be smelted near the mines to reduce their bulk and transportation costs. These metals were then mixed together in distant cities to form bronze.

MAP 7 uses the archaeological record as well as Sumerian documents, such as clay tablets recording commercial transactions, to indicate the full range of trading contacts in this part of the ancient world. It covers many centuries so that not every trade route was actively used at any particular time. The map is limited by fragmentary data and obscure records but future research promises to extend the network to new places and to add to the occurrence of various products. But as it stands, the map gives striking testimony to the contacts that were made, often through traders and merchants, between peoples in Mesopotamia with others in Egypt, Asia Minor, Greece, India, and Central Asia.

Note how the map identifies the Sumerian heartland between the Tigris and Euphrates, just above their delta at the head of the Persian Gulf. A second line marks a surrounding area that was directly influenced by Sumerian culture. This zone of influence extended up river into central Mesopotamia and also into the uplands of Persia. From this center, Sumerian influence, less direct and less powerful, extended via trade routes into three continents. The red lines on the map suggest paths along which people, goods, and ideas moved in both directions.

Most of the goods involved in this commerce would be classified as luxury items – gold, gemstones, and ceramics – but metals, grain, and perhaps even textiles might have passed from traders into the reach of some common people. As a general rule, the more distant the trade the more likely the goods carried high prices, making them accessible only to the wealthy.

Many labels used on the map for general regions rely on modern names to help us locate places. Some arrows have been placed on the trade routes to indicate either the main direction of flow or to suggest that individual traders ventured into regions beyond. We should not think of trade as flowing only in the direction of the arrows. All trading activities took place on two-way routes and people, goods, and ideas went both ways. And trade routes seldom reached a distinct terminus but lost themselves in a network of paths that embraced huge areas beyond the primary route.

Map 8 is the first one in world history to contain a person's name in the title. It is significant because Sargon I, king of the Akkadian Empire, found ways to bond individual city states together into·a unified kingdom, enabling him to develop an imperial state based on conquest. He employed a standing army designed for military conquests at great distances and used art and written accounts to glorify imperial ways.

Because of Sargon's innovations, he is the first person to be known as an individual, the first one about whom we can provide biographical details based on the written record. He was born in 2371 BCE into humble circumstances but became the cup-bearer to the king of Kish, a city-state on the Euphrates river. Eventually he overthrew the ruler and established a new polity based on Akkadian ways. The Akkadian peoples were not Sumerians although they had absorbed Sumerian civilization as nearby neighbors.

Sargon built a new capital for his kingdom at Agade closer to the top of the Fertile Crescent. Although Sargon's capital city of Agade is well know from written records, its exact location has not been definitely established. This factor explains the question mark placed on this map by the cartographer.

The Akkadians under Sargon's leadership then developed an aggressive policy of conquest which first joined the Sumerian city-states into one kingdom and then expanded its jurisdiction to include other people in the Elam highlands to the east and in Syria and along the Mediterranean coast to the west.

Sargon's expansive policies ended in a general revolt in 2316 BCE, but his son was able to restore the Akkadian Empire which lasted for almost two centuries. After this, the Sumerian regional states reestablished themselves, adopting some Akkadian practices which led to a cultural renaissance. It was during this time, about 2000 BCE, that the *Epic of Gilgamesh*, the world's first literary classic, was written down.

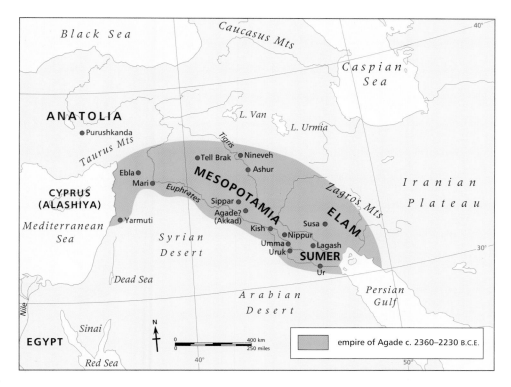

Map 8 Empire of Sargon of Agade, *c*.2320 BCE. It is sometimes pointed out that there was a direct relationship between Sargon's empire and the well-established trade routes pictured on map 7. The king needed revenues to support his army and an extensive system of imperial administration and aggrandizement. Merchants, on the other hand, appreciated imperial protection and the improvement of facilities for the transportation, storage, and sale of merchandise. They were willing to pay a certain level of taxes to secure these advantages, no doubt passing the extra expense on to the consumer in the form of higher prices. The availability of trade goods, finally, was one of the hallmarks of Sargon's empire and one of his claims to fame.

Ancient Egypt, 3100–1070 BCE

A SINGLE MAP often cannot tell the whole story of a region's development. Many maps would be needed to put the narrative of ancient Egyptian civilization into perspective. The earliest chapters would reach back to about 3200 BCE. when the farming communities along the lower Nile valley developed trading contacts with other peoples in Africa and Mesopotamia. Regional kingdoms in Upper and Lower Egypt were united about 3100 BCE. establishing the idea of a mighty, united state that would endure, with several interruptions, for nearly three millennia.

Thirty-one dynasties provided a continuity of rule unmatched elsewhere. Memphis, between the two regional kingdoms, was founded to serve as the capital of the united Egypt, often symbolized by two long-necked beasts with their bodies intertwined. The long stretch of ancient Egyptian history is traditionally divided into three periods. The Old Kingdom, lasting almost a thousand years, to about 2200 BCE, saw the development of monumental building projects such as royal cities, fortifications, temples, and the celebrated pyramids. This period is featured on map 9.

The title of this map is significant because there is more than one territory along the course of the Nile River. This has been true throughout history for several good geographic reasons. The first is carefully documented on the map: the division of the river into segments by extensive cataracts. The Nile steps down from the plateau that characterizes the African continent in a regular series of levels which are numbered as five cataracts. Each cataract separates one navigable stretch of the river from the next. It is not surprising to see that Egypt proper occupies the Nile Valley beyond the first interruption to river traffic. Nubia, south of Upper Egypt above the second cataract, was a distinct land with its own culture and style of civilization.

Map 9 Lands of the Nile: Egypt's Old Kingdom, c. 3100–2200 BCE. Note that Egypt itself was divided into two distinct regions. Lower Egypt occupied the extensive delta lands, spreading out like a great fan reaching into the Mediterranean Sea. Upper Egypt, in contrast was a serpentine strip of land tracing the flood plain of the river. Both regions of Egypt were divided into administrative districts called nomes. Lower Egypt's 22 nomes often used the various branches of the Nile for boundaries. While this was sometimes the case in Upper Egypt, its nomes typically extended on either side of the river, the Nile serving as a link for the nome occupying both banks.

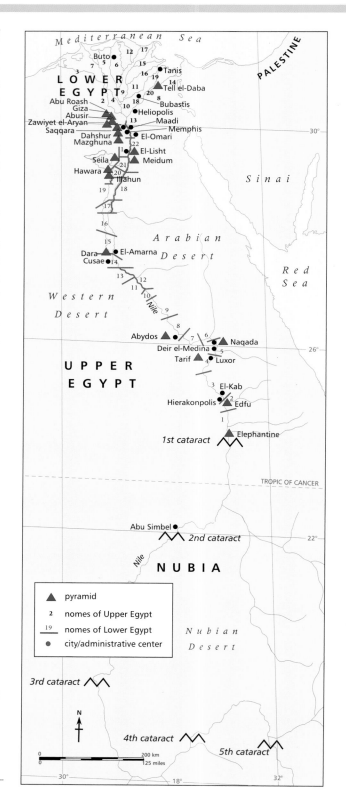

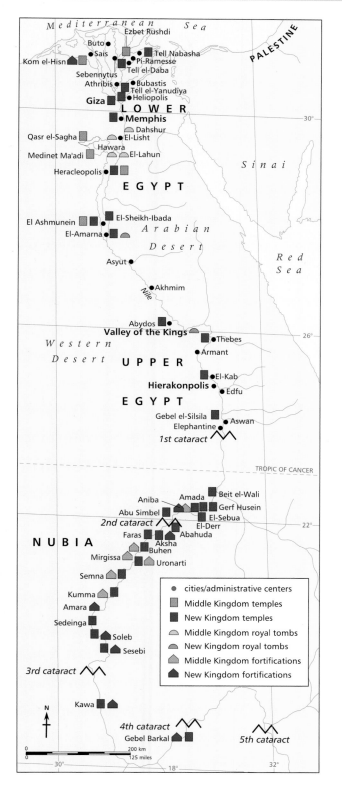

Map 10 Ancient Egypt: The Middle and New Kingdoms

●	cities/administrative centers
▨	Middle Kingdom temples
■	New Kingdom temples
◠	Middle Kingdom royal tombs
◖	New Kingdom royal tombs
⬠	Middle Kingdom fortifications
⬟	New Kingdom fortifications

A second geographic factor also encourages readers to think of the lands of the Nile in the plural. This is the fact that the great river flows in a northerly direction across 32 degrees of latitude, from rainforest and highland sources through steppe and desert lands. Each of these regions developed different ways of living and made different products.

Note that only half of the great river's course is shown on these maps. Above the fifth cataract the river changes character again, splitting into two major streams. The Blue Nile turns to the southeast reaching into the Ethiopian Highlands while the White Nile extends southward all the way to Lake Victoria on the Equator.

Egyptian history looks out into the Mediterranean Sea as well as up and down the great river. Ancient Egypt was connected to Asia by land routes. Ports on the Red Sea also supported an active trade with the Near East and East Africa by way of the Indian Ocean. Relations with these neighboring peoples were not always peaceful.

Conflicts with peoples up the Nile and across the Fertile Crescent provided rhythms to ancient Egyptian history. For example, attacks by invading armies from Asia brought a period of disruption after 2200 BCE, but a unified Egypt on the traditional model was reestablished in the Middle Kingdom period 2040–1640 BCE. Although it lasted only a few centuries, the Middle Kingdom pushed Egyptian settlements south of the first cataract into the tropical region. Another period of invasion, unrest, and dislocation followed on the heels of this expansion.

Around 1570 BCE, however, Egypt was again united and the expansionist impulse was quickened. Egyptian influence spread into the Mediterranean Sea, especially on Crete, and into the Fertile Crescent. Egyptian influence also spread up river into Nubia as far as the fourth cataract. The seat of royal authority shifted south, with New Kingdom royal tombs being located in the Valley of the Kings near Thebes.

Map 10 Ancient Egypt: The Middle and New Kingdoms, *c.*2040–1070 BCE. After 1150 BCE, new invasions coupled with internal strife and social upheaval started Egypt on a long path of gradual decline. The Exodus of the Jewish people occurred near the beginning of this period of decline. The Israelites fled from Lower Egypt across an arm of the Red Sea where the pharaoh's army drowned. A forty-year sojourn in the wilderness of Sinai preceded their entry into Palestine, the Promised Land. Map 21 (see p. 36) portrays the Kingdom of Israel at about 930 BCE.

Early Civilizations in the Indus River Valley and China

LIKE THE NILE RIVER featured in maps 9 and 10 (see preceding pages), the Indus brought a dependable water supply to the dry lands along its course. Because this river flowed in a southerly direction and received much of its flood waters from monsoon rains and snow melt, it was not as gentle and predictable as the Nile which had its sources in the steady equatorial rains which followed the sun northward each spring.

Neither did the Indus descend from its highland sources in a regular series of steps as it made its way to the sea. Instead it took a more wild approach, often shifting its course, finding new channels, and abandoning old ones. The changing nature and less dependable character of the Indus probably led early farming communities along its banks to see it in a way that was different from how the ancient Egyptians viewed the Nile. These attitudes toward the natural environment probably affected how people viewed life itself.

The ancient Indus civilization was based on individual walled cities. Over time these tended to be located away from the river banks to avoid flooding. By 2500 BCE an extensive trading system, probably based on roads as well as waterways, connected these cities with one another. To view map 11 with geographical eyes, keep in mind the rugged mountain barriers of the Hindu Kush and the Himalayas which walled off the Indus Valley to the north and west. Baluchistan is also a rugged highland with few routes to connect its plateau with the Indus Valley. East of the Indus Valley lies the Thar Desert, increasing the isolation of the early Indus Valley.

Note how the Indus River brings together five great streams coming down from the Himalayas. The northwestern branch carries the name of the mother river. The other four tributaries are named on the map. Harappa, the leading city which gave its name to this early civilization, is located on one of these smaller streams, the Ravi.

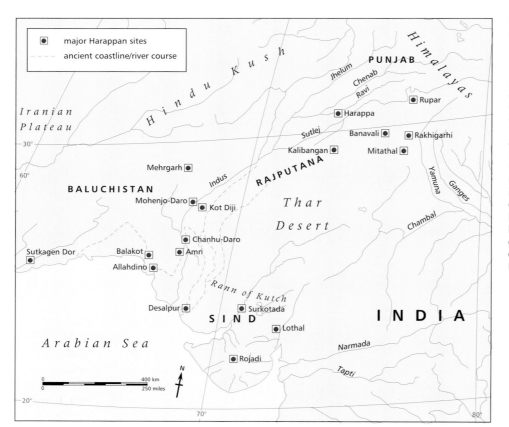

Map 11 Harappan Civilization: Cities of the Indus River Valley, c.2500 BCE. Harappan Civilization lasted over a thousand years. But sometime between 1500 and 1200 BCE, it fell victim to ecological disaster, internal collapse, or destruction by invaders. This magnificent civilization seems to have largely vanished from history, lost and forgotten until uncovered by archaeologists in the nineteenth century. Gradually historians are beginning to perceive links between the Harappan way of life and the cultures which developed later on the Indian subcontinent.

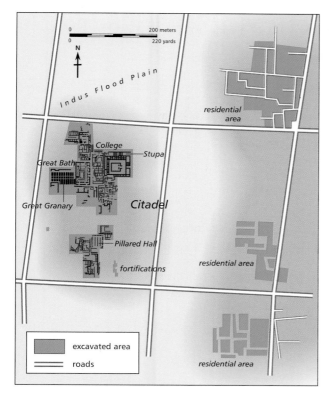

Map 12 Mohenjo-Daro. Harappan Civilization supported two great urban centers along with many smaller cities and towns. Mohenjo-Daro was located near the Indus river about midway between the mountains and the sea. Its water supply and sewage disposal systems were among the most advanced for pre-modern cities. Bathrooms with toilets and showers were commonplace and a large pool at the center of the city was apparently used for ceremonial bathing. Upwards of 40,000 people lived in this thriving center of commerce, manufacturing, education, and administration.

Turning from South Asia to East Asia, we encounter another civilization, not as ancient as the Harappan, but one that was to last even longer – over four millennia.

Someone once characterized a civilization as a successful idea system. The degree of success can, in some ways, be measured in terms of its diffusion over space and its endurance over time. By both measures, the civilization that developed in the rich alluvial soils of the Huang He (Yellow River) about 1800 BCE. is a dominant force in the world's history.

The Shang, a nomadic warrior people, came into a region of agricultural villages along the Ordos bulge of the Huang Ho. They expanded the existing irrigation and flood control devices while developing a writing system that became a hallmark of Chinese culture. As they pushed their control down the river, the Shang came to dominate other

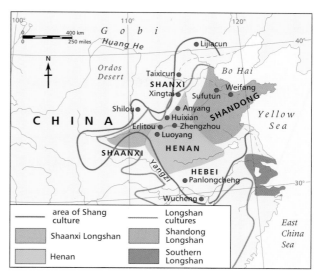

Map 13 Shang China, 1800–1025 BCE. Two great rivers are featured on this map, the Huang He and the Yangzi. Both were included in the Longshan culture area, but only a small segment of the Yangzi was included in the area controlled by the Shang. Note how the regional kingdom at the mouth of the Yangzi maintained its independence during this era. One of the major events in Chinese history in the next era will be the unification of these two great river basins into one political unit.

regional kingdoms that emerged in this period: the Shaanxi Longshan, the Henan, and the Shandong Longshan.

Note that the Shang conquests did not extend to the entire area occupied by the Longshan culture area, but Shang influence extended further to the north and west. Shang rulers did, however, view their capital city as the center of the world and considered their rightful jurisdiction to extend to the ends of the earth. As they integrated neighboring peoples into their empire, Shang emperors used ruling families from the old regional kingdoms as vassals to collect tribute, supply soldiers for the imperial armies, to administer justice, and to keep the peace.

Shang rulers and their attending aristocrats devoted much of their attention to performing rites and ceremonies so that the gods would look with favor on their exploits. Writing may have developed to ensure that these rituals would be performed in the correct way.

The combination of a decentralized political system and a preoccupation with religious ritual by the Shang overlords made it easy for one of the vassal peoples gradually to gain power and eventually depose the emperor. This happened about 1025 BCE when the Zhou, a Turkic-speaking group with origins in Central Asia, founded a new dynasty that was to last for nearly eight centuries.

Classical Cultures in the Americas, 250–1500 CE

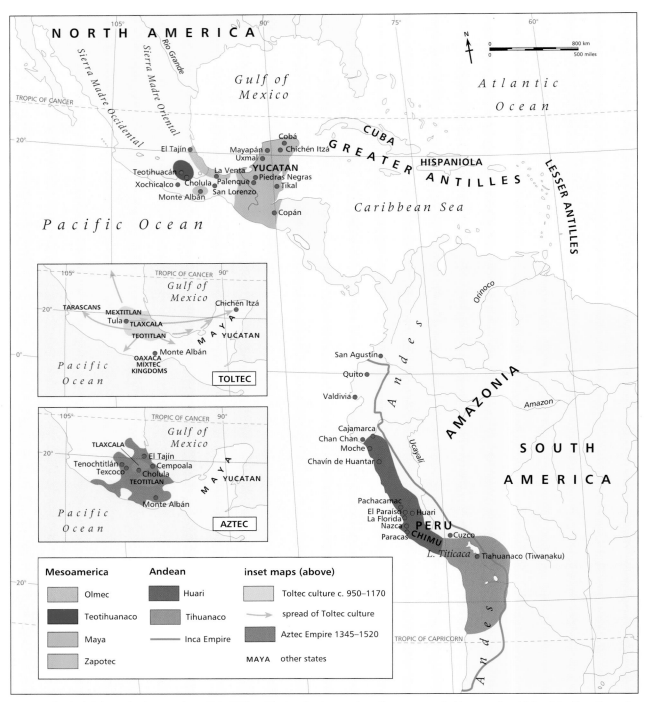

Map 14 Classical Cultures in the Americas, 250–1500 CE. The two inset maps show the same area in Mesoamerica at later dates than the main map. The top inset presents conditions about 1100 CE and the second one advances the calendar to around 1500 CE. Note that Chichén Itza, the Mayan center on the Yucatan Peninsula received influences from the Toltec culture but was not in direct contact with the Aztec Empire.

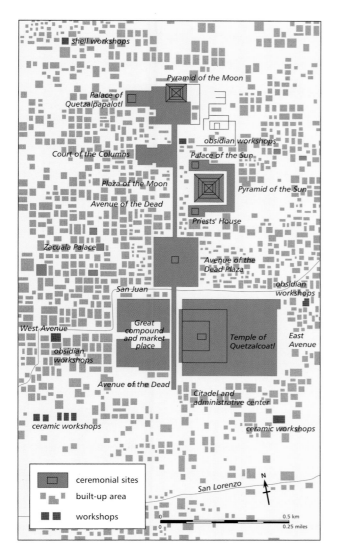

shell workshops

Pyramid of the Moon

Palace of Quetzalpapalotl

obsidian workshops

Court of the Columns

Palace of the Sun

Plaza of the Moon

Pyramid of the Sun

Avenue of the Dead

Priests' House

Zacuala Palace

Avenue of the Dead Plaza

San Juan

obsidian workshops

West Avenue

Great compound and market place

Temple of Quetzalcoatl

East Avenue

obsidian workshops

Avenue of the Dead

Citadel and administrative center

ceramic workshops

ceramic workshops

ceramic sites
built-up area
workshops

San Lorenzo

N

0   0.5 km
0   0.25 miles

Map 15 Teotihuacan, *c.*650 CE. The large city known as Teotihuacan presided over the Valley of Mexico and surrounding areas for at least three and a half centuries after 400 CE. Laid out on a grid pattern and supporting a whole avenue of temples and ceremonial structures, the city probably housed 100,000 people at its height. Workshops scattered throughout the city used resources from many distant areas to produce pottery, jewelry, ceremonial items, and luxury goods. Around 650 CE the city went up in flames. It never recovered and was almost totally abandoned a century later.

A SOCIETY DEVELOPS a classic culture when it gathers together traditional ways of life and expresses their values in such a powerful way that it sets standards of achievement for future generations. The art, literature, and language of that particular time and place become enduring marks of achievement, authoritative examples to guide future developments.

Two different geographical areas served as heartlands for the classical cultures in the Americas. The humid regions in Mesoamerica saw a succession of related civilizations which ended when the Aztec Empire was taken over by invaders from Europe in the sixteenth century. A similar fate met the Inca Empire based in temperate valleys in the Andes mountains. Although there may have been some contact between these two areas of classic civilizations over the centuries, each one developed independently, following its own traditions. Both regions, however, enjoyed a succession of distinctive urban centers, each with its own character.

In the fertile valleys along the western slope of the Andes, early farmers raised beans, peanuts, sweet potatoes, and cotton. Trade with coastal peoples who relied on the sea for much of their livelihood eventually led to a series of small states each with its own distinctive type of pottery. Some time between 1000 and 900 BCE three related changes swept over the region: corn (maize) became a major food crop capable of supporting large populations; a new type of ceremonial religion appeared; and contact between various river valleys became more frequent. A series of distinctive civilizations flourished in the area over the next 25 centuries, sometimes overlapping in time or space, but each with very distinctive features. Archaeologists label these as Chavín, Tihuanaco, Moche, Nazca, Huari, and Chimu. All of them may be considered as precursors to the Inca who after 1200 CE extended their control up and down the Pacific coast.

Corn (maize) originated in Mexico and its advantages as a food crop led to a wide-spread agricultural tradition that dominated Central America and regions beyond from about 4000 BCE and continuing for several millennia.

Around 1200 BCE a ceremonial center at San Lorenzo seems to have set a cultural pattern for urban societies in the region. Archaeologists call this classic civilization Olmec after the rubber trees found in the area. The mysterious decline and fall of the Olmec gave opportunity for other empires to emerge, all owing their basic structure to the classical Olmec tradition. The Maya dominated the Yucatan while a series of peoples rose to pre-eminence in Mexico. The last of these, the Aztec, fell to Spanish invaders in 1520 CE.

The Ancient Near East, 1550–1250 BCE

ONE WAY to put map 16 into perspective is to picture a great hinge at Sinai connecting the African continent to the Eurasian world. This region is sometimes called the Near East, using a Western European viewpoint. The title used here is geographically accurate, but calls on us to use a larger geographical perspective to put it into context.

The map calls on us to use a historical view as well, envisioning the ebb and flow of fortunes which brought constant change to the region. These changes can only be hinted at on a static map, but the cartographer has employed graphic devices to provide a dynamic quality: different colors, distinguishing between core areas and periphery, and overlapping lines of conquest.

The core Egyptian area is confined to the valley below the first cataract, but the early New Kingdom pharaohs extended their control into Nubia, Sinai and the Mediterranean littoral. This line of control could be continued to include the Mediterranean Sea as well. Note how two major Egyptian cities are identified: Memphis, the traditional capital, and Thebes, the new imperial center located far upstream.

The Hittites, who established a cradleland in central Anatolia about 2000 BCE, were originally invaders from the steppes north of the Black Sea. As they pushed outward to include new lands in their territory, they triggered the movement of other peoples, such as the Hyksos who briefly conquered Egypt in 1720 BCE, the Kassites who overran Babylon a century later, and the Hurrians who founded a kingdom in Syria. Unsettled conditions led to an era of small states in the Fertile Crescent, lasting until 900 BCE during which such peoples as the Phoenicians and the Hebrews could establish smaller, independent states. Then the expansion of the Assyrians ushered in a new imperial age (see map 17, p. 32).

Note how the cartographer has designated a core area for each of the four major empires at this time in the ancient Near East. A color code identifies those states which assume two different generalized shapes. Those confined to river valleys by geographic conditions are attenuated, assuming the shape of the river valleys. Both Egypt and Babylonia follow this pattern.

In other geographic situations, the core areas assume a more circular shape, spreading out from a central area more or less equally in all directions. Given a uniform climate and topography, one can posit a circular core area such as the cartographer has drawn for the Hittites.

The imperial holdings of these core states reached out in all directions, often not stopping until they ran into a coastline, forbidding deserts or rugged topography. In general the reaches of the empires tended to repeat the shape of the core areas because these were all land-based empires.

As people from the core areas ventured out into the surrounding territories, their activities followed certain general patterns. Exploration involved the gathering of basic information which led to a discovery of possibilities for expansion. Gathering resources such as metals, salt, and lumber could be quickly undertaken if these activities were not contested by local populations. In many cases, however, the adventurers had to barter to gain the resources they wanted.

Sometimes force was used to seize things of value to take back to the homeland, a process of plundering that was usually limited to a one-time opportunity. If regular trade was the object of expansion, then commercial outposts would be established in the periphery. Some control of the peripheral lands could be asserted if soldiers or other agents of the core area were sent to occupy the outposts. To support these imperial agents, an imperial colony often developed around the outposts, with the implantation of farmers, workers, and agents of the core culture.

The names of various other peoples appear on the map on the periphery of the most powerful empires. Often these were powerful states in their own right, able to resist imperial armies sent to conquer them. As the centuries passed the Medes and the Persians on the Iranian Plateau joined to become the most powerful empire in the region. Meanwhile, around the Aegean Sea, a Greek civilization developed which was able to withstand Persian advances.

Map 16 Empires of South-west Asia, 1500–1250 BCE. The cartographer has called special attention to the battle of Qadesh in 1285 BCE. Fought in Syria, the conflict pitted an Egyptian army against the Hittites. Ramsses II claimed victory, but he failed to dislodge the Hittites from control of the trade routes that connected Egypt and Mesopotamia. Note how all three empires tried to dominate this key area where the Fertile Crescent touches the northeast corner of the Mediterranean Sea.

Palestine is also located between the major cultural cores shown on this map: Egypt, Anatolia, and Mesopotamia. Advantages and disadvantages accompanied such a crossroads location. The Israelites, for example, spent time as exiles in both Egypt and Babylonia according to the biblical record.

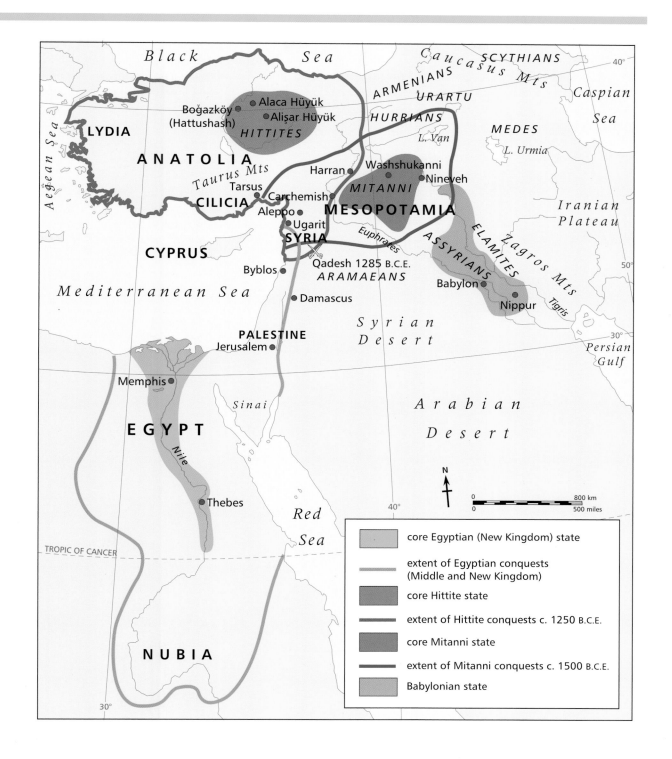

Black Sea

SCYTHIANS
ARMENIANS
C a u c a s u s Mts
URARTU
HURRIANS
Caspian Sea

LYDIA
Boğazköy
(Hattushash)
Alaca Hüyük
Alişar Hüyük
HITTITES
MEDES
L. Van
L. Urmia

ANATOLIA

Aegean Sea

Taurus Mts
Tarsus
Harran
Washshukanni
Nineveh
MITANNI

CILICIA
Carchemish
Aleppo
MESOPOTAMIA
Iranian Plateau

CYPRUS
Ugarit
SYRIA
Euphrates
ASSYRIANS
ELAMITES
Zagros Mts

Byblos
Qadesh 1285 B.C.E.
ARAMAEANS
Babylon
Nippur
Tigris

Mediterranean Sea
Damascus
Syrian Desert
Persian Gulf

PALESTINE
Jerusalem

Memphis
Sinai
Arabian Desert

EGYPT
Nile

N

Thebes
Red Sea
800 km
500 miles

TROPIC OF CANCER

NUBIA

- core Egyptian (New Kingdom) state
- extent of Egyptian conquests (Middle and New Kingdom)
- core Hittite state
- extent of Hittite conquests c. 1250 B.C.E.
- core Mitanni state
- extent of Mitanni conquests c. 1500 B.C.E.
- Babylonian state

The Assyrian and Persian Empires, *c.*911–330 BCE

ASSYRIA, the hilly homeland of the great conquerors of the first half of this period, is in northern Mesopotamia where the Tigris and Euphrates rivers twist away from each other toward different headlands. Here abundant rainfall made the agricultural settlements less dependent on rivers and irrigation to support their crops. Assyrian farmers originally occupied the lands at the top of the fertile crescent, with their religious center, named Ashur after their chief god, located on the Tigris river.

About the year 911 BCE the leaders of the Assyrians started an aggressive program of attacks against hostile neighbors. The success of one foray led to another, and soon Assyria had turned into a military state, sending out armies of conquest in all directions. These military adventures followed the ancient trade routes and, at their greatest extent, embraced the entire arc of productive lands from the Persian Gulf to the Nile Valley.

Although the wheel had been used in Mesopotamia for several thousand years and wheeled carts or wagons date back to the earliest records, vehicles were primarily used to haul such materials as bricks, ores, reeds or foodstuffs. It was not until the Assyrians combined a horse-drawn chariot with archers that the wheel found an effective military application. By sending waves of chariots into the middle of enemy forces, with the archers firing arrows as fast as they could, the mobile forces of the Assyrians were able to terrorize their opponents.

The monarch was the center of the Assyrian world. He owned all the land and everyone, even the highest rank-

Map 17 The Assyrian Empire, *c.*650 BCE, and its Rivals. The most striking images on this map are the colored regions along the northern borders of the Assyrian Empire. These neighboring states were able to contest the imperial armies. In 614 BCE an alliance of Persian and Median tribes with the Babylonians crushed an Assyrian army. But the Assyrians created an enduring legacy in one respect. They collected many documents and records from the regions they conquered, assembling in a central location a wealth of knowledge about the ancient Near East, a "museum" today's scholars use to help reconstruct the story of civilization throughout Mesopotamia.

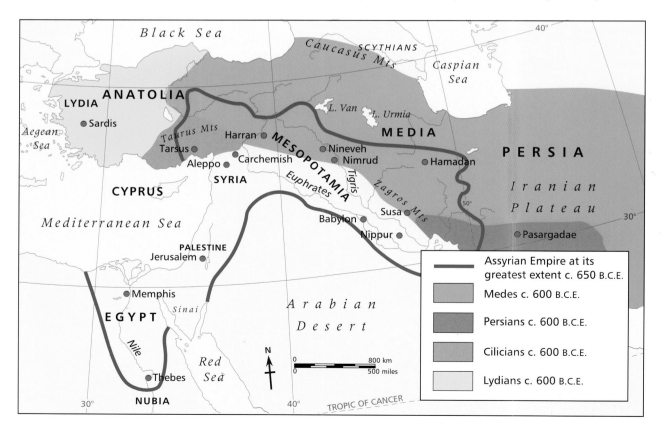

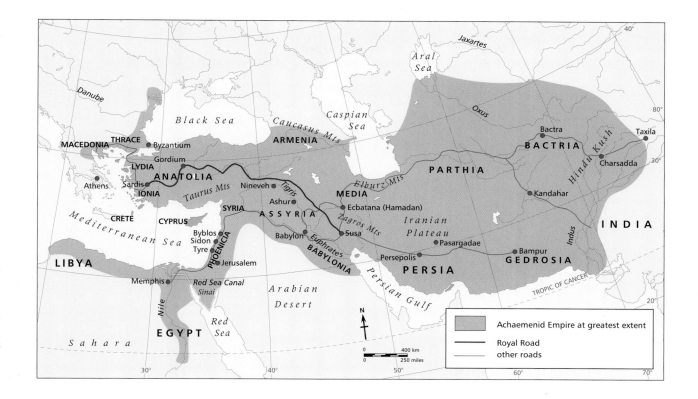

Map 18 Achaemenid Persia. The tomb of Cyrus the Great still stands, a solid and simple stone structure, near the ruins of his palace at Pasargadae. Darius started building a magnificent new palace at Persepolis in 520 BCE. It took three generations to complete the new capital, but it then served for over a century as the scene of resplendent ceremonies each New Year's day when the governors (*satraps*) of the various provinces brought tribute to the emperor.

ing officials, were, in theory, his servants. The hereditary kings were crowned in Ashur where they would also be buried. In between ceremonies, the king was often on tour supervising the administration of a far-flung empire or commanding the armies in battle.

As the riches of the ancient Near East were funneled into the royal coffers, Assyrian kings built a series of royal cities to display their wealth. Nineveh, of Biblical fame, was one of these new cities.

The Assyrian Empire was eventually weakened by internal struggles. Imperial troops withdrew from Egypt to face attacks in the east from Medes and Persians and in the north from Scythians. The Persians dominated their neighbors and soon made an alliance with the Babylonians to defeat the Assyrians. Nineveh fell in 612 BCE.

A generation later an ambitious Persian monarch named Cyrus claimed descent from the legendary hero Achaemenes

and rallied his troops to attack the neighboring states. His success earned him the appellation "the Great" and led to the establishment of the Achaemenid Empire. When Cyrus the Great died in 529 BCE, his empire extended from the Persian Gulf to the Mediterranean Sea. His immediate successors continued pushing outward, adding Egypt, Libya, Macedonia, Thrace, Bactria, and the Indus Valley to the Persian Empire.

To rule such a vast empire, Persian emperors improved transportation facilities such as roads and canals. For example, to facilitate troop movements, the Persians completed an early version of the Suez Canal, a project that had been sponsored by the pharaohs of earlier times. By land and sea the Persians brought troops as well as trade goods from India into the ancient Near East.

Although an invasion of Greece by Persian forces led by Emperor Darius I was defeated by the Greeks at Marathon in 490 BCE, the Achaemenids continued to dominate the region until the Macedonian general Alexander the Great, at the head of a Greek army, defeated the Persians in Syria, Egypt, Mesopotamia, and Persia itself (see map 20, p. 35). When Alexander put himself on the Persian throne in 330 BCE, the age of the Achaemenids came to an end.

The Ancient Greeks

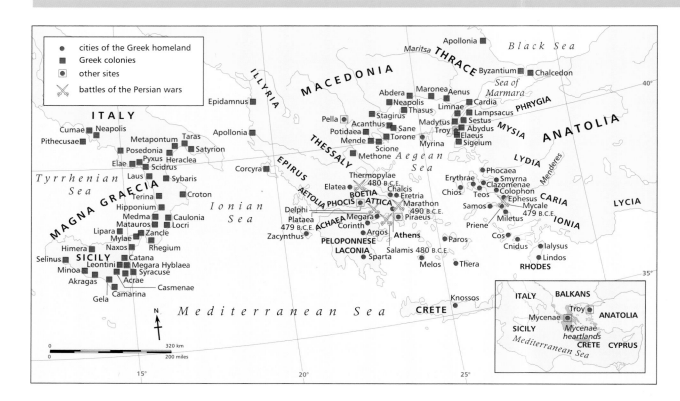

Map 19 Classical Greece and its Antecedents, *c.*2000–479 BCE.
Athens, a port on the Aegean Sea, is the most celebrated city of
classical Greece and is at the center of this map. Its rival, Sparta, is
located inland on the Peloponnese, an irregular peninsula at the
southern tip of Greece. Delphi, the site of the famous oracle, was on
the Gulf of Corinth which separated the Peloponnese from the
mainland. Byzantium and Chalcedon were Greek colonies at the
entrance to the Black Sea. Syracuse became the major city in Magna
Graecia, the Greek region in Sicily and southern Italy.

WITH MAP 19 we are introduced to a new geographic orientation for the study of world history. For the first time the Mediterranean Sea is the dominant feature on the map. Its name, meaning the sea in the middle of the earth, points to the fact that its shores belong to three continents: Africa, Asia, and Europe. This is a point made by the small location map inset at the lower right.

The Mediterranean can also be conceived as a series of smaller seas, some of which appear on this map. Note that it is also connected by the Sea of Marmara to the Black Sea between Europe and Asia Minor (Anatolia).

The lands surrounding the Mediterranean Sea have a similar climate characterized by mild, wet winters and warm, dry summers. The Mediterranean climate produced both shifting wind patterns and similar biological environments around its shores, two key factors in encouraging venturesome people to take to the water and establish overseas colonies.

Three distinct civilizations are portrayed on this map, each of which depended on the Mediterranean for its livelihood. The oldest, the Minoan, was centered on the island of Crete. By 2,000 BCE the Minoans had mastered the Mediterranean Sea and had established trading relations with Egypt, the Middle East, and ports around the Aegean Sea.

About 1450 BCE the Minoan civilization was destroyed by invaders, possibly the Myceneans. Named after the citadel of Mycenae (Troy), this new civilization owed a great deal to the Minoan example, but seems to have been more decentralized, with many centers spread throughout the Aegean region. The Mycenean heartland area is colored green on the inset map.

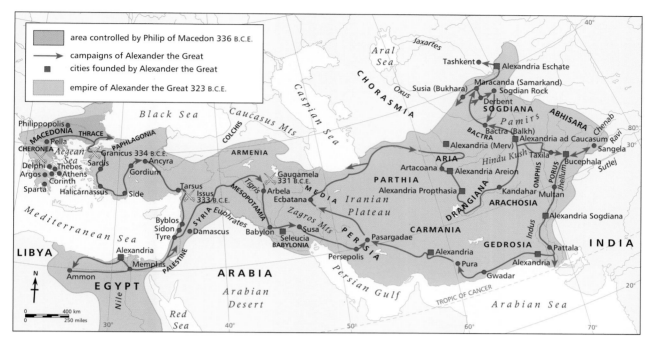

Map 20 The Empire of Alexander the Great, c.323 BCE. It is important to compare the Achaemenid Empire (map 18) with this map. Note especially how the routes used by Alexander in the course of his conquests often made use of the royal roads maintained by the Persian Empire. Both empires included ancient centers of civilization in Mesopotamia, Egypt, the Indus Valley, and Anatolia.

Alexander founded many new cities throughout his empire. Thus this map shows one Alexandria at the mouth of the Nile and another in the valley of the Indus near the site of Mohenjo-Daro (see map 12, p. 27). Sister cities appeared on the Plateau of Iran, in Turkestan and in Afghanistan.

Classical Greek civilization, in turn, was built on Mycenean foundations. As city states around the Aegean prospered from trade, they developed their culture to a high degree at home and, at the same time, expanded overseas, establishing colonies in Italy, Sicily, and the Black Sea region.

In many ways, the power of Greek culture has been exerted in periodic waves on Western civilization. It is said that when Rome conquered Greece, the culture of the captive conquered Rome in return (see map 23, p. 38). The Renaissance in Europe (see maps 53 and 54, pp. 67 and 69) can be characterized as a rebirth of the ideas of classical Greece. Later centuries in Europe and the Americas saw periodic revivals of interest in Greek ways of cultural expression.

And yet, as map 20 makes clear, the culmination of classical Greece was an event that happened east of Eden, on the plateau of Iran, at the Persian capital of Persepolis. Here, after shattering the Persian forces in the great battle of Gaugamela (331 BCE), Alexander of Macedon led his troops into the Achaemenid capitals, seized their treasuries, married a Persian princess, paid his respects at the tomb of Cyrus I, and proclaimed himself the new emperor. History agreed and named him "the Great" as well.

Then Alexander continued to push eastward, eventually conquering the eastern reaches of the old Persian Empire. He wanted to push on, to the Ganges river in India, but his troops refused to go further. Putting Greek leaders in the positions of power from the Adriatic Sea to the Arabian Gulf and from Central Asia to Nubia was an achievement great enough.

Alexander died young in 323 BCE, but not before founding cities throughout his realm which became centers for the dispersal of Greek culture. The Hellenistic kingdoms under Greek leadership which followed then proved that cultural thoroughfares always lead two ways, bringing eastern influences into the Mediterranean world just as they dispersed Greek ideas to Egypt, Mesopotamia, Persia, India, and Central Asia.

Palestine in Biblical Times, 930 BCE–30 CE

THE NARRATIVES told in the bible, containing the holy scriptures of the Jewish and Christian faiths, fit into the pattern of history related on maps 7, 10, 16, 17, 18, and 23. The maps on these pages supplement the preceding ones, highlighting Palestine as a case study of life in the Ancient Near East.

Map 21, which presents the kingdom of Israel in 930 BCE, picks up the account of the Chosen People as recorded in the Torah, or Old Testament as Christians call it. The story begins with the creation of the world and the expulsion of Adam and Eve from the Garden of Eden, located east of Mesopotamia (see map 4, p. 20).

Eventually, after a great flood and the saving of human and animal life in Noah's ark, people dispersed to all parts of the world. Abraham, the founding father of the Jewish people, came from the city of Uruk near the mouth of the Euphrates (see map 7, p. 22). The patriarch received a divine call to come to the Promised Land, Palestine, and probably followed an established trade route across the Fertile Crescent to Palestine.

In a time of drought the descendents of Abraham sought relief in Egypt where eventually they fell into a long period of slavery in the early years of the New Kingdom (see map 10, p. 25). During these centuries, the Egyptian Empire incorporated Palestine and Syria as dependent states (see map 16, p. 31). A period of Egyptian weakness around 1200 BCE permitted the Jewish people to escape Egypt and begin a great exodus from slavery to freedom in a long journey through the Sinai wilderness to Palestine.

In the wilderness wanderings, traditionally lasting forty years, the deity spoke to Moses, the leader of the Exodus, and gave the people a set of laws and guides to proper living which included the Ten Commandments. These stories, precepts, laws, and associated literary texts were collected and elaborated as the twelve tribes of the Jewish people eventually conquered parts of Palestine and were pulled together into a centralized kingdom. Around 980 BCE King David started building a great temple as a focus for the religious life of the Jews. The process continued as his wise son, Solomon, extended the boundaries of the Kingdom of Israel from the tip of the Red Sea to the banks of the upper reaches of the Euphrates.

With the rise of Assyria (see map 17, p. 32), the Kingdom of Israel was pushed back and fragmented into two small kingdoms, both of which were reduced to client states and their leading families eventually taken into exile, first by the Assyrians and then by the Babylonians. The rise of the Persian Empire, with its more tolerant policy toward ethnic groups, enabled remnants of two Jewish tribes to return to Palestine in the reign of Cyrus the Great (see map 18, p. 33).

The Jewish people then enjoyed a degree of freedom as one in a cluster of small states along the coast where the Fertile Crescent met the Mediterranean Sea. They tried to preserve a distinct culture in the days of the Persian Empire and the Hellenistic states which followed the conquests of Alexander the Great (see map 20, p. 35). When

Map 21 The Kingdom of Israel, 980–930 BCE. Note how the River Jordan river rises in the mountains of Phoenicia (now Lebanon) and flows southward in the rift valley, through the Sea of Galilee, eventually releasing its waters, far below sea level, into the salty wastes of the Dead Sea. Jericho, an important settlement dating back to Neolithic times, is situated near the mouth of the Jordan. Jerusalem, the capital of the Kingdom of Israel and a Holy City to three major religions, is located in the uplands west of Jericho.

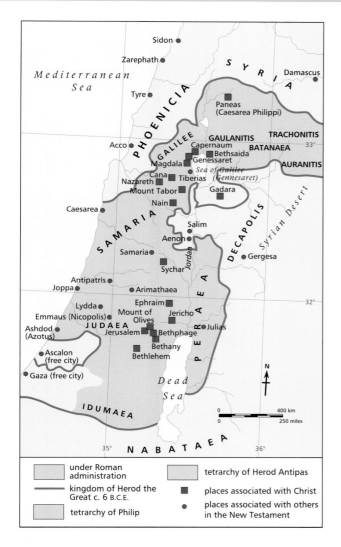

Map 22 Palestine in the Time of Jesus, 5 BCE–30 CE. Mary the mother of Jesus, and Joseph, her husband, came from Galilee in the north of Palestine. Jesus was born while they were on a trip to Bethlehem, "the city of David," located in Judaea, south of Jerusalem. Jesus grew up in Capernaum, near the Sea of Galilee, but his life seemed to revolve around a series of trips taken to the Temple in Jerusalem. His suffering and crucifixion, and then his resurrection and ascension, according to the gospel accounts, all took place in the vicinity of the capital city.

letters, using Greek, the literary language of the Hellenistic world. These writings were then called the New Testament and added to the Greek version of the Hebrew Torah, completing the Christian bible.

Jesus Christ became a familiar name in the Mediterranean world as the message of salvation through him was spread by missionaries (see pp. 48–9). The precise relationship between Jesus as a human being and his Godhead expressed in his messianic function as the Christ became a topic of much debate among early Christian churches.

Some church leaders wanted to emphasize the divinity of the Christ in which the divine appeared in human form but really was not human. Others held that Jesus was basically a man who lived such an exemplary life that God blessed his efforts and eventually took over his being. Jesus, in this view, was transformed into the Christ. In a series of creeds, or statements of belief, the Orthodox Church came to the conclusion that Jesus Christ was both true God and true man, a mysterious incarnation.

The early Christian writings collected in the New Testament did not shed much light on how the human and divine came together in the person of Jesus. Neither did they provide many biographical details about his life. The four gospel accounts, three of them drawing from a common source, were more concerned with the teachings of Jesus and with stories of his healing and concern for others. Only his last days were presented in enough detail to reconstruct a fuller story and the suffering, death, and resurrection of Jesus have become the central event of the Christian religion.

The cross subsequently became the major symbol of the Christian faith. Even here, however, the two aspects of Jesus Christ find full expression. A crucifix, showing a suffering human being on the cross became a widespread devotional item in Christian churches and homes. But a plain cross came to represent the resurrection of Jesus and the triumph of the divine, life victorious after death.

Jesus was born, about 5 BCE, the Roman Empire dominated Egypt, Greece, and Mesopotamia.

Map 22 shows Palestine at this time, first assigned by the Romans to Herod the Great as a client state, and then divided among his sons and Roman officials after his death in 4 BCE. Jesus probably studied the scriptures in both Greek and Hebrew, but he and his fellow Jews spoke Aramaic, a popular tongue in the Near East that was encouraged by Hellenistic kings as a common language.

When Jesus was accepted by his followers as the promised messiah or savior, he was called the Christ. They recorded his life and teachings in a series of gospels and

The Roman Empire

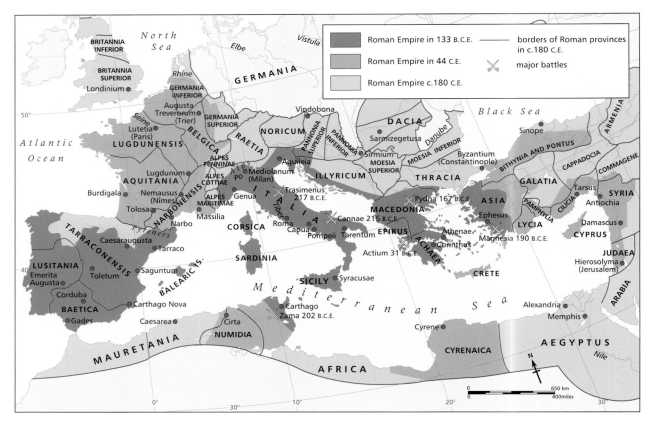

THE ACHIEVEMENT of the ancient Romans was to unite the entire Mediterranean Basin into one polity. The Roman Empire was not built in a day, as the map makes clear by showing how the imperium expanded from 133 BCE to 44 CE and then to its greatest extent in 180 CE.

The traditional date for the founding of Rome is 753 BCE, but archaeological evidence at the site records hilltop farming villages dating back to about the year 1000. By 600 BCE several of these communities cooperated in draining wetlands, the location of which eventually became the Roman Forum. According to tradition the early Roman settlements were ruled by kings. In 507 BCE the monarchy was replaced by a republic which made the government a *res publica*, or public possession, with ruling power vested in a Senate, an Assembly, and two elected consuls.

Soon the Roman Republic joined other agricultural towns in the vicinity to fend off the pastoral peoples who occupied the hills above the Latin plain. This led

Map 23 The Roman Empire, 133 BCE–180 CE. One key to understanding the expansion of Rome is the geographic concept of centrality. This map demonstrates the advantage of the city's location in dominating Italy, and also suggests why, due to its position, Rome came into conflict with both Carthage and the Greek states. The map also shows how Rome's position west of the center of the Mediterranean Sea encouraged its expansion into Europe.

to a series of wars, at the end of which Rome ruled most of the Italian peninsula. Extending Roman citizenship to these conquered neighbors transformed a city-state into a regional power which, in turn, led to a great confrontation with another regional state, Carthage.

The Punic Wars between Rome and Carthage (264–201 BCE) ended in complete victory for the Romans who, in the process, gained an overseas empire in Sicily, Spain, North Africa, and the islands of the western Mediterranean Sea. Turning to the east, Roman armies soon dominated the Adriatic coastal areas and fought a series of wars against the leading states in Greece. Roman officials, trying various ways to keep the peace, eventually decided to turn

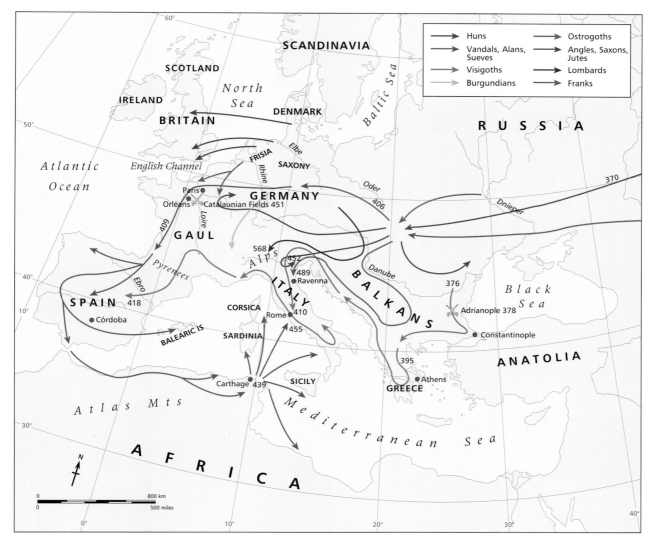

Map legend:
- → Huns
- → Vandals, Alans, Sueves
- → Visigoths
- → Burgundians
- → Ostrogoths
- → Angles, Saxons, Jutes
- → Lombards
- → Franks

Map 24 The Coming of the Barbarians, 4th–6th Centuries CE. This map shows a world in transition. The key indicates that each colored line represents the path or direction taken by a group of people who entered the Roman Empire and eventually settled on its lands. Each migration is divided into segments, occasionally punctuated by dates of arrival or the crossed swords symbolizing a momentous battle.

the overseas lands into provinces. Thus the republic ruled an extensive empire by 133 BCE. A period of civil war followed which eventually led to the consolidation of power in the hands of Julius Caesar, the Roman general who had extended imperial holdings into Gaul (France).

The assassination of Caesar led to a struggle for control of the Empire by several military leaders. Augustus eventually won this contest and established a pattern of government which combined some traditions of the old Roman state with a powerful role for the emper-

or, or "first citizen," backed by the power of the army. Peace and prosperity followed, a period often called the Pax Romana in the Mediterranean world.

The lure of the East that had led Alexander the Great to India also cast its spell on the Roman Emperors and Constantine moved his residence from Rome to a new capital at the gateway to Asia. Constantinople after 340 CE became the major seat of the Roman Empire.

Roman armies soon faced a new problem. For centuries they had managed the migration of Germanic tribes from northern Europe by settling newcomers on the imperial frontier. But just after the founding of Constantinople, a nomadic people from Central Asia entered Europe by way of the lowlands north of the Black Sea. Led by a capable warrior named Attila, the Huns set off a reaction that pushed a variety of peoples across Roman frontiers.

Rome's Successors and the Byzantine Empire

I T IS DIFFICULT to show many historical developments on a single map because complex changes tend to turn the graphic aid into a chaotic mess. A better approach is to use a series of maps of the same geographical area to trace changes over time, each one, perhaps, employing a different emphasis. This map, for example, clarifies the results of the migrations featured on map 24 (see preceding page), but the reader also needs to take account of the movements traced on map 38, The Expansion of Islam (see p. 52), and map 50, The Spread of Christianity (see p. 64), to fully comprehend it.

These four maps should be viewed as a set but they do not follow a strict chronological order. The spread of Christianity began when the Roman Empire was at its height. As new peoples migrated into Europe, they were often met by Christian missionaries. When they settled down to establish regional kingdoms, the Christian church provided institutions to hold society together, blending newcomers and resident peoples into a single community.

A few generations later, however, the Christian peoples, divided into various churches by ethnic, linguistic, and doctrinal differences, were fighting battles with Arab armies spreading the Muslim faith. These are also important factors to consider when studying the end of the Roman Empire and the beginning of the early Middle Ages in Europe.

But in even more maps with greater coverage will be needed to put the story in the informative context of world history. The general flow of people started in the late fourth century CE on the steppes of Eurasia. Their movement paralleled the north shore of the Black Sea and they crossed the Danube into the center of Europe before splitting off in different directions, following the various peninsulas which jut into the Mediterranean Sea. The advance of one group often led to the displacement of others so that the whole map was constantly changing except at the eastern portion of the Mediterranean Sea. In this densely populated region, Roman armies turned aside the

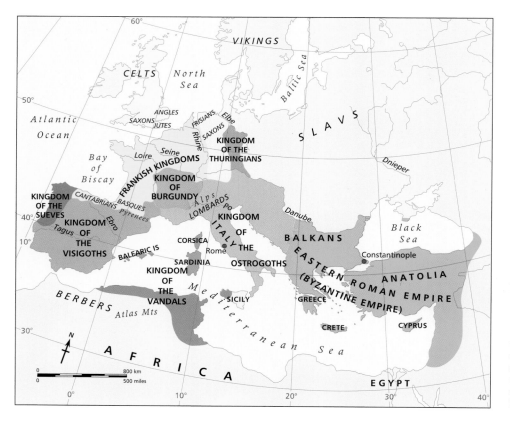

Map 25 Rome's Successors, 455 CE. It is important to put this map in chronological sequence. The precise date marks an attack on Rome by Gaiseric, a Vandal king who brought his forces overseas from Carthage. The subsequent Kingdom of the Vandals was based in North Africa and the islands of the western Mediterranean Sea. Rome, which had been sacked in 410 CE, was sacked again. In both cases imperial officials refused to acknowledge the barbarians as their equals. The great city never recovered its former status, becoming famous for its ruins.

invaders to preserve their empire in the east. Historians later called this remnant the Byzantine Empire (see below). Note that its capital was located at Constantinople on the hinge between Europe and Asia.

The movements in Europe and the western Mediterranean show only one part of a more general phenomenon. Peoples from the steppes of central Asia also advanced on centers of civilization in China, India, and Persia. The Huns, for example, whose movements are traced on map 24 by a purple line, were closely related to the Xiongnu who had earlier attacked China (see map 27, p. 42).

The victory of the Visigoths (West Goths) over the Roman armies at Adrianople in 378 CE was a key turning point in the history of Europe. It changed imperial policy, permitting various tribes to settle in western parts of the Roman Empire. The blending of these new peoples, Roman civilization, and Christianity provided the base from which European civilization would emerge in the coming centuries.

Meanwhile, the Byzantine Empire continued to hold lands close to the sea after the fall of Rome in the West (476 CE). Mesopotamia could be held within a Mediterranean empire only at great effort and expense, and it was soon given up to the Sassanians in Persia. Egypt, however, was retained and beginning in 533 CE Byzantine armies and navies under the leadership of Emperor Jus-

tinian began to take back some of the lost Roman provinces in the West. Map 26 shows the success of these efforts by 565 CE, the year of Justinian's death.

The reconquests in the West, however, were offset by some losses of territory in the Middle East to the Persians and a huge burden of taxes to pay for these wars. After 565 CE the Byzantine Empire began a long gradual decline which did not end until 1453 when the last Roman Emperor fell from the throne following the Ottoman conquest of Constantinople (see map 53, p. 67).

Map 26 The Byzantine Empire, c.530 CE. Belisarius, the brilliant Byzantine military leader under Justinian, defeated the Vandals in 534, returning these and surrounding territories to the Eastern Roman Empire. Then he invaded Sicily and Italy, taking back provinces controlled by the Ostrogoths. Byzantine forces also recovered some territory in Spain from the Visigoths. These Gothic wars ultimately encouraged the growth of regional kingdoms because imperial control proved to be short-lived.

The Eastern Roman Empire at first controlled lands in Egypt, North Africa, Spain, and Italy, but these provinces were lost to local rebellions, to invading peoples from Asia, and then, more extensively, to the expansion of Islam after 632 CE. This map illustrates the process at work, showing Palestine as a Roman (Byzantine) province, but map 50 records a series of battles which turned the Holy Land into Islamic territory between 636 and 644 CE.

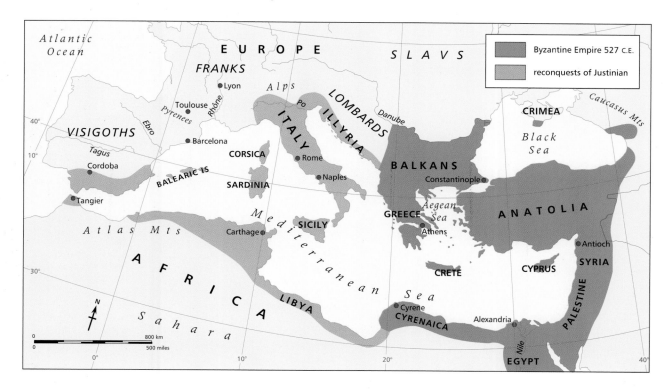

China in the Classical Age

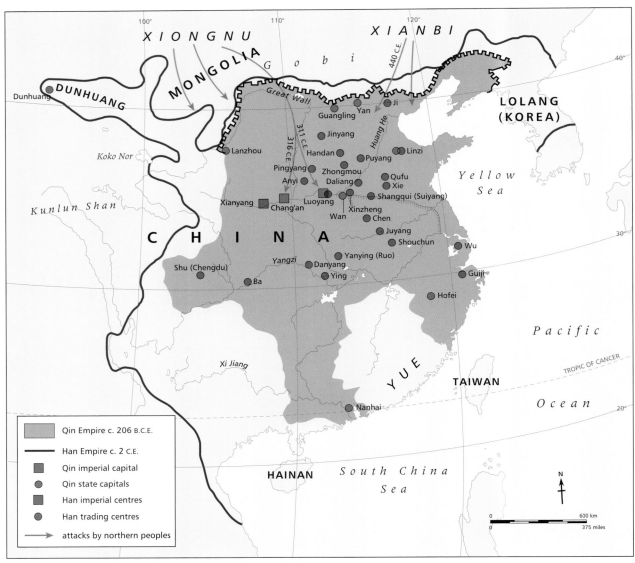

Map 27 Classical China, 221 BCE–220 CE.

Legend:
- Qin Empire c. 206 B.C.E.
- Han Empire c. 2 C.E.
- Qin imperial capital
- Qin state capitals
- Han imperial centres
- Han trading centres
- attacks by northern peoples

CHINA under the rule of the Zhou (1025–221 BCE) exhibited two divergent tendencies. The first was the formation of a common culture as trading networks spread ideas, products, and ways of living throughout the region. At the same time, the area undergoing integration by Chinese culture was politically fragmented into a series of smaller states with shifting boundaries as a result of almost constant wars. The Zhou rulers exercised nominal rule over much of China, but the best description labels this period "the Era of Warring States."

Map 27 Classical China, 221 BCE–220 CE. The Great Wall of China, started on a massive scale under the Qin, was fully developed under the Han. The Han also extended the boundaries of China outward in all directions. The most vulnerable border, however, ran along the northern frontier which divided the nomadic herding peoples of the steppe from the sedentary farming communities south of the wall. As long as the Chinese people behind the wall were able to maintain a united front against enemy attack, they could hold off the nomadic groups that tried to cross the frontier. An internal uprising in 220 CE ended Han rule and soon nomadic peoples broke through the Great Wall.

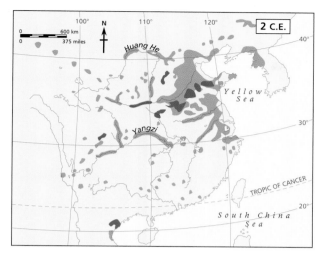

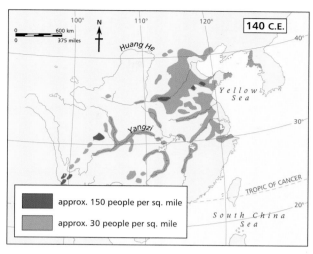

Map 28A Chinese Population Distribution, 2 CE. This map is constructed from data found in the earliest surviving census of Chinese subjects, taken in 2 CE Note how the population is concentrated in the valley of the Huang He. The Chinese also had a notable presence along the Yangzi river and in scattered sites in south and southwest China. The total Chinese population in these records is about 57 million people, a huge number at this early date.

Map 28B Chinese Population Distribution, 140 CE. Also based on census records, this map presents the same data as its mate, 28A, but is based on information compiled 138 years later. The map highlights the expansion of settlement along the Yangzi river and its tributaries as well as a "pulling-in" of outlying settlements in the northwest. In the later Han period the capital was moved to Luoyang on the Huang He, reflecting this shift in population distribution.

The age of conflict was brought to a conclusion by Shi Huangdi who conquered all his rivals and established the short-lived Qin Empire (221–206 BCE). However, its place was soon taken by the Han dynasty which ruled China for over four centuries (206 BCE–220 CE). The Han period saw Chinese culture enter its classical age, but this process was aided by a program of ruthless standardization imposed during the Qin Empire. The Han relaxed this program somewhat, claiming they were restoring the old ways.

At the center of these reforms, and a key to understanding Chinese civilization, was the way early Han emperors developed a bureaucracy to govern the empire. Schooled in the Confucian classics, officials were often recruited from a gentry class just below the aristocracy. They formed a loyal core which maintained the basic structure of Chinese government for 2,000 years.

The careful record-keeping of the Han bureaucracy and the preservation of archives over the next 2,000 years has enabled modern scholars to reconstruct the expansion of Chinese influence in the Yangzi river valley in the first two centuries of the common era. Maps 28A and 28B plot similar data on identical base maps. The outline of coasts and rivers picture the area that later became known as China. The data showing the population density of Chinese subjects has been derived from surviving records of periodic censuses taken by Han officials.

In general these two maps show a shift in population from agricultural areas in the northeast and northwest to the south. In the process, rice-growing increased as new techniques were perfected to take advantage of humid climates and a longer growing season. Farmers sometimes migrated from wheat-growing areas to take up new fields in the rice bowl. In the process, essential elements of Chinese civilization were established.

When viewing these maps one should not think that the Han emperors ruled only small enclaves in the far reaches of the base map. By extending civil administration over distant agricultural colonies, Han officials also gradually brought local princes and neighboring aboriginal peoples into the imperial fold.

Thus the Han Empire around 2 BCE included most of the Korean peninsula, all of the island of Hainan, and reached out with arm-like projections along the coast of the South China Sea and westward along the great central Asian trade route. Actually the Han influence extended even beyond Dunhuang in the far west because Chinese troops "protected" a series of oasis trading centers westward into the Tarim Basin.

The early Han capital, Chang'an (see p. 51), was located in the upland area where the Han River and Huang He come close together. The Han is a major tributary of the Yangzi, thus Han administrators had ready access to China's two great river valleys.

Classical India and South Asia

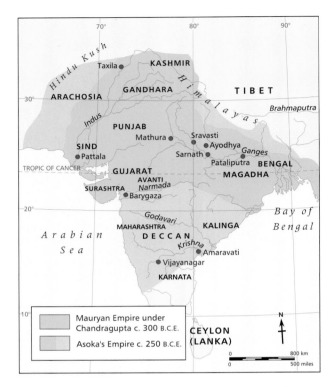

Map 29 Mauryan India, *c.*300–*c.*250 BCE. The Mauryan Empire reached out from the Ganges valley to annex the Indus valley peoples shortly after the death of Alexander the Great. Asoka extended the empire in all directions, but had an even greater impact in spreading the teachings of the Buddha throughout his realm. He had pillars erected at crossroads locations covered with edicts written in stone to proclaim his ideals.

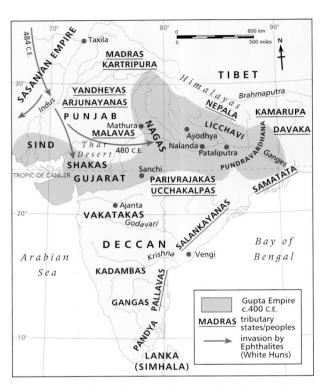

Map 30 Gupta India, *c.*400 CE. The Gupta practice of leaving the administration of the provinces in the hands of local leaders ushered in a period of prosperity and cultural flowering. As time went on, however, local governors grew stronger and were able to challenge the later Gupta emperors, especially after 400 CE when Gupta powers were expended in fighting off Hun invasions from Central Asia (see map 24, p. 39).

THERE is a long stretch of history on the Indian subcontinent about which little is known, in part because many of the texts from the early times have yet to be deciphered. Historians are working to reconstruct the events between the fall of the ancient Indus cities (see map 11, p. 26) and Persian and Hellenistic times (see maps 18 and 20, pp. 33 and 35). In the generation after Alexander, however, information resurfaces with the establishment of the Mauryan Empire by Chandragupta in 324 BCE.

By 240 BCE the Mauryan Empire reached its greatest extent, controlling the great river valleys of both the Ganges and Indus rivers. Of even more importance was the conversion of the emperor, Asoka, to Buddhism. He inscribed his new philosophy on special rock tablets throughout his empire, explaining a policy of nonviolence,

moderation, morality, and tolerance. The Mauryan Empire did not last very long, however, and India again became a collection of small states. Traditional ways reasserted themselves and the old religion regained control of the subcontinent. Now called Hinduism, which means "the ways of the Indians," it blended some new practices with the traditional structure of society.

The Hindu revival covered the subcontinent with Hindu temples and shrines which served as pilgrimage centers. The land's rivers, changed from destructive torrents into life-creating waters as they fell figuratively through the god Siva's hair, became sacred places where worshippers could purify themselves.

The Jain centers on map 32 point to another religion which, like Buddhism, developed out of ancient Indi-

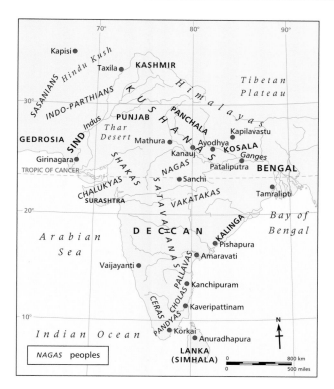

Map 31 Classical South Asia. It is essential to consider the varied cultures of the southern half of the subcontinent in any construction of the idea of Indian civilization. In recent years scholars in the West have become more aware of the importance of Indian Ocean trade routes in world history. When Alexander the Great reached the Indus river, Indian merchant vessels were already employed in centuries-old commerce between their home ports and lands across the Indian Ocean. Hordes of Roman coins uncovered in South Asia attest to the extent of later contacts with the Mediterranean world.

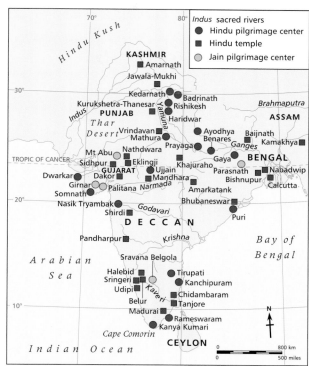

Map 32 Classical Sites of Hindu South Asia. The development of pilgrimage sites and major temples marked the emergence of Hinduism as a religion of the people, not just a preserve of the upper class brahmins. Jainism, dating back to the seventh century BCE, also became a religion of salvation when a great spiritual teacher gathered a group of disciples to found a religious order. The master was called Jina, "the conqueror," and the disciples became known as Jains.

an beliefs. Jainism emphasized the sanctity of all life which led the most devote followers to extreme forms of earthy denial, refusing to eat most foods.

The golden age of Hindu culture and Sanskrit literature took place in the period when the Gupta kings ruled an empire centered in the Ganges valley but also later reaching westward to the Arabian Sea. Samudra Gupta, son of the founder of the dynasty, embarked on a series of military expeditions between 330 and 380 CE. which resulted in a series of stunning victories in the Punjab, along the Bay of Bengal, and in the mountain kingdoms of the Himalayas.

Gupta practice after a military victory was to leave the defeated ruler in power, but turn him into a tribute-paying client (see map 30). A great flowering of arts and letters was encouraged by both Gupta emperors and the rulers of the vassal states, the latter competing with each other in patronizing scholars, writers, artists, and teachers.

After Asoka (*c.*250 BCE), various kingdoms south of the Ganges Valley developed their own local cultures, often based on distinct languages. These so called "ethnic states" included both rich provinces in fertile regions and fiercely independent tribes in the hill country (see map 31). In some ways the Deccan and surrounding areas can be considered an essential part of classical India, adding rich elements to the diverse cultural expressions co-existing on the Indian subcontinent.

The Common Era
The First Fifteen Centuries

CARTOGRAPHICALLY SPEAKING, the first great time period of the common era begins with Ptolemy and ends with Ptolemy, almost fifteen centuries apart. Claudius Ptolemy, who lived in Alexandria in the second century CE, summed up a new approach to constructing a world map developed by Greek thinkers over the previous five or six centuries.

Instead of starting with a cosmological scheme and drawing the earth deductively as it were, the Greeks eventually measured the earth and constructed a grid to represent its surface. They established the position of specific places by estimating and pacing off distances eastward from the lands furthest west (the Canary Islands) and measuring the angle of the sun to get a reading north of the equator. These specific locations were placed on the grid and then lines were drawn to create the natural features. Thus Ptolemy's *Geographia* was basically a book of key places and their positions, including directions on how to construct a graticule or grid that would minimize the distortion of reducing a globe to a flat surface. In effect, it was a set of instructions on how to make a world map.

PTOLEMAIC MAPS

The version shown here, probably based on late Byzantine Ptolemaic maps, was drawn in Florence around 1474 and is now kept in the Biblioteca Apostolica Vaticana in Rome. Each of the continents making up the Old World is clearly labeled. Europe is filled with place names. Africa reaches to the *terra incognita* beyond the Ethiopian interior and the sources of the Nile. Asia's great expanse is criss-crossed by long mountain ranges dividing it into isolated regions.

Note that only 180 degrees of longitude are represented on Ptolemaic maps, suggesting another half of the globe on the other side which is not pictured. The extension of the map northward to include Scandinavia uses data gathered long after Ptolemy wrote his book. On the Florentine map, the Scandinavian protrusion makes it look as if the known world is about to break out of its ancient Greek cartographic shell.

Ptolemy lived in a classical age and his books became classics in the Byzantine and Islamic civilizations. They were lost in Medieval Europe and then rediscovered during the Renaissance in the fifteenth century.

A GLOBAL CLASSICAL ERA

In nearly every geographical region, a classical age appeared between 1000 BCE and 500 CE which would continue to influence people right up to the present and which provide fundamental documents for the study of world history. In Western civilization, the classical foundations were laid in Greece and Rome during this era. Persia connected the heritage of ancient Mesopotamia with later peoples in the Near and Middle East. In South Asia, Buddhism emerged as a major religion and Hinduism developed its set of traditions. China's classical period coincided with the Han dynasty. In the western hemisphere, ways of living which developed in Mesoamerica and along the Andean slopes before 500 CE set patterns for later peoples to follow.

But world history after 300 CE is often characterized by severe disruptions. These occurred because of the decline of old centers of imperial power and the invasion of territories by new peoples from the steppes, forests, and deserts. The whole of Afro-Eurasia seemed to be convulsed by invasions of barbarian peoples and the adjustments demanded as new empires were formulated out of the old.

To focus entirely on the discontinuities, however, would overlook the significant ways in which old patterns persisted and the fact that classical traditions even expanded their domains. The Afro-Eurasian trading networks of antiquity were actually strengthened in this period by technical advances such as high-masted ships on the Indian Ocean, the digging of long canals in China, and an expansion of camel routes across the Sahara. At the edges of Eurasia, Europe and Japan developed distinctive civilizations.

EXPANDING ZONES

The Americas, southern Africa, and Australia remained outside of the world trading system but in the case of Mesoamerica and the Andean slope, the extent of influence for Native American civilizations extended over greater distances. It is appropriate therefore to call this era of world history one of expanding zones of intercommunication instead of the old references to the Dark Ages when historians once believed the lights of classical civilization were being extinguished by the invading barbarians.

The rise of Islam in the seventh century was the most dramatic example of the extension of religious influence over widespread areas of the Old World. Christianity at the same time was expanding north, west and northeast to the edges of Europe. Buddhist ideas were diffused to Southeast, Central, and East Asia. The Hindu tradition flowered in Asoka's India. But the meteoric rise of Islam sounded the theme of expanding zones most dramatically. As Map 38 so strikingly illustrates, Muslim influence spread from its core in Arabia to the Indus valley in the east and the Atlantic Ocean in the west in a matter of several centuries.

Then, in 1206, attention focused on the heartlands of Eurasia as Genghis Khan gathered together Mongol forces and started a wave of conquest which would eventually extend from Eastern Europe to the East China Sea.

Paralleling the land-based empires of the Mongols, Muslim forces to the south used the sea lanes of the Indian Ocean to extend their influence to the East Indies. By the mid-fourteenth century, when Ibn Battuta, the great travel writer, visited cities in Spain, North Africa, the Middle East, India, the East Indies, China, East Africa and along the Niger river, he could feel somewhat at home everywhere in the Islamic world.

GLOBAL INTERACTION IN THE MIDDLE AGES

Europe in the high or late Middle Ages also experienced periods of intensified interaction as trading networks over land and by sea linked its regions together and connected them by way of Mediterranean ports to the Old World commercial system. The traffic sponsored by these linkages unfortunately also brought the Black Death which dramatically cut populations in China, the Islamic world, and Europe as it spread along the routes of commerce.

As the period drew to a close, populations were recovering from the plague and the Mongol conquests, which had run their course. The Ming dynasty reclaimed China and the khanates of central Asia and Persia had become Islamicized, with power generally equally distributed in a series of regional states stretching across Asia. In the Mediterranean region the end finally came in 1453 for the Byzantine Empire, the last vestige of the Roman Empire.

Christianity and Judaism

ONE OF THE followers of Jesus who came to the fore in the early Christian church was a physician named Luke. In the generation after the death of Jesus Luke wrote a gospel, an account of the life and teachings of his savior, which contains the classic story of the birth of Jesus, followed by accounts of his ministry and miracles, suffering and death, resurrection and ascension. Luke then recounted the growth of the early church in a book called the Acts of the Apostles.

The most active apostle, at least according to Luke, was a former persecutor of the Christians, Saul of Tarsus. Saul was a Roman citizen from a commercial city in the far northeast corner of the Mediterranean Sea. Saul was also well schooled in the Jewish faith in which he was raised. He put his learning to good use after encountering the risen Jesus in a vision on the road from Jerusalem to Damascus in Syria. After this encounter Saul's name was changed to Paul and he spent the rest of his life as a missionary carrying the Christian gospel to people in Asia Minor, Greece, Rome, and possibly Spain. He sought both Jewish and gentile converts.

After gathering new Christians together into a local church, Paul would move on to the next city, keeping in contact with the group by way of letters and return visits. Map 33, featuring Paul's recorded journeys, shows how he criss-crossed the Greek-speaking part of the Roman Empire. As local churches treasured his longer letters, or epistles, they shared copies with other churches. These, along with the gospels, became the core of the Christian scriptures, called the New Testament.

When Paul arrived in a city to begin his mission work, he called first on Jewish families. Most of the commer-

Map 33 Paul's Missionary Journeys, *c.*46–64 CE. The early Christian churches in Asia Minor were strung like beads along overland trade routes. The seven churches of Asia identified on the map refer to the work of John, another disciple of Jesus. John wrote a gospel, plus several short epistles and the celebrated apocalyptic book of Revelation. This latter work, which was placed at the very end of the New Testament, begins with letters to the seven churches of Asia.

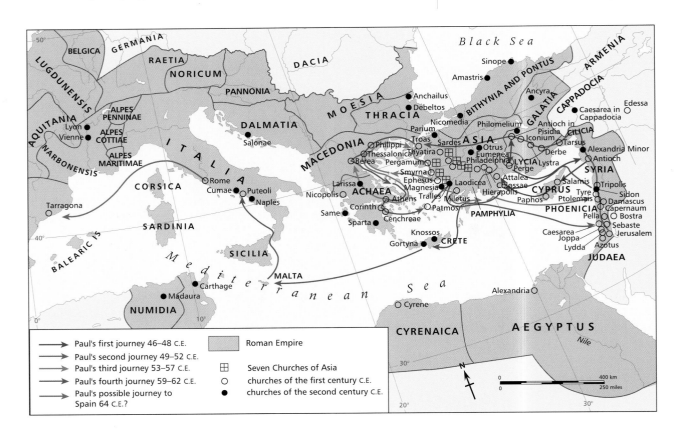

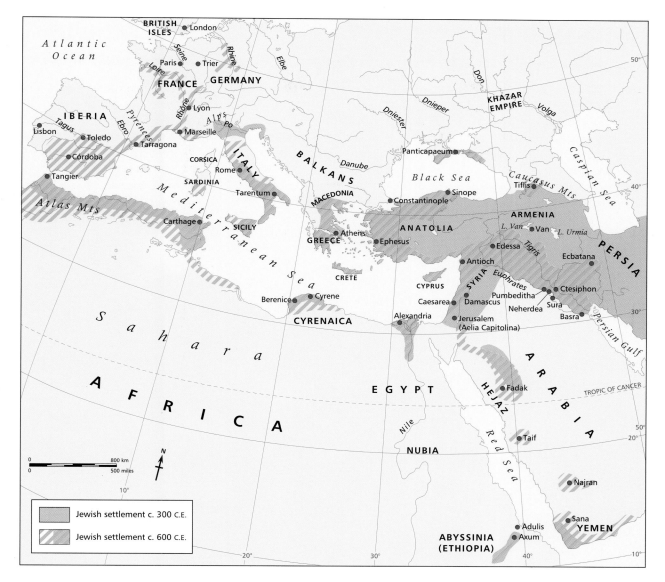

Map 34 The Jewish Diaspora, 66–600 CE. The dispersal of the Jewish people throughout the Near East, Europe, and parts of Africa continued a pattern of movement and forced migration described in the Hebrew Bible. During Hellenistic times, Jewish families often engaged in trade and settled in cities and ports throughout the Greek-speaking world. With the rise of Rome and Carthage in the western Mediterranean, Jewish colonies could be found in today's Algeria and in southern Italy. Jewish people also made their way along trading routes paralleling the Red Sea.

cial centers in the Mediterranean world in the first century CE had a Jewish community. But troubled times were just ahead for both Christians and Jews in the Roman Empire. Because of their strong religious convictions, and their monotheism, clashes with imperial authorities upholding the state religion became commonplace, especially when Roman emperors began behaving more like oriental potentates than "first citizens."

Paul was executed in Rome, apparently during the reign of Nero, around 67 CE. The apostle Peter, one of the original twelve disciples of Jesus, and the traditional leader of the Christian church at Rome, also became a martyr about the same time.

Meanwhile, back in Palestine, many Jewish people rose in revolt against the Roman overlords in 66 CE. The Romans put down the uprising and destroyed the Temple at Jerusalem in 70 CE. Resistance however continued until the year 135. On each occasion, imperial authorities systematically expelled Jewish families from Palestine, augmenting the Diaspora.

China Under the Sui and Tang Dynasties, 581–906 CE

THE DISINTEGRATION of the Han Empire in China in the third century CE was due to both internal weaknesses and external attacks which led to a series of regional states with shifting boundaries. Some of these kingdoms followed the traditional Chinese pattern, governed by an emperor claiming broad territories and administered by a bureaucracy educated in the Confucian classics. In recognition of the persistence of some elements of Han civilization, this period is sometimes called the "Era of the Six Dynasties" (220–581 CE).

In other kingdoms, however, especially in the north and west, different cultural influences were stronger. Here invading peoples took control and turned to new ways of governing. It is in this climate that Buddhism gained a foothold in China against the inveterate Confucian outlook.

Toward the end of the sixth century CE, one of the regional kingdoms was able to bring a semblance of unity to China as it extended its rule to Korea and Southeast

Map 35 China under the Sui and Tang Dynasties, 581–906 CE. The intense development of the extensive coastal plain of northeastern China, along the Yellow Sea, is clearly shown by the cluster of major prefectures on this map. Note how the important canals dug during the Sui dynasty served this area (see map 37). One of the most significant roads in the Tang period connected the port of Guangzhou with Chang'an, the Tang capital city, permitting commercial goods from the Indian Ocean trade to reach the emperor. Products from Africa, India, Malaya and the East Indies traveled over this route.

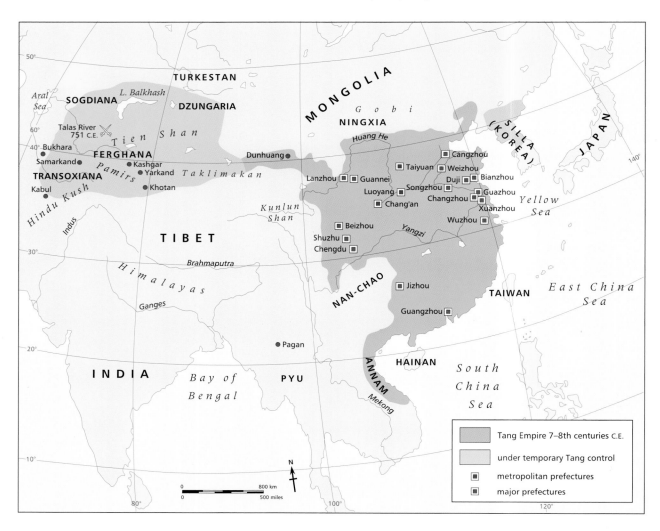

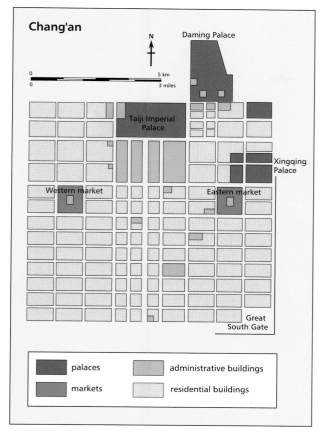

Map 36 Chang'an. The Tang built their new capital city in the Wei valley, recalling the first Han administrative center (see map 27, p. 42). The location provided ready access to the concentrations of people served by the canals on the plain, the rice paddies along the Yangzi River and in south China, and also to the silk road across central Asia along which the Tang armies marched. Goods sold at the city markets thus came from every part of Asia, as well as from India, Africa, and even Europe. Chang'an had a population of about a million people when it served as the Tang capital.

Asia. To solidify its center, the new Sui Dynasty rushed to complete the Grand Canal connecting the Huang He and the Yangzi rivers. But the pace of expansion and the drive toward unification led to discontent, revolts, and, eventually, a state of anarchy. In 618 CE a military family, the Li, established order and created the Tang dynasty which would rule China until 906 CE.

The Li clan had roots in the Turkic peoples who invaded northern China several centuries earlier. Li officers intermarried with daughters of Chinese officials, gaining a cosmopolitan outlook that enabled them to combine the best of both worlds. This gave them an important military advantage when they placed advanced weapons such as the Chinese crossbow in the hands of expert horsemen from the steppes of Central Asia. By 650 CE the Tang had the mightiest armies on earth and were pushing westward across the Great Silk Road, eventually controlling territories reaching to the gates of Bukhara and Kabul.

In 751 CE Chinese forces engaged Arab armies on the Talas river in Central Asia, fighting to a draw. This marked the extent of advance by both civilizations. Note that this battle is also located on map 38 (see p. 52) outlining the early expansion of Islam.

The expansion of Chinese influence under the Sui and Tang can be traced by the use of paper in various parts of Asia. An invention first used by the Han bureaucracy in the second century BCE, paper was soon used throughout China, appearing in Dunhuang by 366 CE. Chinese interest in eastward expansion toward Korea and Japan brought paper to these regions by the early seventh century. By the end of that century the paper trail had extended across Central Asia to Samarkand.

The Arabs may have been introduced to paper as a result of the battle on the Talas river, for that very year paper is mentioned in historical records at Baghdad. Over the next three centuries it would spread westward across the Islamic world. Slowly paper was introduced to Europe by way of Spain and Italy.

Map 37 The Canal System of the East China Plain, *c.*700 CE. The extent of the canal system on the East China plain reached several thousand miles under the Sui emperors. The canals were augmented by a system of imperial roads which reached in every direction, providing China with an integrated transportation system. The Grand Canal, from Luoyang to Hangzhou, connected China's two great river systems. Major portions of this great waterway were dug in a seven-year period by forcing all common people along the route to do their share, a total of five or six million workers.

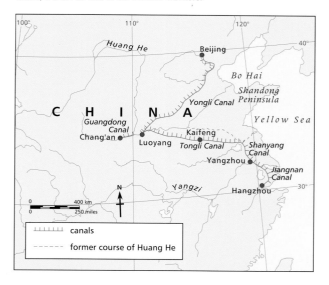

The Creation of the Islamic World after 622 CE

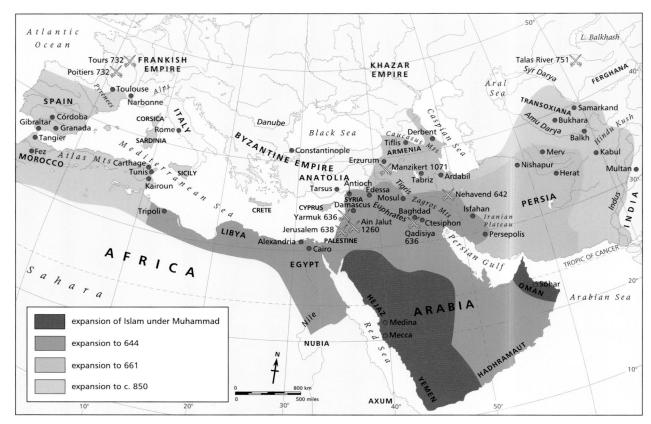

THIS MAP presents the rapid expansion of Muslim territory from 622 to about 850 CE. To trace these developments one must start on the Arabian Peninsula. Mecca, a commercial center on a trade route that paralleled the Red Sea, connected the Mediterranean basin with the Indian Ocean. It was also a place of pilgrimage for local Arabian tribes who had enshrined their gods in a famous sanctuary, the Ka'ba.

Muhammad the prophet, a former trader, received messages from an angel calling for submission to the one true god. At first the call to become *muslim* ("submission" in Arabic) was rejected by the people of Mecca. In 622 CE Muhammad was forced to flee to a neighboring town which received him. The place of refuge was renamed "the city of the prophet," or Medina.

The event marked the beginning of the Muslim calendar and started the spread of the faith which soon covered extensive areas in Arabia. After the prophet's death in 632 CE, successors to his leadership (caliphs) contin-

Map 38 The Expansion of Islam, 622–c.850 CE. In 732 CE Frankish armies were able to stop the Muslim advance into Europe. Note how sea power enabled the forces of Islam to wrest control of the islands in the western Mediterranean Sea from the Byzantine Empire after 756 CE. By this time the Abbasid clan had seized power from the Umayyads, forcing the latter to set up a new caliphate in Spain. The Abbasids then built another new capital eastward at Baghdad. By 850 CE Bukhara and Samarkand on the Great Silk Road had become Muslim cities and the new religion was poised to cross the Indus into South Asia.

ued to advance the faith, conquering Egypt and Mesopotamia by 644 CE. Then another clan took over the caliphate, extending the conquests even further, and built up the empire's sea power. Continued disputes over the succession of leadership slowed down the expansion. Then the new Umayyad dynasty moved its capital from Arabia to Damascus to facilitate expansion to the east.

By shifting the political center of the Islamic world from the Hejaz to a more central location in the Near East, the new caliphs picked up locational advantages at the

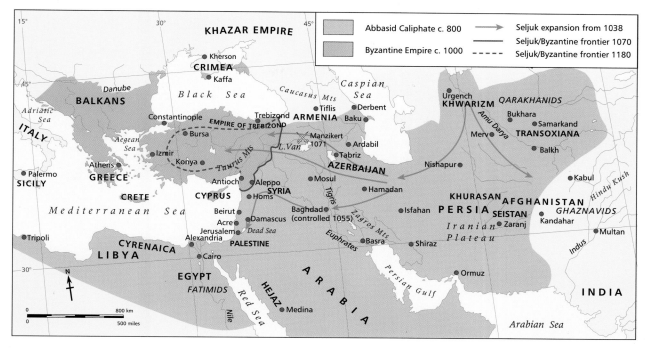

Map 39 The Byzantine Empire and Islam, c.800–c.1200 CE. The Byzantine Empire served as a bulwark against Islamic expansion for centuries. It was gradually forced to give ground in the Near East and eventually in Asia Minor as well.

same time they escaped the bitter rivalries of the original Arab followers of Muhammad. From Damascus the Umayyads developed an administrative structure that paralleled earlier Roman and Persian examples.

Fearing the loss of the purity of the original caliphate, the followers of the family of Ali contested the leadership of the Umayyads. Ali, a cousin and son-in-law of Muhammad, had taken his place in a ruse that enabled the great prophet to avoid assassins in Mecca and escape to Medina. Ali was passed over when a caliph was appointed after Muhammad's death. He later claimed the title, but was cut down by zealots in 661 CE who objected to his agreement to mediate the struggle with the Umayyads.

From then on, the Shi'a, the supporters of Ali, formed a branch of Islam that eventually centered in Persia. Over the centuries the Shi'a community developed distinct beliefs, ceremonies, and legal traditions that set it apart from the majority of Muslims, called the Sunni, which originally supported the Umayyad caliphs.

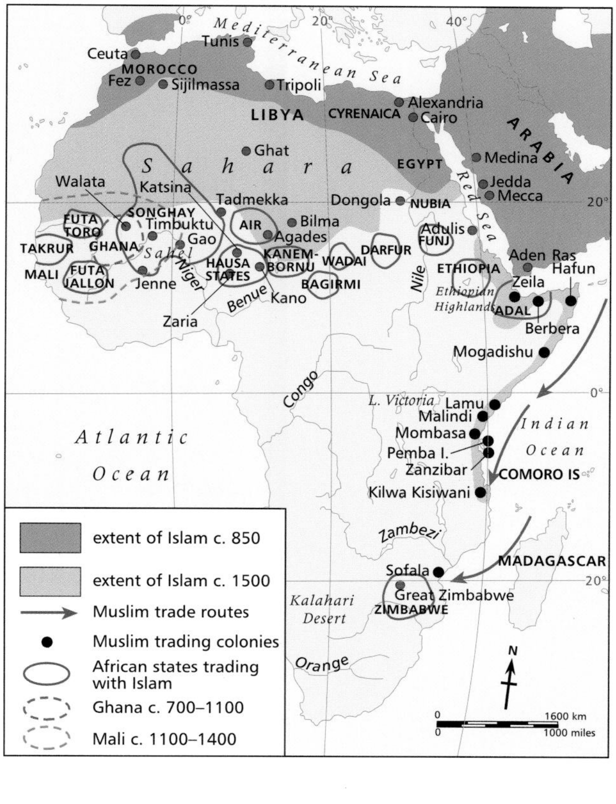

Map 40 Islam in Africa. Muslim forces took control of Egypt and Libya by 644 CE, a scant dozen years after the death of Muhammad. Two centuries later they had spread westward across the entire Mediterranean shoreline. Then various expeditions took Islam across the Sahara to the trading cities at the southern edge of the desert. Meanwhile Muslim trading colonies were being established along Africa's coast on the Indian Ocean. Here the Swahili language was used to facilitate commercial transactions. Swahili was a Bantu language which gradually incorporated a large number of Arabic words and was written in Arabic script.

The Spread of Islam to South and Southeast Asia

T HE STORY of the spread of Islam to the Indus valley, on to the Indian subcontinent, and then to Southeast Asia and the East Indies began after the landmark battle on the Talas river in 751 CE. (see map 35, p. 50). Here a Chinese army of the Tang Empire was stopped in its westward campaign by Muslim forces under the rule of a provincial commander based in the far northeastern province of Muslim lands. As the Chinese gradually pulled back from the interior basin, which drained into the Aral Sea, Turkic peoples made their way south across

Map 41 The Expansion of Islam in South and Southeast Asia to 1600 CE. Muslim traders entered China in this period by land and by sea. Islamic influence spread eastward into the cities of Central Asia along the routes of the Silk Road, eventually reaching as far east as Lanzhou on the headwaters of the Huang He and at the very end of the Great Wall.

Other Muslim traders came to China by sea, using the Strait of Malacca to sail from the Indian Ocean into the South China Sea. Both Canton and Fuzhou had long established Islamic quarters.

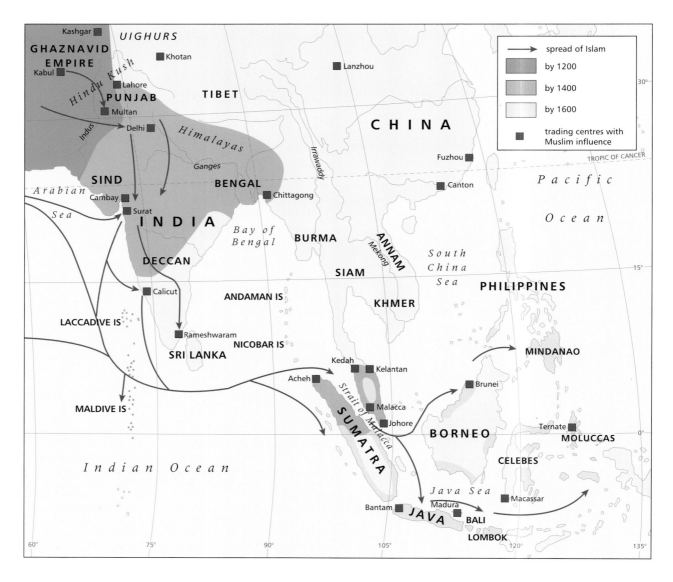

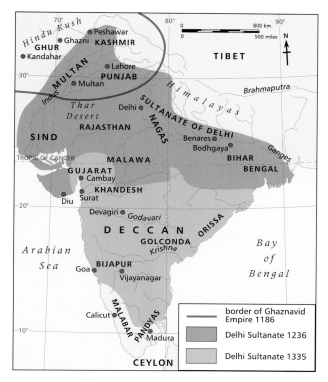

Map 42 The Delhi Sultanate, 1211–1526 CE. The Muslim advance into India took advantage of the diversity of the Hindu states which were divided and engaged in constant internal struggles. Islamic emphasis on one god and the unity of the faithful gave their leaders an advantage in the rise of the Delhi sultanate. Delhi, the capital city, was placed in a strategic location controlling the major route between the upper Indus river basin and the Ganges river valley.

these lands to settle on the borderlands of the Abbasid caliphate centered in Baghdad.

Gradually the Turks became assimilated into the Abbasid Empire, soon serving as the backbone of the army. By 1055 CE the Abbasid caliph recognized a Turkish general as sultan, or military chief, who held power alongside the caliph. Soon the Turkish sultan had more power than the caliph who became a mere figurehead.

Several branches of the Turkic peoples then sought riches and power by attacking neighboring states. The Saljuqs turned westward and defeated Byzantine forces as they took over Asia Minor (see map 39, p. 53). The Ghaznavid clan, meanwhile, struck out to the east into Afghanistan and the Indus valley. Eventually they established a sultanate with its capital at Delhi. From this base they conquered the lands drained by the Ganges river and soon claimed to rule all of northern India.

The Turkic invaders of India first sought booty from both the palaces of local rulers and the temples or shrines located in Buddhist and Hindu religious centers. The Turks sometimes slaughtered local officials and religious leaders, encouraging the people to abandon the old polity and convert to Islam. But as the power of the Delhi Sultanate reached deeper into India, it met with less and less success. Buddhist and Hindu communities remained intact, blunting the Islamic advance to the east.

Here the Muslim traders on the Indian Ocean took over, spreading their faith by establishing commercial outposts in Malaya and the East Indian islands. The expansion of Islam in Southeast Asia was a gradual affair, gaining a foothold along the Strait of Malacca by the twelfth century, and then spreading throughout the tropical islands over the next four centuries.

Meanwhile the Delhi sultanate progressed through five dynasties, finally expiring in 1526 CE. Map 42 shows the empire at its greatest extent, around 1335 CE. At that time, most of India was ruled from strongholds scattered throughout the subcontinent from which imperial authorities extracted taxes and tribute from the local population.

Although as many as one quarter of the Buddhists and Hindus in India eventually converted to Islam, they often brought many elements of their old beliefs into their new faith. In some areas, Muslim practices and beliefs exhibited a new diversity and honored mystical approaches to the faith.

Hindu communities in India were able to accommodate themselves to Muslim rule much more successfully than Buddhist areas. The latter were almost completely eradicated by Turkic forces, which seemed to take special delight in destroying Buddhist libraries and monasteries throughout India. Thus the Buddhist presence in the land of its birth was greatly reduced.

The Mongol World

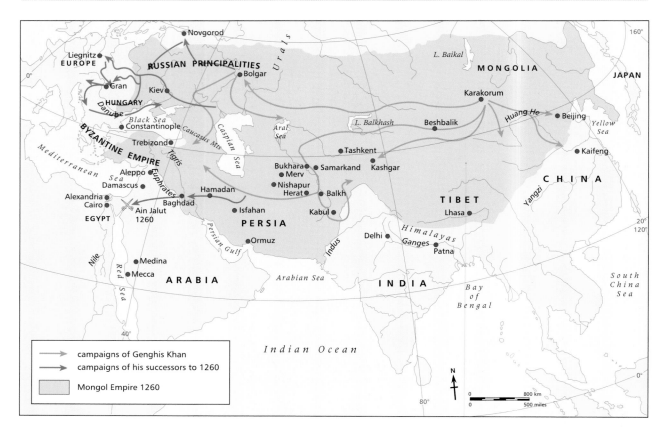

Map 43 The Mongol World, 1206–1260 CE. Note that the Great Khan controlled parts of northern China from the days of Genghis Khan's earliest victories. The map shows that Mongol rule extended only to the upper Huang He and the north China plain around Beijing. At the time, however, Kublai Khan, a grandson of Genghis, was besieging cities along the Grand Canal. Mongol forces, after a long, difficult campaign that lasted nearly 35 years, finally deposed the last emperor in the Song dynasty and reunited Chinese lands in 1279. Kublai and his family took the name of Yuan as emperors of China. At Beijing they planned a great capital which later became known as the Forbidden City.

THE MONGOLS were a group of people from the steppes of Central Asia. Like the Scythians of ancient times and the Huns and Turks of more recent ages, the Mongols were nomads who pastured their herds on far-flung grasslands in the heartlands of Eurasia. Settlers in favored locations in this vast region had learned to coexist with these nomads by offering tribute to the horsemen in return for protection. Because the size of these payments was enhanced by commerce, Mongol policies encouraged long distance trade and ushered in a flowering of activity along the Great Silk Road which provided a backbone for their lands.

Because of their warlike activities, one group of Mongols received so much tribute that they decided to make conquest their first order of business. Their khan, or leader, was given the name Genghis, and eventually led his warriors back and forth across the continent in the process of building the most extensive empire the world had ever seen. His successors carried Mongol campaigns west-

ward into the heart of Europe and to the shores of the Red Sea.

By 1260, 33 years after the death of Genghis Khan, Mongol rule extended across Eurasia. Some regions were under the control of Il-khans or secondary khans who ruled independently but owed allegiance to the Great Khan in Mongolia. By then the Mongols occupied the leadership positions in the army and in the government, with most of the soldiers and officials being recruited from the subject populations.

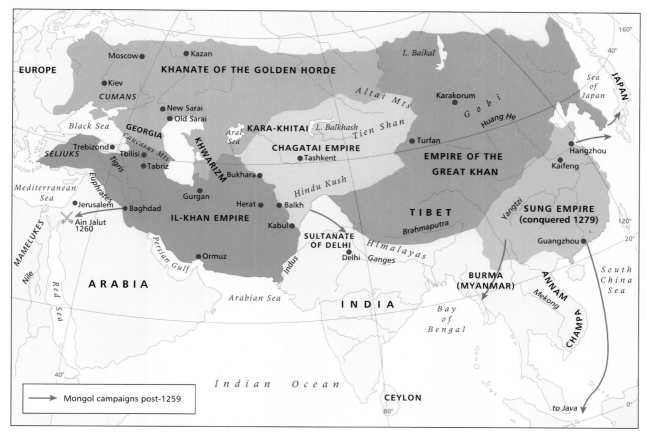

Map 44 Mongol Successor States, *c.*1260–*c.*1360. The death of Mongke, the grandson of Genghis Khan, in 1259 led to the formal division of Mongol territories into separate regional empires. Borders and relative power shifted often in the next century, but China remained the largest and most populous empire in the world, the Mongols calling themselves the Yuan dynasty.

In 1258 a grandson of Genghis Khan seized Baghdad and killed the last Abbasid caliph. Mongol fortunes declined several years later at the hands of the sultan of Egypt.

Less than a century later the Ming dynasty had chased the Mongols out of China. Meanwhile, a Turkic leader came to dominate the Near East. Around 1370 CE Timur the Lame built a capital at Samarkand and then started a series of campaigns that eventually expanded his territory into an extensive empire. Timur's armies eventually sacked Delhi, invaded the Ottoman Empire, and weakened the Golden Horde in southern Russia. At his death in 1405 he was planning an invasion of China. His empire soon disintegrated, with power passing to three notable centers of rule: the Ottomans based in Asia Minor, the Safavids in Persia, and the Mughals in India.

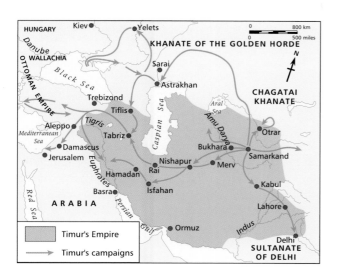

Map 45 The Empire of Timur, 1405. Timur seems to have had two personalities. One appreciated cities, with their great buildings, fine gardens, and centers of learning. For example, he spent several days discussing affairs with the great Islamic scholar Ibn Khaldun. The second persona was that of a ruthless conqueror who took great pleasure in destruction and the suffering of others. Timur's death in 1405 ended the period of history when nomads from the steppe lands shook the foundations of civilizations throughout Eurasia.

World Trade Before the Global Age, 400–1400 CE

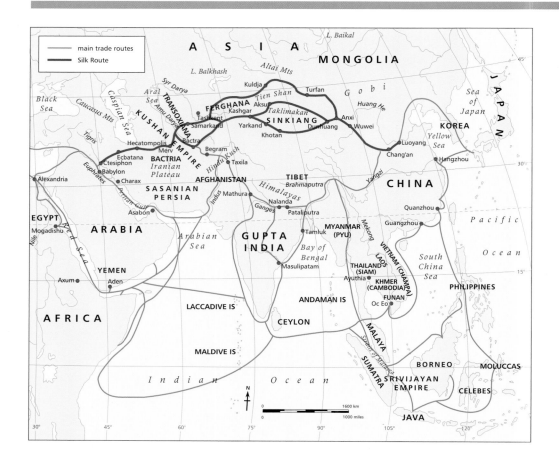

WHEN ONE tries to put together the entire sweep of history in the Afro-Eurasian world for the first 15 centuries of the Common Era, it is natural to think about trade routes. Empires rose and fell, Islamic civilization emerged and matured, dynasties came and went in China, but basic patterns of commerce endured throughout the period.

There were, of course, major disruptions in the flow of commerce. And most of the goods traded found their way only into wealthy homes. It was a rare occurrence when the stirrings of commerce were felt by the common folk. And yet, in spite of interruptions and the selective nature of the trade goods, the enduring silk road across Central Asia, as well as the persistent trade routes across the Mediterranean Sea, the Indian Ocean, and the South China Sea provide a continuity to help us see 15 centuries as parts of a common era.

Map 46 Asian Trade Routes, c.400 CE. Sometimes rivers showed the way for important commercial routes and at other times they seem to have had little influence on the overall pattern of long-distance trade. The Nile is presented here as a major route only as far as the first cataract when the passageway took a sharp detour across the desert to the Red Sea. The Euphrates, Ganges, and Irrawaddy rivers, in contrast, guide major commercial arteries for almost their entire length.

Map 46 presents the major routes in Asia around the year 400 CE. It is difficult to pin an exact date on this map because of constantly shifting patterns and commercial centers. The placenames do not all fit one particular year, but it is important to see the patterns, both by land and sea, east and west, north and south. The point is that no region touched by these commercial routes could be totally isolated from the others. Outbreaks of the plague, the dissemination of technology like the manufacture of paper, and the use of silk cloth throughout the ecumene demonstrate that truism.

And the trade went on year after year. As Columbus and his colleagues set off on their voyages of discovery in the late fifteenth and early sixteenth centuries, the world's trading spheres continued to function without noticing the momentous events characterized by the year 1492. Note that transatlantic voyages are not indicated on this map, nor is the Atlantic Ocean employed as a major avenue of commerce anywhere except in Europe. The color code also makes it clear that world trade around 1500 CE was really a series of separate systems, often connected, but sus-

tained largely by exchange within the region's own spheres rather than depending on interaction with other regions.

The Mesoamerican trading zone focused on tribute payments which sustained the Aztec Empire, but its routes also extended way beyond the boundaries of Aztec control. Commerce in the Inca/Andean sphere was encouraged by a series of magnificent roads, paved and properly graded. Note how this system extended over 30 degrees of latitude and had two major arteries: a low route along the shore and a high road along the Andean slope.

The Arab-dominated Indian Ocean system connected merchants on all three continents that made up the Old World. The Red Sea and the Persian Gulf provided ways for Indian Ocean ships to reach far north of the Tropic of Cancer with their cargo and passengers. Indian Ocean merchants also had well established connections with sealanes along the Chinese coast and in the Mediterranean Sea. The Saharan routes, both north-south and east-west are shown as extensions of the Indian Ocean system because most of the trade was in the hands of Arab merchants. The coastal trade in the South China Sea appears on the map as an integral part of the trans-Asian commercial system that reached from Japan all the way across Asia.

Map 47 World Trade Routes, 1100–1500. The European trading zone had a definite north-south orientation with four major passageways: (1) from Constantinople north through Kiev; (2) from Venice at the head of the Adriatic Sea over the Alps to Germany and the low countries; (3) another leg of the above route which took different passes across the mountains from Genoa in the western part of the Mediterranean; and (4) the north and western coastal trade which connected the commerce of the Baltic and North Seas with that of the Mediterranean world.

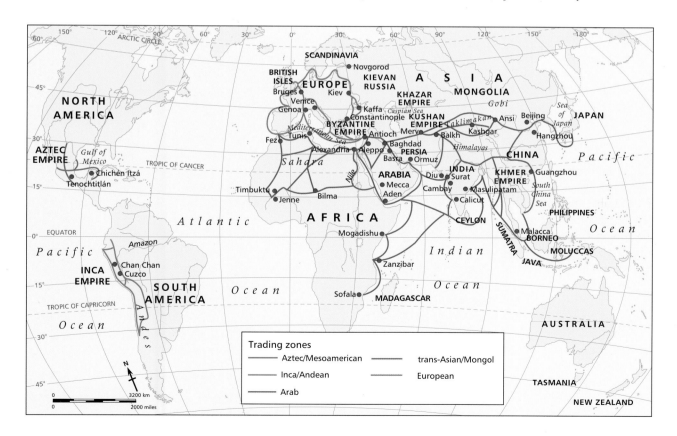

The Americas, 1000–1520 CE

THE AMERICAS in the five centuries before contact with the Old World were filled with numerous peoples speaking a great variety of languages and following diverse cultural traditions. In two general locations agriculture had supported large populations for a thousand years, producing two classical civilizations which continued to flourish throughout this period.

In Mesoamerica, the narrowing band of land connecting North and South America, a single empire never united the entire area. The ancient Maya peoples continued to occupy a belt of land southward from the Yucatan Peninsula as they had for centuries. But Mayan political organization was characterized by a variety of small city states which competed with each other but never coalesced into a unified empire.

The Aztecs, however, were aggressive imperialists who migrated from the north into the valley of Mexico, constructing twin capital cities on islands in the shallow waters of Lake Texcoco where Mexico City thrives today. The militaristic Aztecs soon subjected nearby peoples and controlled an extensive trading network in the region.

Along the western slopes of the Andes in South America another aggressive people, the Inca, put together a vast empire in little more than a century, from around 1380 to 1493. The Inca were a pastoral people with enormous flocks of llamas and alpacas. From their capital at Cuzco, just northwest of Lake Titicaca, they sent out military expeditions to add additional regions to their empire. Their practice was to leave the old ruling families in place to administer their conquests, taking the children of the former rulers and images of their local gods back to Cuzco as hostages.

Macchu Picchu ("old peak") was an Inca fortress in the Andes which was so well hidden that later Spanish invaders never found it. Although located only 50 m (80.5 km) from Cuzco and covering an area of 5 sq. m (8 sq. km), this major urban centre was not rediscovered until 1911 when a shepherd led an archaeologist to the site, then covered with dense vegetation.

Although only a portion of the lands on this map are highlighted, the blank spaces were filled with hundreds of different peoples, most of whom relied on an agricultural base for their economies. On Hispaniola and Cuba, for example, the Tainos, whom Columbus met in 1492, were one of at least three groups who inhabited these major islands. The oldest inhabitants, in the western portion of Cuba, had come from Middle America thousands of years earlier. The Saladoids, who arrived later, apparently pushed the first people out of Hispaniola and most of Cuba about 600 CE. The newcomers brought a farming culture from South America to the islands. The Tainos, who probably descended, at least in part, from the Saladoids, were an advanced agricultural society, raising cassava, sweet potatoes, peanuts, pineapples, cotton, tobacco, and a variety of other plants.

Trading networks also helped new ideas spread across the continents. Contact by sea between Peru and the west coast of Mesoamerica probably occurred on a regular basis between 300 and 900 CE. The islands of the Caribbean Sea encouraged sea-faring people to venture to new areas. In the northern coastal regions of South America and throughout the great basins of the Orinoco and Amazon rivers, a multitude of tribal groups lived in rainforest villages. Although these peoples had contact with Andean civilizations, the restricted amount of available land and the leaching of the soil by the constant heavy rains prevented large agricultural surpluses. As a result, populations were scattered and low in density.

Many peoples living in North America more directly felt the influence of the Mesoamerican civilizations, but probably by land routes rather than by sea. Maize, the staple crop of the Aztec and their predecessors in Mexico, had become widely cultivated by 1500, reaching as far north as the growing season permitted.

The immense temple mounds characteristic of Mesoamerican civilizations were also duplicated in North America along the Mississippi and on the Gulf Coastal Plain. Some of these temple-mound sites had been abandoned by 1500 CE, especially in the upper Mississippi valley, and different cultural traditions had taken their place. But the dense populations needed to support the temple towns were often intact in 1500 in the southeastern part of North America. These populations were probably decimated by the European diseases that reached them indirectly after 1500.

Map 48 Precolumbian America, *c.*1500. At first, the Incas pushed north all the way to the equator. After 1471 they turned to the west and south, eventually ruling an empire extending over 27 degrees of latitude, roughly the distance from Hudson Bay in Canada to Cuba.

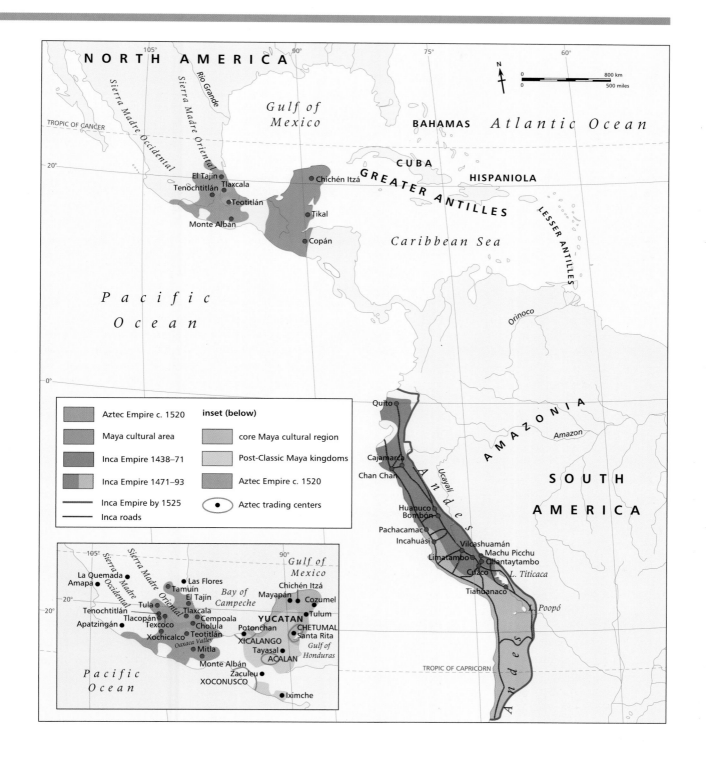

NORTH AMERICA

105°   90°   75°   60°

N

800 km
500 miles

Sierra Madre Occidental   *Sierra Madre Oriental*   *Rio Grande*

Gulf of Mexico

TROPIC OF CANCER

BAHAMAS   *Atlantic Ocean*

20°

CUBA   **HISPANIOLA**

El Tajín
Tlaxcala   Chichén Itzá   **GREATER ANTILLES**
Tenōchtitlán
Teotitlán   **LESSER ANTILLES**
Tikal
Monte Albán   *Caribbean Sea*
Copán

Pacific Ocean

0°

Orinoco

Quito

AMAZONIA   *Amazon*

Cajamarca

Chan Chan   **SOUTH AMERICA**

Andes   *Ucayali*

Huánuco
Bombón

Pachacamac
Incahuási   Vilcashuamán
Limatambo   Machu Picchu
Ollantaytambo
Cuzco   L. Titicaca
Tiahuanaco

Legend:
- Aztec Empire c. 1520
- Maya cultural area
- Inca Empire 1438–71
- Inca Empire 1471–93
- Inca Empire by 1525
- Inca roads

inset (below)
- core Maya cultural region
- Post-Classic Maya kingdoms
- Aztec Empire c. 1520
- ● Aztec trading centers

Inset map:

105°   90°

Sierra Madre Occidental   *Sierra Madre Oriental*   *Gulf of Mexico*

La Quemada   Las Flores   Chichén Itzá
Amapa   Tamuín   Mayapán   Cozumel
El Tajín   *Bay of Campeche*
Tula   Tlaxcala   Tulum
Tenōchtitlán   Cempoala   **YUCATAN**
Tlacopán   Cholula   Potonchan   **CHETUMAL**
Apatzingán   Texcoco   **XICALANGO**   Santa Rita
Xochicalco   Teotitlán   Tayasal   *Gulf of Honduras*
Oaxaca Valley   Mitla   **ACALAN**
Monte Albán   Zaculeu
XOCONUSCO
Pacific Ocean   Iximche

20°

L. Poopó

TROPIC OF CAPRICORN

Andes

Africa, 1000–1500 CE

THE BASE for this map is a simple outline of the African continent and the lands, seas, and islands that surround it. To the east is the Atlantic Ocean whose currents and winds as well as a smooth regular coastline did not encourage contact between places along the littoral. The Mediterranean Sea to the north is more irregular and in some areas enjoys a salubrious climate, but the Sahara in historic times has constantly expanded northward toward the sea, limiting the continent's productivity in the north. The valley of the Nile, however, cutting through the desert, has been one of the world's most productive agricultural regions for many millennia.

The Red Sea, over 1,000 miles (1,600km) long, separates Africa from Arabia but brings the Indian Ocean almost up to the Mediterranean Sea. The Indian Ocean on the continent's east coast, has some fine ports, a variety of off-shore islands, and a favorable pattern of winds and currents. These maritime advantages have connected East Africa to the trading system of the Indian Ocean almost since the very beginning of world trade. It is no accident that Madagascar shares its language, many food plants, and other cultural traditions with Southeast Asia.

The Equator, crossing Lake Victoria in East Africa, divides the continent into two unequal parts. The smaller portion in the southern hemisphere is the more forested region, but it also includes the Kalahari Desert. Africa north of the Equator is dominated by the Sahara, a forbidding desert that stretches across the entire continent. The Sahara forms a cultural as well as a physical divide. The peoples north of the Sahara are oriented to the Mediterranean Sea and gradually became Muslim.

Although most of Africa is in the tropics, and hence has hot climates, these are moderated by relatively high elevations, especially in East Africa. The continent is mostly elevated on plateaus, which provide little room for coastal plains. Africa's rivers thus fall over rapids near their mouths, blocking passage to the interior.

The empires of the period 1000–1500 CE, which are the focal points on this map, are concentrated along the southern boundary of the Sahara. Extensive grasslands encouraged the herding of animals and offered ease of transport across long distances.

Many cities that were prominent in the period 1000–1500 CE are located by red dots. Note that three major empires in West Africa are indicated by the colored

Map 49 African Kingdoms, 1000–1500 CE. Africa's vegetation east of the Great Rift Valley followed a different pattern. The empire of Zimbabwe, for example, occupied the plateau above the rainforest areas near the coast. Zimbabwe is located in southeast Africa across the Mozambique Channel from Madagascar. With the increased elevation, a mixed tropical forest turned into the savanna. The different ecosystems produced a variety of products and the local economy centered on farming and the herding of cattle. The great stone buildings and towers of Great Zimbabwe, however, reflected the city's role in international trade, exporting salt, copper, and gold from nearby mines.

lines showing their approximate limits. These overlap because one empire succeeded the other in dominance as the centuries passed. Note how the Almohad Empire shifted around 1140 to become more of a Mediterranean state as its predecessor waned in the western Sahara.

The blue lines outline other major states in Africa that arose from time to time. Not all of these states existed at any particular date, and it should be emphasized that throughout this period people lived in all parts of the continent. Even the blank spaces on the map were inhabited by vibrant cultures, except in the most forbidding portions of the desert.

To make the dry bones of this basic information come to life, consult map 47 which shows the world-wide trade routes around 1350 CE. Note how Africa was connected to the Mediterranean world by caravan routes across the Sahara and also involved in the flourishing Indian Ocean commerce.

Another way to put this map into perspective is to note the various vegetation zones into which Africa is divided. Start at the equator in the Congo Basin where it crosses the 20th east meridian. From here the tropical rainforest extends in every direction until the savanna belts take over. These grasslands are broken by lines of trees following along the watercourses. Oyo, Ife, and Benin are prominent rainforest city-states on this map. Most of the states, from Takrur in the west to Ethiopia in the east lie in the transition zone where forest lands merge into grasslands in the savanna. Some, like the Air, were almost entirely located on the steppes that ring the deserts. The steppe landscapes are characterized by short, bunched grasses and very few trees.

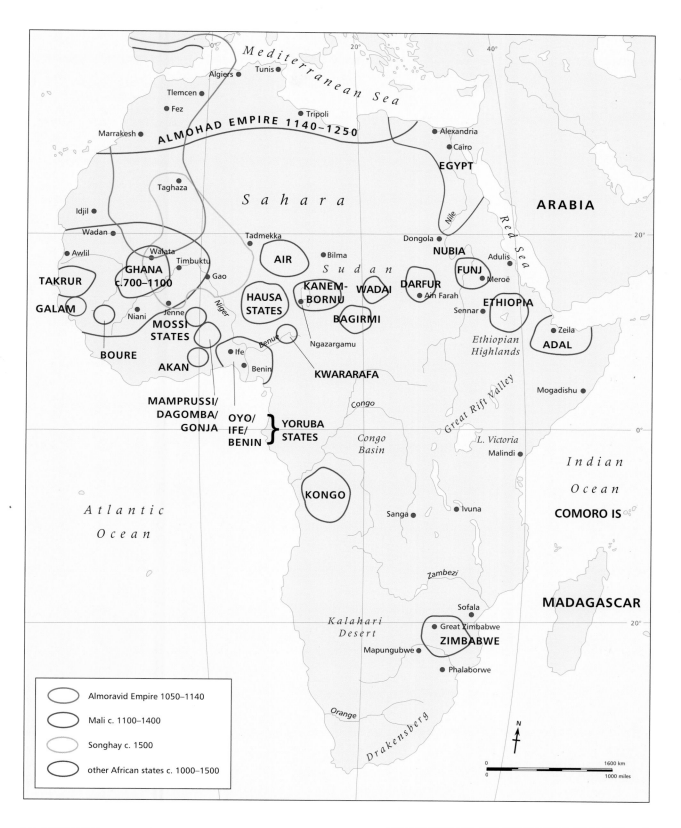

Mediterranean Sea

Algiers
Tunis
Tlemcen
Fez
Tripoli
Marrakesh

ALMOHAD EMPIRE 1140–1250

Alexandria
Cairo

EGYPT

ARABIA

Sahara

Taghaza

Idjil

Wadan
Tadmekka
Dongola
NUBIA
Adulis
Red Sea

Awlil
Walata
Timbuktu
AIR
Bilma
FUNJ
Meroë

TAKRUR
GHANA
c.700–1100
Gao
Sudan
HAUSA
STATES
KANEM-
BORNU
WADAI
DARFUR
Aïn Farah
ETHIOPIA
Zeila

GALAM
Niger
BAGIRMI
Sennar
ADAL

Niani
Jenne
MOSSI
STATES
Benue
Ngazargamu
Ethiopian
Highlands

BOURE
AKAN
Ife
Benin
KWARARAFA
Mogadishu

MAMPRUSSI/
DAGOMBA/
GONJA
OYO/
IFE/
BENIN
} YORUBA
STATES
Congo
Great Rift Valley

Congo
Basin
L. Victoria
Malindi
Indian
Ocean

KONGO
Sanga
Ivuna
COMORO IS

Atlantic
Ocean

Zambezi

MADAGASCAR

Sofala

Kalahari
Desert
Great Zimbabwe
ZIMBABWE
Mapungubwe
Phalaborwe

Orange

Drakensberg

N

0   1600 km
0   1000 miles

Almoravid Empire 1050–1140

Mali c. 1100–1400

Songhay c. 1500

other African states c. 1000–1500

Europe and Its World Relations, 600–1350 CE

THE MAKING of modern Europe depended on four major historical developments. The first was the classical heritage of the Mediterranean world as expressed in Greek and Roman civilization. The Judaic-Christian perspective constituted the second and map 50 traces the diffusion of Christianity in Europe between 600 and 1200 CE.

Map 50 The Spread of Islam and Christianity, 600–1200 CE. Records indicate that Irish monks were commonplace travelers in Europe between 500 and 950 CE, reaching southern Italy, the Danube valley, the Baltic region, and the North Atlantic. According to legend, St. Brenden even reached a new land across the Atlantic Ocean.

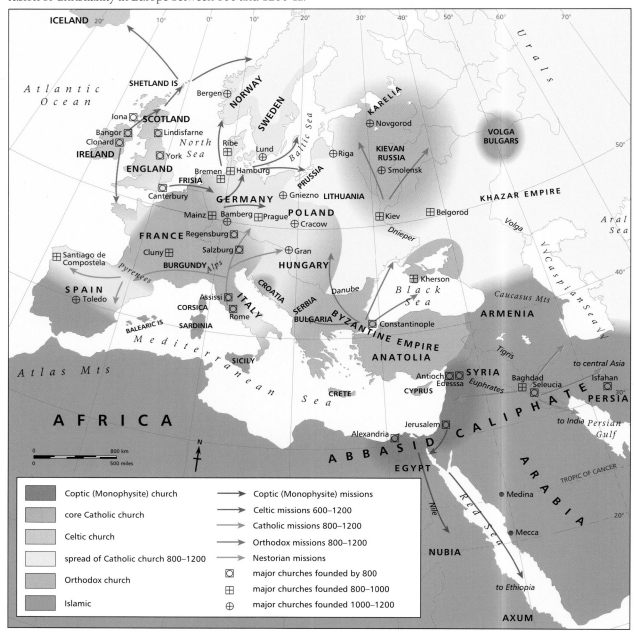

Legend:

- Coptic (Monophysite) church
- core Catholic church
- Celtic church
- spread of Catholic church 800–1200
- Orthodox church
- Islamic

- → Coptic (Monophysite) missions
- → Celtic missions 600–1200
- → Catholic missions 800–1200
- → Orthodox missions 800–1200
- → Nestorian missions
- ◻ major churches founded by 800
- ⊞ major churches founded 800–1000
- ⊕ major churches founded 1000–1200

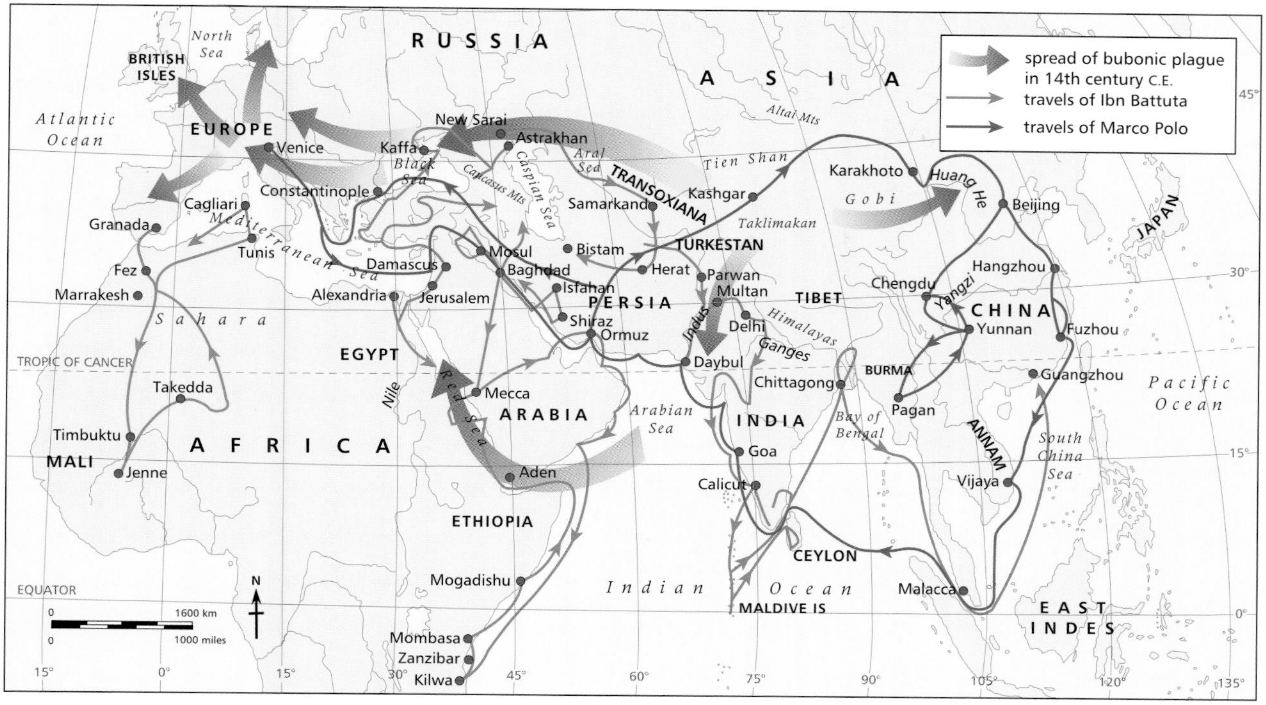
spread of bubonic plague in 14th century C.E.
travels of Ibn Battuta
travels of Marco Polo
RUSSIA
ASIA
EUROPE
BRITISH ISLES
North Sea
Atlantic Ocean
Venice
Kaffa
Black Sea
New Sarai
Astrakhan
Caspian Sea
Aral Sea
Caucasus Mts
Altai Mts
Tien Shan
TRANSOXIANA
Kashgar
Karakhoto
Huang He
Beijing
JAPAN
Gobi
Taklimakan
Samarkand
Constantinople
Cagliari
Granada
Mediterranean Sea
Tunis
Fez
Marrakesh
Sahara
Damascus
Mosul
Bistam
TURKESTAN
Baghdad
Herat
Parwan
Multan
TIBET
Chengdu
Hangzhou
Yangzi
CHINA
Yunnan
Fuzhou
Alexandria
Jerusalem
Isfahan
PERSIA
Shiraz
Ormuz
Indus
Delhi
Himalayas
Ganges
EGYPT
Daybul
Chittagong
BURMA
Guangzhou
Pacific Ocean
TROPIC OF CANCER
Takedda
Red Sea
Nile
Mecca
ARABIA
Arabian Sea
INDIA
Bay of Bengal
Pagan
ANNAM
South China Sea
Timbuktu
AFRICA
MALI
Jenne
Goa
Aden
Calicut
Vijaya
ETHIOPIA
CEYLON
EQUATOR
Mogadishu
Indian Ocean
Malacca
MALDIVE IS
EAST INDIES
N
1600 km
1000 miles
Mombasa
Zanzibar
Kilwa
45°
30°
15°
0°
15°
30°
45°
60°
75°
90°
105°
120°
135°

Map 51 The Afro-Eurasian World during the Mongol Peace, 1260–1400 CE. The adventures reported by Marco Polo and Ibn Battuta combined travel by land and sea. Marco Polo used the silk road route to go from the Middle East to China. Ibn Battuta, who was mostly interested in visiting Muslim areas, used the Indian Ocean sea lanes. Ibn Battuta's last trip was by caravan across the Sahara to Mali, then the most powerful state in West Africa.

The third ingredient was the blending of Germanic, Slavic, and other peoples into a continental cultural system. The fourth element is more difficult to define simply. It combines the development of an economic system, the use of a scientific outlook, and the adaptation of technological advances picked up from other civilizations.

At any rate, Europe emerged from the Black Death in the fifteenth century (see map 51) to become the main force shaping world history in the next five centuries.

An account of the rise of Europe to a prominent role in world history thus must take notice of multiple developments over many centuries. Map 50 features the year 600 to illustrate the spread of Christianity. The map tells many stories. The first is how the advances of Islam after 622 CE severely cut down the early Christian presence from the Pillars of Hercules in the west to the Caspian Sea in the east. Some Christian populations did remain in Muslim regions, but they were soon reduced to minority status.

Another story is the gradual split of the European Christians into the Greek-speaking Orthodox and the Latin-based Roman Catholic wings. Both sent missionaries northward into pagan Europe, converting various peoples. In the process, Rome, having lost its imperial power, regained status as the religious capital of Western Europe.

Map 51 picks up the story in the thirteenth century and needs a broad canvas to show how long distance trade flourished when the Mongol khanates controlled the heartlands of central Asia.

This map also shows some of the results of the Mongol "peace" and the increased trade and travel that accompanied it. Three separate movements are marked on the map: the spread of bubonic plague by fleas on rats infesting the cargo of trading expeditions; the travels recorded by the Christian adventurer Marco Polo between 1271 and 1295; and the similar journeys made by the Muslim lawyer Ibn Battuta between 1325 and 1355. Each of these movements has an important place in world history.

The bubonic plague had spread across Eurasia centuries earlier, but Europe had not experienced the Black Death since about 700 CE. It is thought that the increase in commercial travel led to infected rats finding their way across Asia on the Great Silk Road. From cities along the route the plague reached into their hinterlands, causing more deaths and cultural disruption than the terror wrought by the Mongols.

Europe in the Fifteenth Century

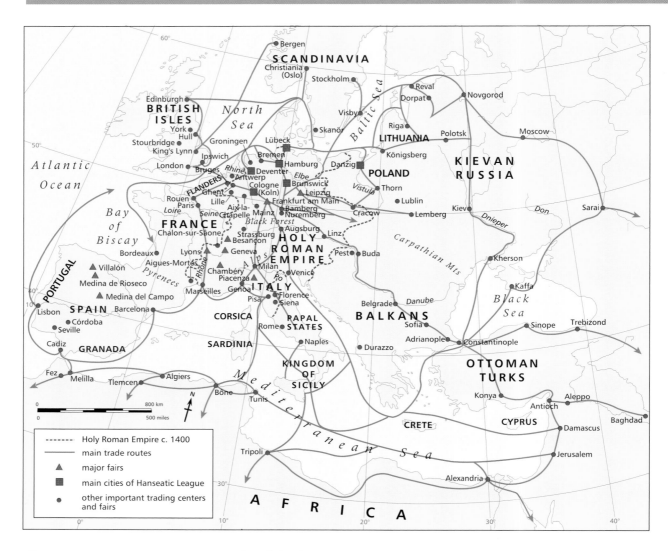

Map 52 **Medieval European Trade, *c.*1400 CE.** The two most important Mediterranean ports for European trade were Venice, at the head of the Adriatic Sea, and Genoa, which dominated the coastal trade in the western Mediterranean area. Both cities maintained close links with Constantinople, Alexandria, Antioch, and other ports along the eastern shore of the Mediterranean. Italian ships also ventured out into the Atlantic Ocean to reach Bordeaux and Flanders.

N THE FIFTEENTH century new cultural developments in Southern Europe recaptured the spirit as well as many literary and artistic treasures of ancient Greece and Rome. It seemed like a rebirth, or a Renaissance, to many pundits of the time who looked askance at the intervening centuries which they labeled the middle ages. Others were more critical, calling the era between antiquity and the enlightened fifteenth century "the Dark Ages."

Yet, as always with history, the situation was not so simple. The classical world in the Mediterranean did not die out with the Barbarian invasions, but gradually evolved, at varying rates of speed from place to place. There was also the expansion of civilization northward as Christianity extended throughout the continent by 1200 CE (see map 50, p. 64). As forests were cleared and roads were cut, towns and trade opened up links to larger intercontinental patterns. Map 52 makes this point dramatically.

To place this map into its world-wide context, compare it with map 47 (p. 59) which shows the major routes of Afro-Eurasian trade and map 33 (p. 48) which traces the routes of travel in the classical age. What the map of medieval European trade really shows, therefore, is how the long-established world trading system was extended to include all of Europe in the five centuries after the year 1000.

The lines running off the map to the east roughly trace the arteries of international commerce reaching out to the Red Sea, the Persian Gulf, and the Great Silk Road. Routes south from the African ports along the Mediterranean Sea, although they carried lesser amounts of trade, should be kept in mind eye to complete the connections between European commerce and the greater world system. Conspicuous by its absence, however, is any indication of trading activity westward across the Atlantic.

In Europe itself, a key to commercial activity can be found in the major fairs staged by cities in the middle of the continent. Here merchants with goods gathered from the Mediterranean ports exchanged them for products from northern and north-western Europe. Roads through Moscow, Kiev, and Constantinople witnessed similar activities taking place in eastern Europe, but using a different system to effect the exchange.

Map 53 European States in 1453 CE. In 1453 Constantinople finally fell to the Ottoman Turks, destroying the last vestige of the Byzantine Empire. Although the Holy Roman Empire in central Europe still recalled the imperium that held sway throughout the Mediterranean lands at the beginning of the Common Era, it was a faint shadow of classical times. Strong new monarchs in France, England, and Spain would soon rule the day. But in 1453 much of Europe still was ruled by an assortment of polities: dukedoms, city-states, principalities, khanates, knighthoods, and the like.

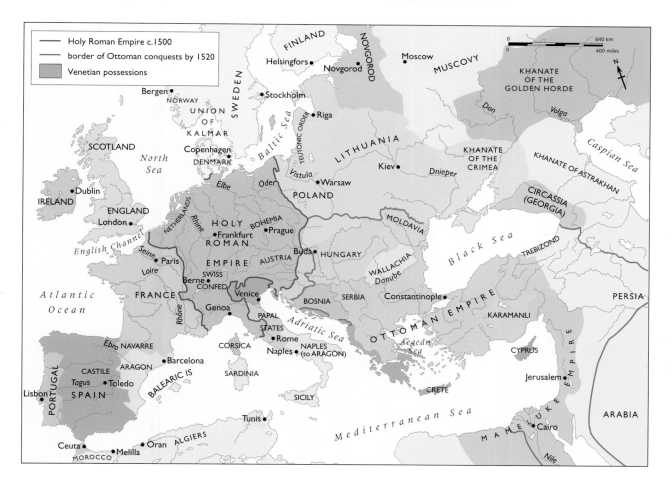

European States in 1526 CE

THERE ARE three ways to view any historical map and number 54 in particular. The first, as a statement of conditions at a particular date, demands that the reader look at the map in the context of its time. The second is to see the map as the culmination of a series of historical developments, to search for past traditions which still show up on the map. The third angle of vision considers the map as a baseline on which to construct future developments.

As a report on conditions in Europe in 1526 this map emphasizes how territories were amassed into larger empires and dynastic holdings. Thus Danish possessions dominated the northern reaches of the Baltic Sea until 1524 when Sweden gained its independence after a civil war in Denmark. Another important development, in 1526, was the decision of the Teutonic Knights, a military and religious order, to follow the lead of Martin Luther in religious affairs. Their influence in the Baltic area soon brought many of the commercial centers into the Protestant fold. Meanwhile, the Holy Roman Empire collected a host of small polities in central Europe, both Roman Catholic and Protestant, into a single unit. Venetian possessions looked to the Mediterranean Sea. The most important holdings scattered throughout Europe belonged to the Hapsburg rulers.

Developments in Hapsburg lands have dictated the exact date of this map. In 1526 the Holy Roman Emperor, Charles V, and Francis I, king of France, signed the so-called "Peace of Madrid" in which Francis relinquished claims to lands in Italy and acknowledged the Hapsburg Emperor as the master of Italy. In the same year Ferdinand of Austria was elected King of Bohemia, planting the seeds for a multi-ethnic empire centered in Vienna that would last until the twentieth century.

Meanwhile, in neighboring Hungary, the ruler Louis II was killed as his army was decimated by the Ottoman Turks. Indeed, the most powerful ruler in the region in 1526 was probably Suleiman I, whose armies would soon be marching toward Vienna. Other Europeans called him Suleiman the Magnificent, awe-struck by the splendor of his court. In his own provinces, however, he was known as Suleiman the Lawgiver, in recognition of the legal edicts, often of an enlightened nature, which he used to rule his empire.

The map shown here also seems to look to the past. The very name of the Holy Roman Empire recalled the unity which ancient Rome gave to the classical world fifteen centuries earlier (see map 23, p. 38). Even though Constantinople, the later Roman capital in the East, fell to the Ottoman Turks in 1453, and was renamed Istanbul by the conquerors, Europeans still used the old name for the city, hence it appears on this map (see also maps 26 and 53, pp. 41 and 67).

The extensive holdings of the Ottoman Empire also recall earlier movements of Turkish peoples into Europe and the Near East. The Ottomans, named after their leader, Osman, migrated from Central Asia and settled in Anatolia during the thirteenth century. In 1352 they gained a foothold in Europe which they expanded over the centuries to the territories shown opposite. The unsuccessful Turkish siege of Vienna in 1529 marked the high tide of the Ottoman advance into Europe. After that, Suleiman I turned his attention elsewhere, conquering Baghdad in 1534 and adding the ancient lands of Mesopotamia to his empire.

The Ottomans, forced to turn back from Vienna by the Austrians, established a settlement on the Danube river at Buda in Hungary where Europeans learned about two food plants from the New World which the Turks were already planting in their fields: peppers and maize. When maize was introduced into England in 1529, it was called "Turkish corn". Meanwhile, paprika (a spice made from dried peppers) soon became an essential ingredient in Hungarian cuisine.

Europe experienced many changes in 1526. In the previous year the religious reformer Martin Luther had married a former nun, Katherine von Bora. Then, in the year illustrated on this map, Luther translated the mass into German so that Christian congregations could conduct worship services in their own tongue instead of the traditional Latin of the ancient Roman church. That same year Albrecht Dürer, a supporter of Luther and a major figure of the Northern Renaissance, painted a celebrated portrayal of *The Four Apostles* that he presented to the city of Nuremberg for the edification of its people. Perhaps with one eye on the westward-advancing Turkish armies, Luther published his now famous hymn, *A Mighty Fortress is Our God*, in 1529.

Map 54 European States in 1526 CE. The siege of Vienna by the Ottoman Turks in 1529 would soon strike horror into the hearts of Europeans. Here the two great powers, the House of Hapsburg and the forces of Suleiman the Magnificent, one Christian and the other Muslim, would meet in a head-on clash. The Hapsburg lands were spread throughout Europe: in Spain, the low countries, Italy, and central Europe. Looking to the future, the duchy of Muscovy would soon expand in all directions, eventually to be bounded by the Baltic and Black seas, and the Arctic and Pacific oceans.

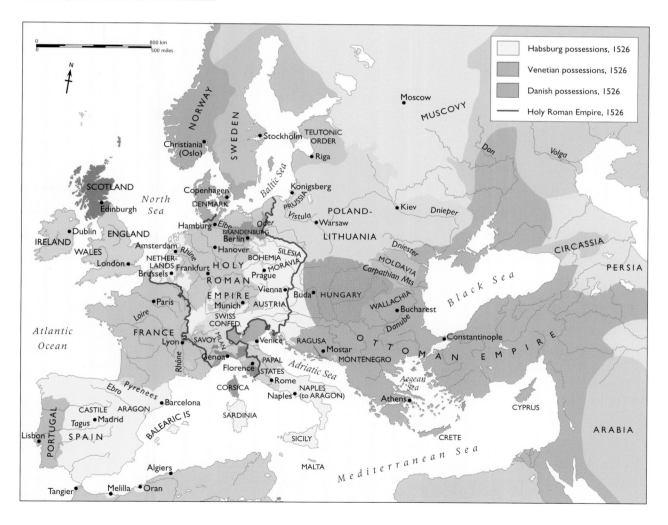

	Habsburg possessions, 1526
	Venetian possessions, 1526
	Danish possessions, 1526
	Holy Roman Empire, 1526

The Early Global Age
1500–1900

ONE WAY to define the term "global age" is to consider how and when European explorers discovered that there was only one world ocean. A surrounding ocean sea had been pictured on the earliest world map from Mesopotamia (see p. 14), but it was not until several millennia later that Magellan's crew made their epic voyage around the earth.

Another way to define the global age is to contrast how cartographers constructed world maps before and after 1500. In the earlier period they often started with a preconceived idea of how the earth looked, drew an outline of this ideal shape, and then fitted geographic information gained from actual experience into the general schema. Their maps were made deductively and were not helpful for navigating the oceans.

THE AGE OF DISCOVERY

The age of discovery transformed cartography. Recovering the Ptolemaic tradition (see p. 46), world maps began to be constructed inductively, starting with a grid and then locating individual places on it based on personal experiences and careful observation. Only after specific places were recorded would the general outlines of the continents be sketched in to provide a telling image for the points of reference.

The new maps could be used for navigation and Mercator's classic projection facilitated that very use. By 1600, every informed person in Europe had seen a map of how the world really looked, and model globes were being set up in many of the towns and cities for public viewing. Individuals were soon able to purchase reasonably priced small atlases and "pocket maps" for family use. In a cartographic sense, the global age had arrived. But in another way, a truly global age had to await more efficient means of transportation and communication. Each century saw some major improvements along these lines, but the major breakthrough occurred at the end of the era, in the nineteenth century.

THE WORLD INDUSTRIALIZES

The nineteenth century has been called the "Age of Invention," the "Age of Improvement," and the "Age of Progress." At the root of these hopeful terms was the Industrial Revolution, a new approach to the manufacturing of goods which began around 1750, primarily in England. During the nineteenth century the Industrial Revolution transformed the economies and societies of Europe, North America, and eventually Japan, giving these nations a decided advantage in world affairs.

The economic and military power reaped by industrial societies created an unequal world system: "have" nations set against "have not" peoples. In some ways, world history after 1800 is the story of the domination of the globe by the industrial powers and the reaction to that domination by the rest.

As its root, the industrial revolution involved the employment of water, steam, and electrical power to run machines to increase the quantity and quality of goods used by people. It transformed not only the way people made goods but also how they acquired their livelihood, how they lived, and how they thought about things. The industrial society put new demands on people as it regimented life and they, in turn, often reacted by seeking their own space and time, promoting individualism.

The wealth used to make the machines and to erect the factories in which they were housed was called capital because it became an investment made with the hope of receiving more money back at a later date as profits. The profits, in turn, were derived from the sale of the finished goods in markets so that the money received was greater than the costs incurred. The Industrial Revolution and capitalism as a way of organizing an economy went hand in hand.

The nineteen century was also a time of political change on a global scale. Former European colonies sought self determination and the New World was transformed by political revolutions which led to new, independent nations. The European imperial powers turned to other areas to exploit as sources of raw material or as markets for their manufactured goods. The element of competition built into world trade led to a scramble for territories, partitioning Africa and much of Asia as well. The whole movement was often justified, in the end, by ideas of progress and of the "white man's burden" to bring the improvements of industrialism to other societies.

OLD AND NEW WORLD VIEWS

As people in various parts of the earth entered the global age, they did so in their own way, bringing along many ways of life and habits of mind from their traditional cultures. There were continuities as well as changes, adaptations as well as transformations. The Chinese map shown opposite, illustrating what we call the Eastern Hemisphere and drawn around 1790 (currently housed in the Staatsbibliothek in Berlin), is a case in point.

Chinese maps traditionally paid careful attention to scale and were presented as works of art. They were often produced by provincial authorities in response to requests form the central administration or were produced as legal or military documents. European cartography also came to China in various ways, but it often coexisted with the traditional maps.

In this example a hemispheric map based on a Western example was used as a decorative preface to a long scroll portraying the coastline of China in traditional style. Note how the Chinese cartographer has transformed the image into a work of art by animating the shapes and delicately coloring the map. The coastlines seem to reflect the wave pattern in the seas and the rivers are often relocated to energize the lands. Following China's examples, these rivers tend to flow across the continents in an eastern or western direction.

The seas are colored green on both the hemisphere and the strip map of the coastline which follows it. China's zone of influence is given a golden color and surrounded with an abundance of islands to indicate its friendly seas. The Atlantic Ocean, in contrast, seems barren and forbidding. The Americas, situated in the other hemisphere, are washed by both the Friendly Ocean and the Barren Ocean in this view. Though the New World's lands are not pictured in this map, they held the keys to the world's situation in the coming era.

The World in the Age of European Expansion, 1500–1600

WHAT WAS the state of the world when Columbus returned to Europe in 1493 and reported the discovery of a new route to India and new islands? Map 55 takes one way to illustrate this by considering how the various peoples on the earth fed themselves around 1500, when Europeans were about to explore overseas.

Only the very cold polar regions and some parts of the deserts were uninhabited in 1500. Almost all of the islands able to sustain society had been discovered and put to use (see map 3, p. 19). St. Helena in the South Atlantic, site of Napoleon's exile, is one of the exceptions.

There were four major ways in which communities could feed themselves. The oldest was to hunt, fish, and gather foodstuffs from the natural environment. Groups of people learned to exploit a great variety of ecosystems to survive in hunting-gathering economies.

Another tradition, herding societies, had almost always had contact with settled communities with whom they traded to obtain certain goods.

The development of agriculture from various centers around the globe (see maps 4, 5 and 14, pp. 20 and 28) caused the populations of economies based on farming, the third tradition, to increase in size, especially when the plow was put to use under animal power. Hand cultivation, combined with herding or hunting and gathering was able, in favored locations, to support urban centers of notable size in the Americas and in sub-Saharan Africa.

Plow cultivation, underpinned by trade with herding, gathering, and extractive economies, supported developed economies from Europe and the Mediterranean region to Persia, India, China, Japan, and Southeast Asia.

All of these regions, as well as the savanna empires in Africa and certain trading cities on Africa's East Coast, were part of a series of interconnected trading systems (see maps 46 and 47, pp. 58–9).

Map 56 summarizes the story of world exploration between 1400 and 1600. The key traces the featured routes in chronological order. Thus the story starts in China where

Map 55 World Economies c.1500. This map shows the approximate boundary of areas known to educated Europeans on the eve of that continent's Age of Discovery. By the late fifteenth century Portuguese expeditions had reached the Cape of Good Hope. Centuries earlier Norse adventurers had established a settlement in Greenland. Trading contacts along the Great Silk Route and via the Indian Ocean brought Europeans knowledge of peoples throughout the temperate and tropical lands of Asia. Much of this knowledge, however, was obtained second-hand and therefore often mixed with legends and tall tales.

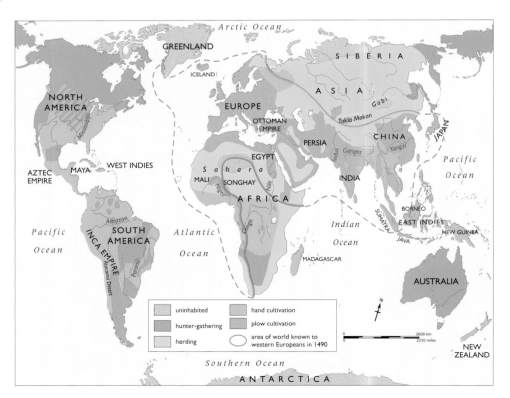

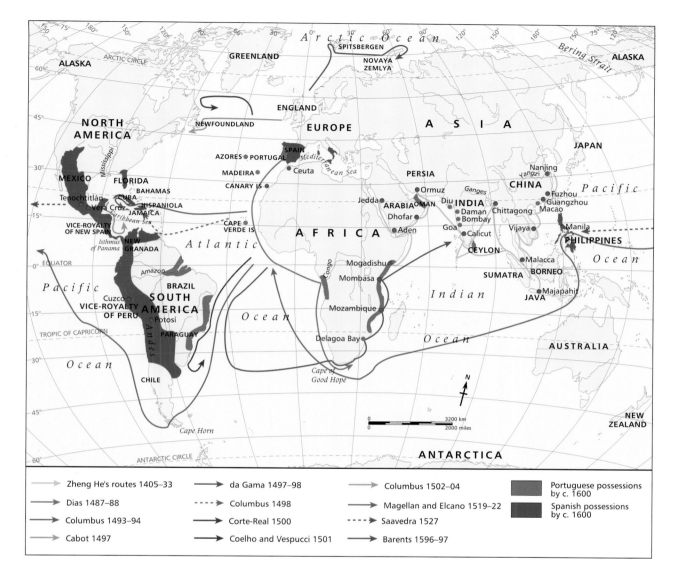

→ Zheng He's routes 1405–33	→ da Gama 1497–98	→ Columbus 1502–04
→ Dias 1487–88	--→ Columbus 1498	→ Magellan and Elcano 1519–22
→ Columbus 1493–94	→ Corte-Real 1500	--→ Saavedra 1527
→ Cabot 1497	→ Coelho and Vespucci 1501	→ Barents 1596–97

Portuguese possessions by c. 1600
Spanish possessions by c. 1600

the celebrated admiral Zheng He led several huge expeditions across the Indian Ocean (1405–33). In the service of the Ming emperor, these voyages were apparently designed not only to add to the court's knowledge of distant places, but also to extend Chinese power and influence. Arab merchants had also established several Chinese cities as routine ports of call and African traders could regularly be seen in Guangzhou (Canton), and Fuzhou.

The great breakthrough for Portuguese exploration was to round the Cape of Good Hope and find the passageway connecting the South Atlantic to the Indian Ocean. Vasco da Gama was able to follow up on this important discovery and reach India five years later, aided by the Arab pilot he met en route. Soon the Portuguese expe-

Map 56 World Explorations, 1400–1600. The voyages of Columbus are the most celebrated voyages of discovery. Two of his four expeditions are traced on this map, but all of them followed the same basic route southwest from Spain via the Canary Islands to the belt of westerly winds near the 15th north parallel. Columbus, thinking he was off the coast of Asia, called the people he found there "Indians," but he had only reached about 90 degrees west, about 150 degrees of longitude short of his goal.

ditions regularly hired pilots on the east coast of Africa to help them cross the Indian Ocean. After all, experienced sailors knew the wind patterns that were essential for a timely voyage. A century after da Gama's return the Portuguese possessed key stations along the entire route on both coasts of Africa as well as in India and China.

European Trading Empires, 1500–1700

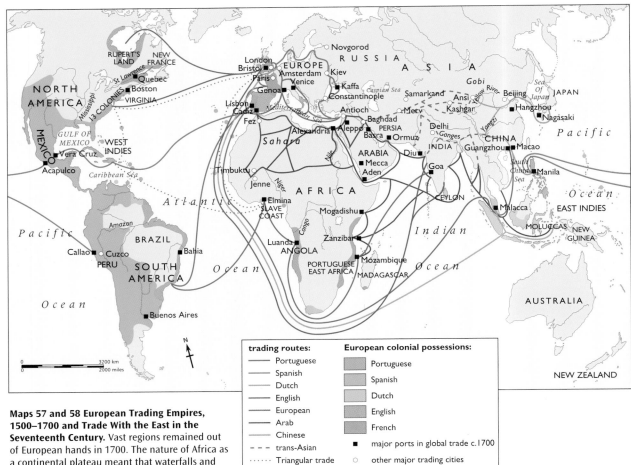

Maps 57 and 58 European Trading Empires, 1500–1700 and Trade With the East in the Seventeenth Century. Vast regions remained out of European hands in 1700. The nature of Africa as a continental plateau meant that waterfalls and rapids blocked penetration up its rivers from the oceans. This factor, along with the European vulnerability to tropical diseases and the strength of African states in the interior, kept most of Sub-Saharan Africa free of European control. The powerful regional states in South and East Asia (see map 49, p. 63) also restricted the Europeans to a few stations along these coasts. Australia, difficult to reach by sailing across the Indian Ocean because of the wind patterns, was not discovered by Europeans until 1627 and it waited until 1788 for the first European settlement.

O NE WAY to understand the trade routes shown here is to trace the pattern of winds and currents that channelled sailing vessels into particular paths. Because the winds often shifted with each season, especially in the Indian Ocean, geography often dictated the timing as well as the direction of a voyage.

To understand the location of the various imperial possessions, however, some history must be added to the basic geography. The Portuguese established the first European sea-born empire (see maps 55 and 56, pp. 72–3) as they explored the coasts of Africa and then crossed both the Indian and South Atlantic Oceans.

Spain, following the voyages of Columbus, soon established the largest European empire, dominating the Americas west of the 60th meridian. Note that this is about 15 degrees west of the so-called Line of Demarcation agreed to in the Treaty of Tordasilles between Portugal and Spain in 1494. Spain also

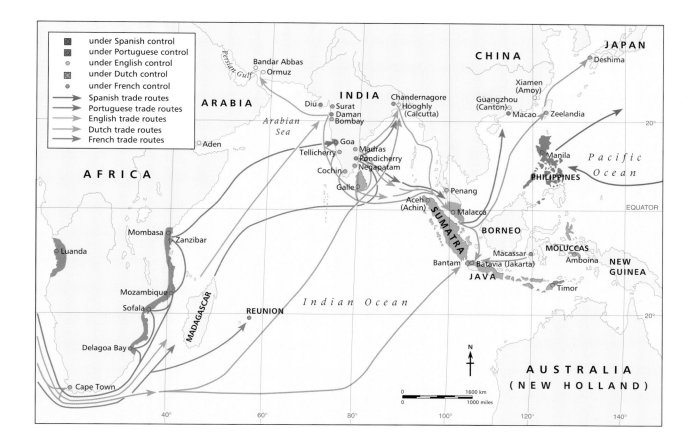

seized the Philippine Islands in East Asia and developed a far-flung commerce across the Pacific Ocean.

Meanwhile, the French and the English, both late-comers to the overseas imperial game, staked out claims along the coastal areas of North America. The Dutch also tried to maintain trading posts in North America along the Hudson River, but were forced out by the English; and so New Netherland then became New York. However, the Dutch were very successful in competing with the Portuguese in the Indian Ocean, claiming the Cape of Good Hope, Ceylon, and some islands in the East Indies.

The map above, showing European trade with South and East Asia in the seventeenth century, highlights the competitive nature of the enterprise. Indeed the series of routes, color-coded by nation, swinging around the Cape of Good Hope, resembles a chart of a horse race. Conflicts and accommodations between the seaborne trading empires soon funnelled the contestants to different ports in the Indian and Pacific oceans.

Navigation acts, trade regulations, tariff policies, and a variety of other devices were then used by each impe-

rial power to keep trade between the mother country and its overseas trading posts within the empire. Fierce competition, however, characterized the oriental trade conducted by the various imperial powers and other parts of Europe, such as Germany and Italy.

Another complicating factor in the commerce of the Indian Ocean and the China Seas was the persistence of the traditional trade carried on by indigenous peoples in these areas. The production of cotton cloth in India, for example, was a major factor in the subcontinent's trade with cities along Africa's Indian Ocean Coast and with trading centers fronting on the Arabian Sea and the Persian Gulf.

Indeed a focus on European trading routes across the Indian Ocean should not distract one's attention from the changes being wrought on the Indian subcontinent at the same time. In 1523 the Mughals, composed of Turkic and other Islamic peoples and led by descendants of Genghis Khan, invaded India and conquered the subcontinent, organizing it into provinces and districts which facilitated cultural and commercial contacts across the land.

Early Modern Europe, 1550–1750

Map 59 The Reformation in Europe, c.1565. Many of the cities on this map recall significant events in the religious developments of the time. Rome, of course, was the seat of the papacy. Wittenberg and Geneva served as home bases for Luther and Calvin respectively. Trent was the site of the church council which defined the Roman Catholic faith. Worms, on the Rhine, was the site of the last major attempt to keep the Protestants in the Roman Catholic fold in 1557.

AMONG THE CHARACTERISTICS of modern times are the dominance of nation-states in the political realm, the expansion of commerce, the rise of industry, the growth of cities, and an increasing diversity of religions. The maps on these pages catch the evolving nature of these developments in the period from 1550 to 1750.

Map 59, showing the Reformation in Europe around 1565, uses a variety of political designations to provide names for the various parts of Europe. Thus there are empires of different types, monarchies, principalities such as Transylvania, and even a confederation in Switzerland. Italy was more of a geographic designation than a political name at the time. Spain was likewise a general term coalescing into a kingdom after the union of Aragon and Castile.

The colored divisions on the map do not represent political entities but rather the religious tendencies of the various regions, often generalized, as they were around 1565, the year Pope Pius IV died. In 1564 he had presided over a Church Council in the city of Trent which defined, over a period of years, what the Roman Catholic Church believed and practiced. Such a statement was needed to specify orthodoxy in the wake of the Protestant reforms.

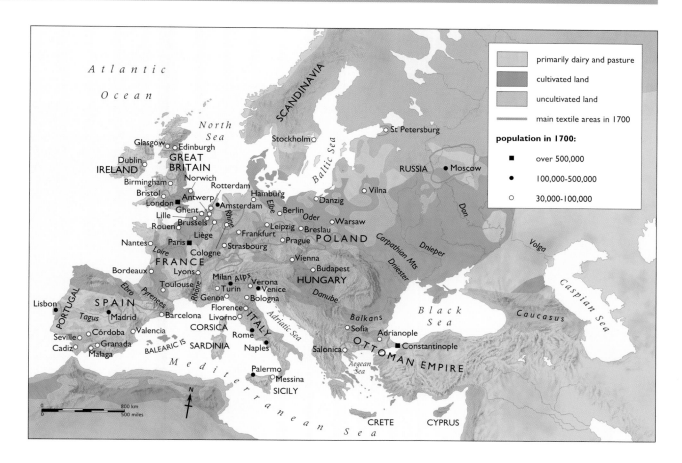

Map 60 European Commerce, Industry, and Urbanization, 1550–1750. The concentration of cities in certain areas is one indicator of the level of economic development in that region. More interesting, however, is the way large cities were spread out across the continent by 1750. Major overland trade routes connected these cities with one another. Maps 57 and 58 (pp. 74 and 75) complement this map by showing how sea-borne commerce connected port cities with each other and with far-flung lands across the oceans.

Protestantism had more than one spokesman. The followers of Martin Luther were numerous in the German-speaking areas, in the Baltic region, and in Scandinavia. John Calvin, based in Geneva, took a different approach to religious reform, and Protestants who followed his lead were scattered in geographic pockets from Scotland through Switzerland to Eastern Europe. Martin Luther died in 1546 and John Calvin was buried in 1564, so this map illustrates the situation just after the passing of Protestantism's first generation of leaders.

In England the Anglican Church assumed a national character and broke away from the pope in Rome. In Eastern Europe Orthodox Christianity, based on the Greek tradition, was the major religion. However, with the fall of Constantinople, its major center, to the Ottoman Turks in 1453, the Orthodox Church was losing ground to the advancing Muslim faith on the Balkan Peninsula.

The appearance of the religious map of Europe would shift again over the next century, especially in central Europe where the Thirty Years' War (1618–1648) devastated the Holy Roman Empire and surrounding areas. In some areas, south of Frankfurt, for example, the population fell by two-thirds during the course of the war. Other areas of Europe, however, maintained a steady growth between 1550 and 1750 due to textile manufacturing, mining, commerce and the growth of cities. Both Paris and London had, by 1750, populations approaching one million inhabitants.

Eurasian Empires, 1300–1700

I T IS IMPORTANT to remember that the celebrated voyages of discovery in the centuries after 1400 did not immediately affect most people. Their lives were influenced more by the series of land-based empires which were spread across Eurasia. Each of them had connections by land to the Great Silk Road as well as by sea to Indian Ocean commerce. They inherited the world system set in place by the Mongol Peace (see map 51, p. 65) but a series of developments turned the focus of each state inward. The various khanates still protected the avenues of commerce across Central Asia, but a series of powerful regional states extended from the Adriatic Sea to the Ganges delta.

The Ottoman Empire originated in Anatolia, gradually conquering neighboring territories until it had major interests along the Black, Mediterranean, Red, and Caspian seas as well as the Persian Gulf. In 1453 Ottoman forces brought about the end of the Byzantine state when they captured Constantinople.

The Safavid Empire included the block of land between the Tigris and Indus rivers, forming a greater Persia. The boundary between Ottoman lands and Safavid territories became more than a political boundary as the leaders of each state came to champion a different branch of the Muslim faith. In 1501 the Shah of Persia proclaimed

himself the only true leader of the Muslim community, elevating the Shi'a sect to a position of power. Safavid leaders then tried to stamp out all vestiges of the rival Sunni Muslim community.

The Ottoman leaders, in contrast, took up the defense of the Sunni and even extended their empire in a long strip along the Red Sea to control the holy places of the Muslim faith. Since 1501 the boundary between Shi'a and Sunni lands has been a significant cultural and political divide.

In India, the Muslim empire established in 1530 often favored the Shi'a when it needed help from its Safavid neighbors, but eventually it became an orthodox Sunni state. This Mughal dynasty ruled many Hindu peoples, who became restless when the state tried to enforce religious purity in any Muslim form.

The Ming dynasty in China began in 1368 when an army led by a former Buddhist monk was able to advance against the Mongol overlords and eventually to drive them

Map 61 Eurasian Empires, 1300–1700. Each of these Eurasian empires faced internal problems or threats from its immediate neighbors which increased its isolationism. About 1500 this inward-looking tendency aided the expansive efforts of Europeans who arrived in the Indian Ocean and the South China Sea in quest of fortune and fame.

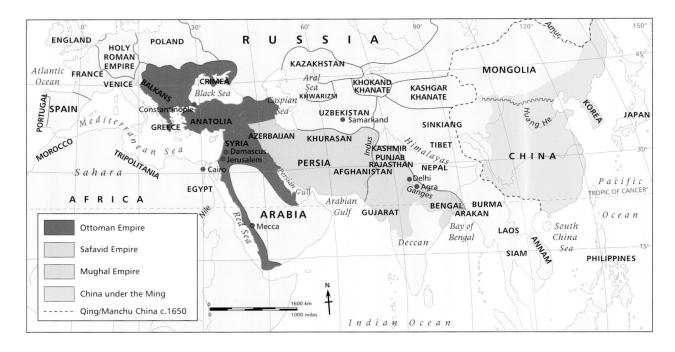

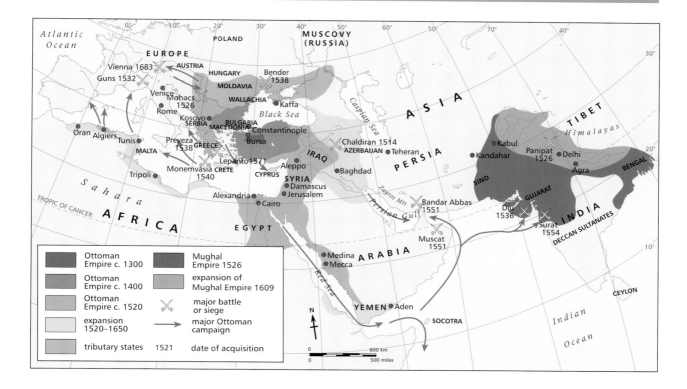

Map 62 The Expansion of the Ottoman and Mughal Empires, 1300–1700. The Mughals were a mixture of Mongol and Turkish peoples who invaded northern India in 1526, soon extending their rule from the Indus river to the Ganges Delta. The Ottoman force that attacked the Mughal port city of Surat in 1554 struck the terminal of three major Indian trade routes which reached north to Kabul, northeast to Delhi and east across the Deccan to the Bay of Bengal.

out of China. As the Ming rulers concentrated on preventing another Mongol invasion, they turned away from global contacts of the earlier period, deciding not to follow up on their voyages of discovery into the Indian Ocean (see map 56, p. 73).

Map 62 illustrates how the Ottoman and Mughal empires expanded in stages over the course of the centuries. A military victory by Osman and his band of migrating Turks led to the establishment of a core area for the future empire on the hinge that connected Asia and Europe along the waterway between the Black and Aegean seas. A century later the Turks had taken over most of Anatolia and had also acquired lands across the Dardanelles in continental Europe itself.

The fall of Constantinople in 1453 was part of an aggressive push outward in which Ottoman forces conquered Greece, Syria, Palestine, and Egypt. Between 1529 and 1683 Ottoman forces arrived several times at the gates of Vienna, but were never able to overrun the city. The key to stopping Ottoman advances into Europe was probably the crippling of its Mediterranean fleet in the battle of Lepanto in 1571, in which a coalition of Christian forces led by Venice and Spain sank 117 Turkish ships.

Even so, the strength of the Ottoman Empire was so great that a rebuilt fleet captured Cyprus a year later. At the same time Ottoman fleets in the Indian Ocean attacked coastal cities and provinces from Africa to India.

The strengths that allowed the Ottoman Empire to expand in such a systematic way in its early days and then to endure into the twentieth century have always fascinated historians. Some have pointed to the weakness of the Byzantine Empire and the feebleness of neighboring states. But contemporary scholars also emphasize the Ottomans' ability to incorporate dozens of different cultures in their empire and to inspire loyalty in these subject peoples.

The African Slave Trade

THE SLAVE TRADE was the primary engine driving the African diaspora which took millions of black people away from their homelands and sent them to the Mediterranean region, the Near East, and especially to the Americas.

The trade in slaves from sub-Saharan Africa dates back to ancient times. Black slaves could be found in the cities of the Roman Empire and in later years slaves from East Africa became cargo on ships plying the trade routes in the Indian Ocean (see maps 46 and 47, pp. 58–9). But after the 1520s the African slave trade took on a new scale and dimension as it turned its focus across the Atlantic to supply the labor demands of European colonies in the Americas.

At first the trans-Atlantic trade was small and experimental. Laborers were imported from Angola to Brazil where the Portuguese were developing sugar plantations. Native American peoples, who often succumbed to Old World diseases, were found to be less satisfactory as work-

Map 63 The African Slave Trade. Note that most of the slaves who came to the areas which became the United States had homelands in West Africa. In addition, they often spent some time in the West Indies before arriving on the North American mainland. Most slaves in Brazil came from other regions of Africa.

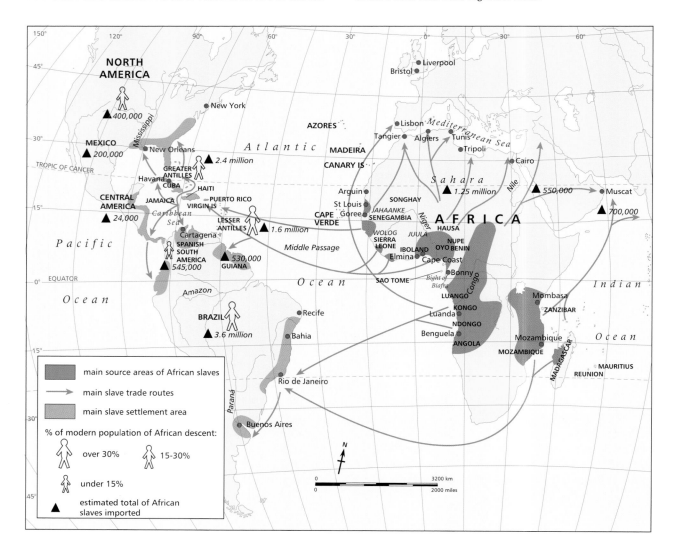

ers on the sugar plantations than the African slaves. European demand for sugar encouraged the rapid expansion of the New World plantations, especially in the West Indies.

Plantations in the Americas owned by Europeans and worked by slaves from Africa became an integral part of a three-cornered commerce across the Atlantic. Ships left European ports with trade goods bound for African trading stations where they exchanged their wares with African merchants for slaves captured from villages in the interior. The middle passage then brought the cargo of slaves to America where they were sold. Sugar as well as other products were carried back to Europe to complete the voyage.

A close inspection of map 63 will indicate how much of the slave trade was tropically oriented. The African sources of the slaves were almost entirely within fifteen degrees of the equator. The destinations of the slaves in the New World were also primarily between the Tropic of Cancer and the Tropic of Capricorn. Only about 5 percent of the slaves brought to the Americas were originally sold in the temperate latitudes.

The first African slave to be sent across the Atlantic sailed in 1502, but up to 1575 the number of forced immigrants remained small. Then the traffic started to increase, reaching totals of 40,000 to 60,000 each year throughout the eighteenth century. Some estimates indicate that as many African slaves crossed the Atlantic as did migrants from Europe.

In Africa, the slave trade was completely in the hands of African traders who quickly adapted to new markets by erecting slaving forts along the continent's Atlantic coast at such places as El Mina, Bonny, Luanda, and Benguela.

In the New World, slave societies were able to maintain much of their African culture. When emancipation came in the nineteenth century, African survivals in language, cooking, clothing, religious practice, dance and music grew strong enough to influence the emerging modern American culture. In the twentieth century these African survivals had such a bearing on the definition of American culture that if their influence were removed, in critical areas such as music, American culture as we know it would be unrecognizable.

The most illuminating and shocking sources of information on the slave trade come from the personal accounts of Africans who were themselves sold into slavery. One of the most famous accounts comes from Olaudah Equiano, who was born in the interior of West Africa about 1745. Equiano was part of a large family with five brothers and a sister. Ironically, his father also owned slaves according to the custom of the region. When he was eleven years old, learning to be both a farmer and a warrior, Equiano was kidnapped, along with his sister, while their parents were away working in the fields.

After passing through the hands of several masters in Africa, including one position where he worked for a blacksmith, Equiano was eventually carried onto a slave ship bound for the West Indies. Flogged for refusing to eat, he soon learned the horrors of the Middle Passage and the ready use of violence by the masters to discipline both cargo and crew.

Arriving at Barbados, some old slaves were brought on board the ship to pacify the newly arrived Africans. Taken on land and sold to a planter, Equiano was filled with surprise as well as terror as he saw the New World for the first time. Struck at first by the sight of houses of several stories made of brick, he was "still more astonished on seeing people on horseback."

Fellow slaves from other parts of Africa soon told him that horses were also used in their home continent, horses "much larger than those I saw." The note of pride for his homeland that is later found in his writing no doubt helped sustain Equiano, who used his intelligence to learn how to beat the system, eventually purchasing his own freedom. He then became an active member of the antislavery movement in England, where he wrote his autobiography.

Thus Equiano participated in several major historical movements of his day. He was a member of a forced migration of Africans to the Americas. He worked in a plantation economy centered on sugar, which created a flourishing transatlantic economy in the eighteenth century. Finally, he became a leading figure in the Abolition Movement, the leading reform movement in the nineteenth century.

The Americas in 1750

THE MIDDLE of the eighteenth century is a good point at which to survey the extent of European domination of the western hemisphere in the Early Modern period. One empire or another had claimed almost the entire sweep of the continent, even though people speaking European languages would not visit some remote regions until the twentieth century.

When viewing the way the Americas are carved up on this map the reader should keep in mind that the colors represent European claims rather than areas actually dominated or controlled. Indeed, most of the Americas in 1750 remained the homeland of indigenous peoples who, by that year, had been decimated by the spread of Old World diseases to which they had little resistance. In some ways this historical map is made possible only by this great tragedy which led to, by some estimates, a 50 to 90 percent decline in the populations of the native peoples.

Traditional cartography illustrates the rival imperial claims put forth by seafaring European nations. Spain was the first to arrive and Santo Domingo on Hispaniola is the oldest permanent settlement by Europeans in the Americas, dating from 1496. From this beachhead, Spanish *conquistadors* soon moved onto other islands, and then pressed into the mainland. After Hernan Cortes and a small pack of followers toppled the Aztec empire in Mexico, other "conquerors" fanned out into Panama, Peru, and North America.

By 1750 Spain in the Americas consisted of the Vice-Royalties of New Spain, New Granada, and Peru, with outlying areas along the Rio de La Plata and in Florida, as well as the original islands in the Caribbean. Of these, Cuba was the largest.

Other European colonizing nations, although arriving much later, had, by 1750, also taken over islands in the Caribbean. The French even established Haiti on the western part of Hispaniola. The British controlled Jamaica, the Bahamas, and several other islands. The Lesser Antilles were divided between France, Britain, the Netherlands, and Denmark. Although small, these islands played a major role in imperial economies as producers of sugar and rum.

In South America, France, and the Netherlands claimed sections of the Guiana coast, but most of the continent was divided, almost equally, between Spain and Portugal.

In 1750 the two Iberian nations signed a treaty which discarded the ancient Papal Demarcation Line of 1494 and agreed to the boundaries shown on this map. These new lines were, however, discarded a decade later when Spain nullified the treaty.

Colonial boundaries were just as fluid in North America. The "Thirteen English Colonies" were the most populous European outposts, but they were confined to the area east of the Appalachian mountains. French settlements and claims traced a broad arc from the Gulf of St. Lawrence in the north to the mouth of the Mississippi in the south. France also named and claimed Louisiana, west of the Mississippi.

Britain commanded the vast northern reaches of the continent starting with Newfoundland in the east, running across the Hudson Bay Company's holdings, and including a vast, vaguely defined region called Rupert's Land. On the basis of voyages made by Vitus Bering, Alexei Chirikov, and their successors, beginning in 1741, Russia claimed the coastal areas of the North Pacific. Spain, in turn, took up much of the remainder of North America, claiming as its own a few long established, but sparsely populated frontier settlements strung out from Florida to California.

Conflicts in North America and rivalries in Europe led these empires into a long series of wars, which would reach their culmination in the Peace of Paris in 1763 at the conclusion of the Seven Years War. A British victory led to the elimination of the French from mainland North America. Louisiana was assigned to Spain, and the British gained control of Florida. This arrangement would not last very long. Soon the American Revolution rearranged the map of North America. When Napoleon, who "secretly" had regained control of Louisiana, agreed to sell it to the newly independent United States, a new empire started expanding across the continent, a development illustrated in map 73 (see p. 93).

Map 64 The Americas in 1750. By combining this map with the previous one (see p. 80), one can grasp the process of creating multicultural societies in the western hemisphere. American colonial societies included a continued indigenous presence – especially strong in Mexico, Peru, and other areas, settlers from a variety of European nations, and slaves forced to leave various parts of Africa to work in the New World. Thus the four Atlantic continents interacted with one another, bringing various peoples together to create multi-ethnic societies in the Americas.

GREENLAND

RUPERTS LAND

*area disputed
by Russia
and Spain*

*Hudson
Bay*

NEWFOUNDLAND

NOVA
SCOTIA

LOUISIANA

Ohio

•Boston

THIRTEEN
COLONIES

•Jamestown

*Atlantic
Ocean*

Rio Grande

Mississippi

FLORIDA

VICE-ROYALTY
OF
NEW SPAIN

*Gulf Of
Mexico*

HAITI
(France)

CUBA (Sp.)

SANTO
DOMINGO
(Sp.)

GUADELOUPE (Fr.)

Mexico City •

•Belize
(GB)

Caribbean Sea

MARTINIQUE (Fr.)

CURAÇAO (Dutch)

Orinoco

NEW GRANADA

GUIANA

*Pacific

Ocean*

Amazon

VICE-ROYALTY OF PERU

B R A Z I L

Lima •

Paraguay

•Rio de Janeiro

CHILE

RIO DE
LA PLATA

•Buenos Aires

the "Thirteen Colonies" (British)

other British territory

French

Spanish

Portuguese

Dutch

Russian

Amerindian peoples

N

0   2400 km
0   1500 miles

Europe in the Age of the French Revolution

WHEN DRAWING a map of the French Revolution and its implications it is difficult to know where to begin or how much of the world to include. The concepts of liberty, equality, and citizenship had deep roots and the movement which gave rise to demands for these rights would soon spread beyond French borders and engage the attention of most of Europe. For this reason two maps are needed, one of France itself and another of the entire continent. Even these, however, seem too restrictive.

Map 65, for example, includes just the northern tip of Corsica, an island in the Mediterranean Sea that France purchased from Genoa in 1768. The Italian city-state was willing to sell the rebellious island which had been demanding its freedom ever since 1755 when it staged one of the earliest independence movements in modern Europe.

After the outbreak of revolution in Paris in 1789, the whole of France was soon involved, as the map makes clear. Leaders in the provinces either remained loyal to the monarchy or supported the Revolutionary forces. Mean-

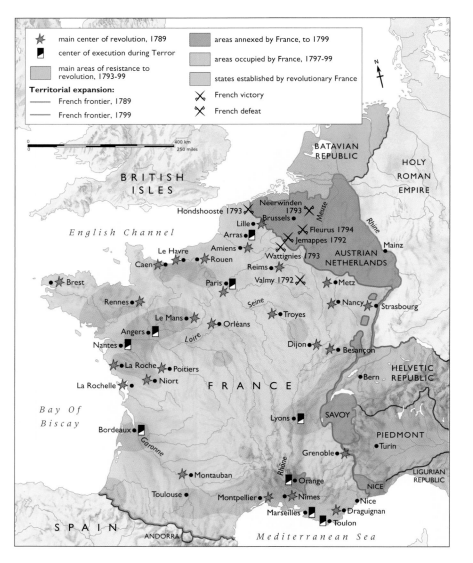

Map 65 The French Revolution, 1789–1799. The French Revolution, drawing inspiration from the thinkers of the Enlightenment, tried to apply reason to build a new society, replacing the *ancien régime*, in which power lay with the Church and the nobility. As new currents of thought swept away past structures, some cities embraced the Revolution with great fervor, but in others, conservative elements fought back. Neighboring peoples were attracted to the new ways at the same time that their nervous governments were attacking the forces of change. A map must have a dynamic character to portray these movements and tensions.

Map 66 European States in 1795. In 1795 the Third Constitution in France established a new government, the Directory. Spain, Austria, Prussia, and other continental states then made peace with France. Poland disappeared from the map as its three aggressive neighbors divided its remaining territories among themselves. Belgium became part of France and the Netherlands became the Batavian, or Dutch, Republic. The Ottoman Empire in 1795 had entered a period of decline and would soon lose some of its holdings.

while, peasant revolts destroyed feudal society at the same time that the middle class was reorganizing France's government, society, and culture in the capital city.

When outside forces started coming to the aid of counter-revolutionary factions in France, control of the Revolution passed to more radical forces. Soon France was at war with her neighbors. Early defeats led to the execution of the king, Louis XVI, and, soon afterward, the period known as the Reign of Terror. But citizen soldiers turned the tide in France's favor and by 1795 the new republic's boundaries were extended (see map 66).

At this point some Corsican local interests made another bid for independence, but the movement failed and was soon forgotten as a Corsican gained fame in the Revolutionary armies: in 1796 Napoleon Bonaparte married Josephine Beauharnais, took command of French troops in Italy, and repeatedly defeated Austrian armies. In 1798 he sailed with an army to Egypt, conquering the country in the Battle of the Pyramids. Then the English took control of the Mediterranean Sea, isolating the French troops. Napoleon left them behind, escaped, and returned to Paris. The following year he overthrew the Directory, a government of five directors set up in 1795 at the end of the Reign of Terror. When Napoleon crowned himself Emperor, the French Revolution came full circle and Europe entered another imperial age (see map 69, p. 88).

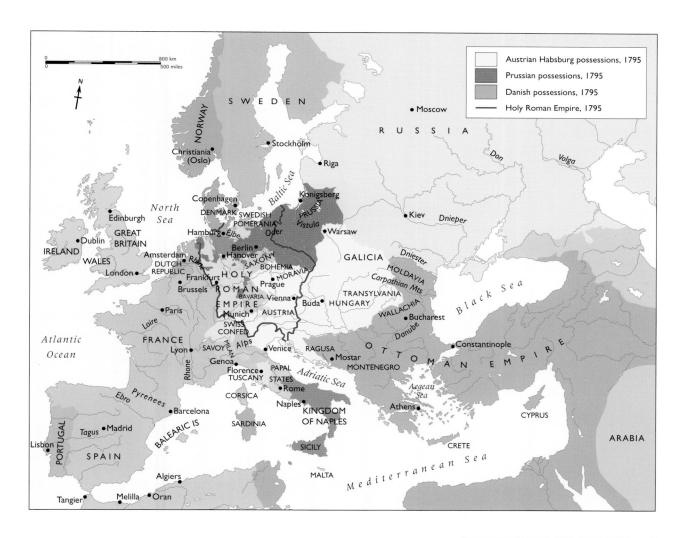

The British Empire in the Nineteenth Century

"THE SUN never sets on the British Empire." The boast was literally true as territories in Africa, India, Australia, and New Zealand were added to the holdings Britain retained in North America after the American War of Independence. The maps shown here trace the expansion of these imperial interests in the early part of the nineteenth century.

Map 67 illustrates how British power expanded in India up to 1805. Both the British and the French followed the early Portuguese example and tapped into the robust trading activities of the Indian Ocean of which the Indian subcontinent formed the major pivot. The European practice was to demonstrate military power, then secure permission from the Mughal rulers to build a fortified trading post on a suitable harbor along the coast. European agents would then purchase goods from local traders such as spices, cotton cloth, Chinese silks, and porcelain to store in the trading castles, waiting for ships to arrive to take the products back to Europe. By 1805, coffee and tea had become key items in this trade.

The East India Company was a huge capitalist enterprise that ran this profitable trade for England. As Mughal power weakened and regional princes gained independence, the English and French companies entered into a series of alliances with regional states. Fighting other Europeans both on land and at sea, and entering the struggles between Indian states, eventually led the English East India Company to rule large areas in India from a base in Bengal, largely by employing Indian troops called sepoys.

Map 68 traces the expansion of British India showing how by 1830 the East India Company controlled almost the entire coastline. India was by then the most valuable part of the Empire and the British took control of a series of islands to serve as way stations between Britain and India. Additional islands and coastal territories were secured in the Mediterranean Sea, in West Africa and along the sea-lanes that connected the Indian and Pacific oceans.

The inset maps detail how British interests also expanded in Australia, New Zealand, and South Africa. The Portuguese probably came across the continent of Australia as early as 1520, but it was not until a Dutch ship arrived in 1606 that Europeans seriously started to explore the southern continent. First called New Holland, Australia waited until 1788 for its first major European settlement, a colony mostly made up of prisoners from England.

Gradually English settlement spread along the continent's east coast, reaching inland after 1830. Soon British settlers spread out to new areas in Australia and arrived in New Zealand. In the latter case their advance was contested in the Maori wars of the 1860s, paralleling the struggles in the West of the United States.

The British Empire in South Africa was established in Cape Town, a way station on the important sea route from Europe to India. The Dutch had founded Cape Colony but lost control of the port, leaving it to establish some settlements further to the east. Gradually these European outposts expanded to grab the best farming lands from the native peoples. The discovery of diamonds in 1866 and then of gold 20 years later set off an explosion of imperial interest in the region which led to the Boer Wars between Dutch farmers and the British government.

Map 67 British Power in India to 1805. The Treaty of Paris (1763) removed France from being a major imperial power in India as well as in North America (see map 64, p. 83). After surrendering to French and American troops at Yorktown, Virginia, a move that would soon bring the American War of Independence to a close, Lord Charles Cornwallis became governor-general of British India (1785–93) where he successfully defended the empire in the Mysore War and published a code of laws that led to substantial reforms.

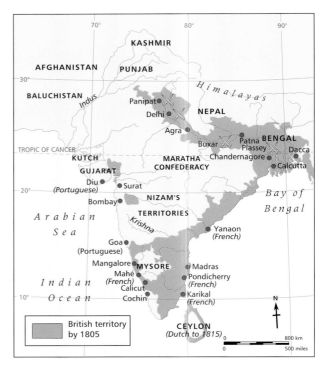

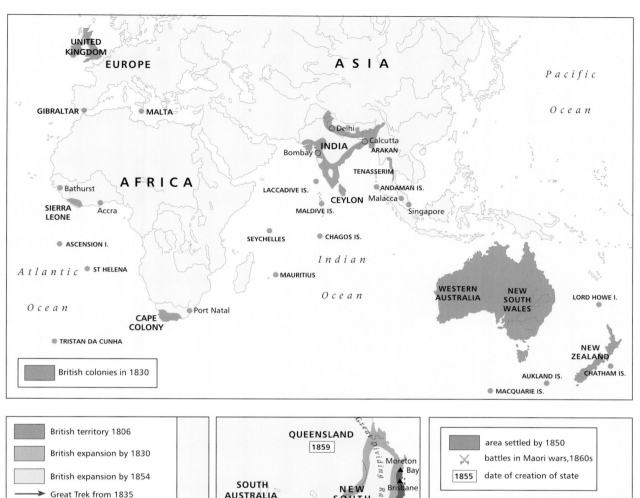

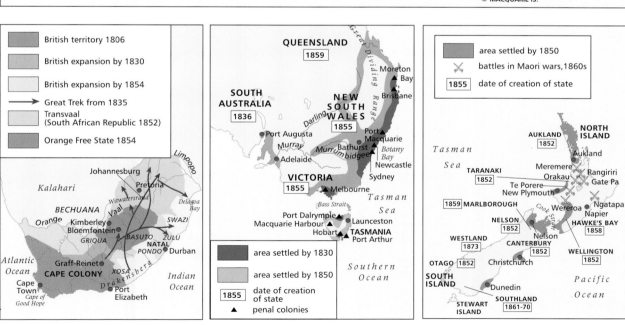

Map 68 The British Empire in Afro-Eurasia and the Pacific to 1860. The expansion of the British Empire in Africa, South Asia, and the South Pacific in some ways compensated for its loss of the thirteen colonies that became the United States following the American Revolution (1776–83). The process hastened the development of the British Empire into a world-wide entity. The top map emphasizes the importance of islands which served as way stations for British commercial and military ships. The larger scaled maps at the bottom portray the advance of English settlements from coastal regions into interior lands.

The Age of Napoleon

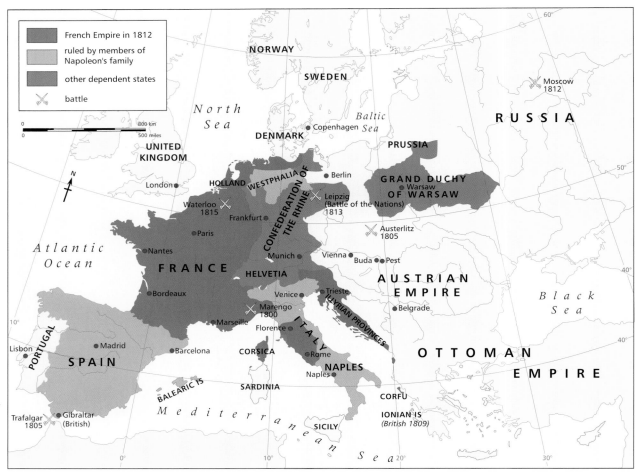

Map 69 The Napoleonic Wars and Empire, 1800–1815. The annexations of border areas by France, the placing of Napoleonic family members on various European thrones, and the creation of dependent states in central and eastern Europe all served to spread Napoleonic institutions and laws throughout the continent. As a product of the Revolution, Napoleon used concepts from the Enlightenment and employed much of the Revolutionary rhetoric in his edicts.

IN 1804, the year he crowned himself emperor, Napoleon issued a codification of French laws. The Code Napoleon, inspired by liberal ideals, became the legal standard for French-speaking areas around the world. The military forces led by Napoleon were also transformed by Revolutionary ideas. The obligation of all citizens to serve the state led to universal conscription and the new citizen armies reached unprecedented size. This numerical advantage balanced their inexperience when they met the professional armies of other states. The enthusiasm of the citizen armies also gave France an advantage in the early battles. At Marengo in 1800 Napoleon's troops defeated the Austrian army and claimed Italy. Five years later they again reduced Austrian and Russian forces at Austerlitz. However, in the same year (1805) Napoleon was forced by the British Navy to give up a planned invasion of England. The Royal Navy followed up its advantage by defeating a combined French and Spanish fleet at Trafalgar near the Strait of Gibraltar. France was henceforth limited to being a continental power.

The decline of Napoleon's power started in 1812 when he took a gamble and marched an army of 600,000 troops into Russia. Russian resistance and the onset of winter soon sent the French armies into retreat. Eventually only a tenth

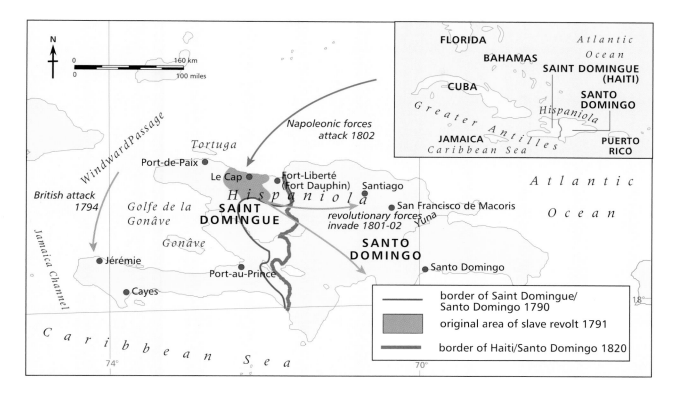

N

0   160 km
0   100 miles

Windward Passage

British attack
1794

Jamaica Channel

Napoleonic forces
attack 1802

Tortuga

Port-de-Paix ●

Le Cap ●   ● Fort-Liberté
              (Fort Dauphin)   Santiago

Hispaniola

SAINT
DOMINGUE   ● San Francisco de Macoris
                revolutionary forces *Yuna*
Golfe de la   invade 1801-02
Gonâve

Gonâve   SANTO
                                  DOMINGO
● Jérémie
              Port-au-Prince ●   ● Santo Domingo

● Cayes

C a r i b b e a n   S e a

74°   70°

FLORIDA   *Atlantic*
                           Ocean
     BAHAMAS   SAINT DOMINGUE
                         (HAITI)
CUBA   SANTO
                         DOMINGO
Greater   *Hispaniola*
Antilles
JAMAICA   PUERTO
Caribbean Sea   RICO

Atlantic

Ocean

18°

border of Saint Domingue/
Santo Domingo 1790

original area of slave revolt 1791

border of Haiti/Santo Domingo 1820

Map 70 Revolution in Haiti, 1791–1804. When the French Revolutionary government abolished slavery in 1794 there were about 500,000 slaves in Saint-Domingue. The white population numbered only 40,000 with a free black population of 30,000. Some slaves, however, had become maroons, living in a state of freedom in the hills away from the plantations. These maroon colonies served as instigators for the slave revolts that came to a head in 1791, several years before the French Assembly voted for emancipation. British troops landed in 1794 to put down these local revolts, hoping to gain control of the island.

of the soldiers survived the long march home from Moscow. France's neighbors then united to defeat the remaining French armies in the Battle of the Nations near Leipzig (1813). After a brief exile, Napoleon returned in a last attempt to regain power, meeting his Waterloo in 1815.

By the turn of the century Napoleon had given up dreams of a renewed empire in the New World. The French National Assembly under the leadership of Robespierre had abolished slavery in all the French colonies in 1794. The owners of the sugar plantations of Saint-Domingue opposed the emancipation. When Napoleon came to power in 1799 he reversed the decision on slavery and dispatched

troops to recapture Saint-Domingue and other islands. Led by Toussaint L'Ouverture, black forces defeated the French and yellow fever completed the job. The republic of Haiti gained its independence in 1804. These troubles in the West Indies led Napoleon to decide to sell Louisiana to the United States in 1803 (see map 73, p. 93).

The Haitian experience is instructive in several ways. It is connected very directly to the rhetoric of the French Revolution. It also showed the way for a whole series of independence movements in Latin America that would take up the energies of the next generation of Latin American leaders. The success of a slave uprising leading to national independence after struggles against French, Spanish, and British armies is an inspiring tale.

But the final achievement of democracy and economic development was long delayed. The fighting ruined the irrigation system which was the lifeline of the economy. A general proclaimed himself emperor, only to be killed a few years later by his own soldiers. Economic and political setbacks made regular appearances as Haiti faced problems which continue to this day (see map 101, p. 133).

Europe in the Nineteenth Century

ALTHOUGH the Congress of Vienna in 1815 tried to restore Europe to the way it was before the French Revolution, it proved impossible to turn back the clock. The quest for liberty, equality, and fraternity continued to propel the forces of change throughout Europe. Map 71 shows some major flash points of liberal revolts in the period 1815–47.

Changes started as early as 1817 when the Ottoman Empire was forced to grant partial freedom to the Serbs. By 1820 a revolt in Spain forced the king to restore the constitution of 1812. Then a revolution broke out in Portugal followed in 1821 by the outbreak of the Greek war for independence. While the Greeks were fighting for their freedom, the Spanish and Portuguese colonies in the

Americas declared their independence. And so it went, year after year of struggles, defeats, victories, and treaties.

The climax came in 1848, the year of revolutions. A revolt in Austria forced the resignation of Prince Metternich, a leading architect of reaction. In France, a revolution brought a new republic and Louis Napoleon was elect-

Map 71 Europe, 1815–1871. This map focuses the reader's attention on the liberal, national, and Socialist uprisings between the Congress of Vienna and the Franco-Prussian War. The latter ended with a revolutionary commune taking over Paris and its suppression by the National Assembly which had accepted the German peace terms. Pockets of unrest were scattered throughout the continent, with Great Britain facing the Tipperary insurrection in 1848 and continuing discontent in Ireland throughout the period.

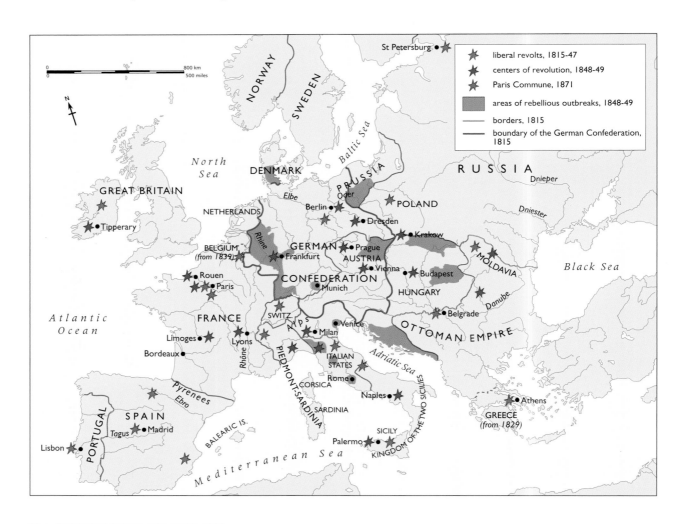

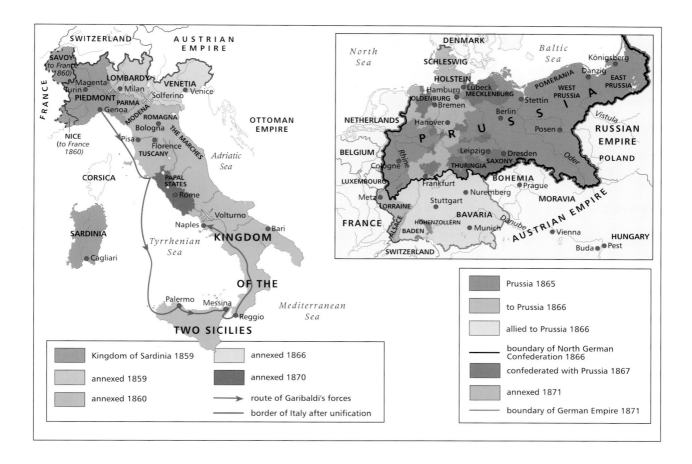

Legend (Italy map):

Kingdom of Sardinia 1859

annexed 1859

annexed 1860

annexed 1866

annexed 1870

→ route of Garibaldi's forces

— border of Italy after unification

Legend (Germany map):

Prussia 1865

to Prussia 1866

allied to Prussia 1866

—— boundary of North German Confederation 1866

confederated with Prussia 1867

annexed 1871

—— boundary of German Empire 1871

Map 72 The Unification of Italy and Germany. Giuseppe Garibaldi (1807–82) was a soldier of fortune and an ardent Italian nationalist. He led a small army, which wore distinctive red shirts, against the forces of a repressive government in Sicily and southern Italy. When he reached Naples he joined forces with Vittore Emmanuele II, the king of Piedmont and Sardinia, who had won victories in central Italy. Over the next decade additional lands were added to this core and Italy became a unified state.

ed president. Once again, slavery was abolished in the French colonies. In Rome, Pope Pius IX was forced to flee in the face of a violent uprising. Sicily, Naples, Milan, Venice, Prague, and Budapest all witnessed fighting between the forces of conservatism and those of change. Then the revolts spread throughout Germany.

In the midst of the revolutionary fervor of 1848 Karl Marx and Friedrich Engels wrote the Communist Manifesto. The next year Richard Wagner took part in an uprising in Dresden, forcing him to flee from Germany as the conservative forces gained control. A decade later, Charles Darwin published the controversial *Origin of Species* in London, somewhat removed from the revolutionary struggles on the continent, but part of the intellectual ferment ushering in modern times.

The French Revolution's emphasis on fraternity, and the rise of nationalism from a variety of other sources, led to the unification of both Germany and Italy. In Italy, a movement to remove foreign control and unite the various principalities into one liberal state met one setback after another (notably in 1820, 1830, and 1848) before the pieces were gradually put together between 1859 and 1870.

The movement toward German unification told a similar story. Frustration in 1848 and 1849 over the inability to found a liberal state led to a different approach, the formation of a German state, not by speeches and elections, but by "blood and iron." The words were those of Otto von Bismarck, the prime minister of Prussia. Between 1864 and 1870 he waged wars against Denmark, Austria, and France, using the power and nationalist fervor that came with victories to create a new German Empire, a unified state replacing the Holy Roman Empire and its successor, the German Confederation.

The Expansion of the United States and the Formation of Canada, 1803–1905

THE UNITED STATES emerged from the War of Independence (1775–83) with favorable boundaries extending from the Great Lakes south to Spanish Florida and then from the Atlantic Ocean west to the Mississippi river. The Appalachian mountains had restricted the original English settlements to the coastal regions, encouraging the development of a sufficient population density to stimulate economic development, so that the colonies could consider autonomy. By achieving both independence and possession of the western lands in the Treaty of Paris (1783), the new nation acquired the potential to become a first-rate power.

In many ways the securing of the territory west of the Appalachians was the key to the expansion of the United States across the continent. It was in this region that the new nation worked out two key policies that guided its later expansion. The first, established in the Land Ordinance of 1785, set up a process for the systematic survey, division, and sale of newly acquired lands by the Federal government. It provided a simple, clear way to turn land into a commodity, an essential ingredient in a capitalist economic system.

The second crucial determinant of American expansion was a decision to create new states in the western lands which could have a republican government and be admitted to the federal union on equal terms with the original states. This was a simple solution to the problem of an empire held by a democracy. It was most fully articulated in the Northwest Ordinance of 1787, which looked ahead to the eventual creation of five new states north and west of the Ohio river.

Both the Land Ordinance and the Northwest Ordinance were set up by the Congress operating under the Articles of Confederation, the first constitutional arrangement for an independent United States of America. This document was soon replaced by the Constitution, adopted between 1787 and 1789, which continued the land and territorial policies established beforehand. Then, in 1803, the United States made a decision which from that date forward cast the fledgling Constitution in a new light. The Federal Government assumed the unspecified power to expand the nation to new lands across the Mississippi river.

The purchase of Louisiana from France in 1803 occurred when Napoleon was thinking about invading England instead of maintaining a distant colony on the North American grasslands. By obtaining the mouth of the Mississippi, the United States also acquired a major presence on the Gulf of Mexico, a status enhanced when it took over Florida from Spain in several installments ending in 1819. Meanwhile a series of territorial adjustments (1818–46) between the United States and Britain led to the extension of the Canadian border along the 49th parallel all the way to Boundary Bay on the Pacific Ocean. The Oregon Country thus became part of a new American northwest.

After the Mexican Revolution brought independence to its southern neighbor, the United States encouraged the revolt of Mexico's Texan province, recognizing the Lone Star Republic's independence in 1836. Nine years later Texas was admitted into the union, enlarging the US presence on the Gulf of Mexico and claiming the Rio Grande as its southern boundary. These aggressive moves soon led to conflicts with Mexico which mushroomed into war and the eventual occupation of Mexico City.

In the subsequent peace treaty, Mexico was forced to yield California and the lands eastward as far as Texas. The Gadsden Purchase extended the American southwest and also carried with it the right for the United States to construct an interocean railroad across Mexico near the 94th meridian. Thus the 1853 treaty was part and parcel of the drive to the Pacific.

If the United States had followed up on the Gadsden Purchase treaty and built a railroad across the Isthmus of Tehuantepec in the 1850s, the subsequent history of North America might have changed dramatically. This provision of the treaty was formally annulled in 1936 as part of America's Good Neighbor Policy.

The purchase of Alaska from Russia in 1867 was viewed as folly by many Americans at the time, not realizing how important the vast northern land would be in the air age. With Alaska and the later annexation of the Hawaiian Islands, the United States established itself as a major power in the Pacific world.

Canada also became a continental nation but it took a different route, remaining within the British Empire. The problem facing British North America in 1763, when

Map 73 The Expansion of the United States and the Formation of Canada, 1803–1905. The political map of North America differs from that of Europe (see map 71, p. 90) in that many of the boundary lines are meridians or parallels, features of mental geometry rather than the actual landscape. The international boundaries of the United States west of the Great Lakes and the Rio Grande are mostly straight lines drawn on a master map rather than boundaries that were developed from geographical features or historical developments. The state boundaries in the Trans-Mississippi West and the provincial borders in Canada are also dominated by straight lines and right angles. In the United States, only a few western states use rivers or a mountain crest to define the majority of their borders.

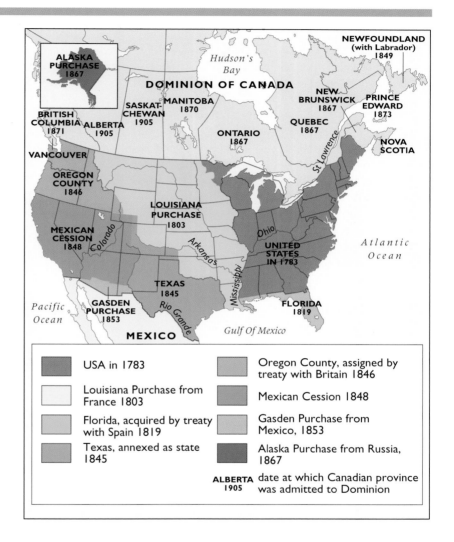

the British took over French holdings, was that it consisted of three distinct parts: a French speaking population in Quebec; a sparsely populated Upper Canada on the Great Lakes which soon filled with English-speaking settlers, many of them Loyalist refugees from the American Revolution; and the maritime areas which remained five separate colonies.

Scattered rebellions in both Quebec and Upper Canada in 1837 pushed the British government into action. A report by Lord Durham in 1839 recommended a unified Canada that would be largely self-governing in local affairs, with foreign policy and defense matters remaining under the control of the Britain. The Canada Act of 1840 put these recommendations into practice, a pattern that was later followed in South Africa, Australia, and New Zealand (see map 68, p. 87). During the American Civil War (1861–5), fears of an invasion led to further discussions eventually resulting in the British North America Act of 1867 which established a Canadian Confederation. Gradually the various provinces joined the Dominion of Canada, a federal state with a parliamentary form of government which owed allegiance to the British monarch.

European Imperialism, 1815–1870

AS RAILROADS marked the spread of the industrial revolution on land (see maps 76–78, pp. 96–8), so steam ships enabled the spread of industrialism overseas. The use of steam engines to power boats made ocean shipping regular and dependable. Steam ships were also much larger and the cost of cargo per ton-mile dropped dramatically. But the full advantage of large ocean liners would not come until the end of the century.

The time period of map 74 encompasses the gradual conversion of sail power to steam power, but the map does not yet reflect the full impact of industrialism. Maps 79 and 80 (pp. 99–101) will show Africa filled with colonies and much of Asia carved up into spheres of influence. What we witness here is a world in transition.

The western hemisphere is filled with symbols designating anti-colonial revolts which led to independence in most parts of Latin America as illustrated on map 75.

The Texan and Californian revolts against Mexico were staged or abetted by citizens of the United States and both the Lone Star and Bear Flag republics soon became American states. The formation of the Confederacy by the slave-owning states is also classified here as an attempt to throw off the yoke of union in defense of local rights.

In Africa, many of the old trading stations along the coast remained in European hands. Note, however, how the Ottoman Empire had expanded along the Mediterranean shore and up the Nile Valley. The British pres-

Map 74 European Imperialism, 1815–1870. The Suez Canal between the Red and the Mediterranean Seas was completed in 1869. Built by the French, the waterway was dedicated by Empress Eugénie, consort of Emperor Napoleon III. The same year the United States opened the Transcontinental Railroad which made it possible to travel across North America by train. Both of these events would help push the powerful nations of the world into a new phase of imperialism (see maps 79 and 80).

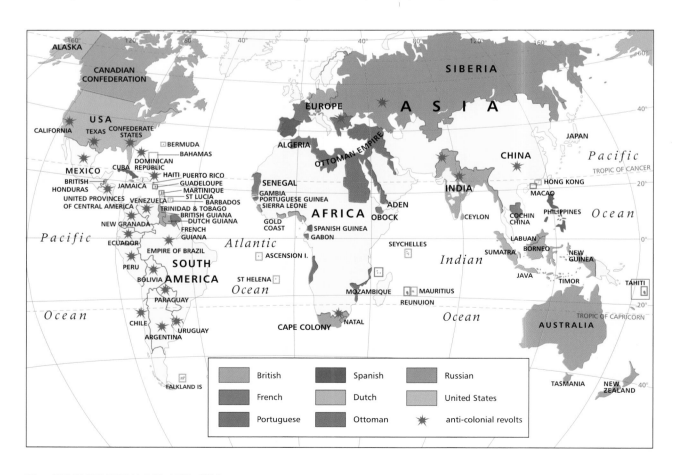

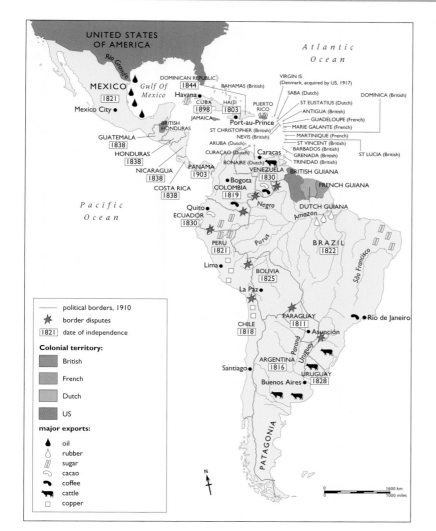

Map 75 Independence in Latin America, 1804–1898. The British, French, and Dutch colonial holdings remained in place during the upheaval, Britain actually extending its empire by taking the Falkland Islands from Argentina in 1833. Spain retained only two colonies in the Americas: Cuba and Puerto Rico. The inclusion of major exports on the map serves as a reminder that political freedom was not necessarily accompanied by economic independence. The new nations of the Americas often played colonial roles in North Atlantic economic systems.

ence in South Africa pushed the earlier Dutch colonists inland, provoking the Bantu peoples who were crowded out as a result.

In South Asia the British added to the lands under the control of the East India Company, triggering outbursts of violence as local groups resisted. After the suppression of the Indian mutiny of 1857–9, India became a crown colony. Britain's presence in South Africa, India, Burma, and Australia made it the dominant power in the Indian Ocean.

Map 75 documents a generation of change, 1804–1838, when most of the European holdings in South and Central America gained their independence.

Using the earlier American and French Revolutions as examples, and taking advantage of the weakened state of Spain and Portugal as a result of the Peninsular Wars waged by Napoleon, the Europeanized elite classes in the Latin American colonies achieved political independence following a series of military campaigns in the decades after 1810. Britain supported these independence movements for its own commercial ends, using its sea power to prevent the Iberian nations from reclaiming their colonies. The United States also announced its support of Latin American independence in the Monroe Doctrine of 1823.

The Industrial Revolution in Europe

THE INDUSTRIAL revolution was rooted in changes in the sources of power used in the production and transportation of goods. As machines – such as the steam engine – and techniques were invented to increase the productivity of power sources, a new way of life dependent on manufactured goods was born. Four essential components of this revolution are featured on these maps: iron ore, which supplied the metal for boilers, machine parts, wheels, and tools; coal, which provided a fuel that made steam engines efficient to use; industrial centers, which collected workers, machines, power sources, raw materials, and storage facilities at one place and on a scale large enough to promote economic efficiency; and the development of the railroad, which provided a way to assemble production materials at one site and then to distribute the products made there to consumers in a wide area.

1850 was a pivotal year in the story of European industrialism. Developments in Britain over the previous cen-

Map 76 Great Britain Industrializes, 1750–1850. During this 100-year period the British leaped ahead of Europe as forerunners for the Industrial Revolution. Britain's location, insular setting, natural resources, trading empire, large population, and capitalist mentality, all encouraged the development of an industrial society. London remained the great metropolis, but other cities such as Manchester, Birmingham, Sheffield, Newcastle, and Glasgow became famous as industrial centers.

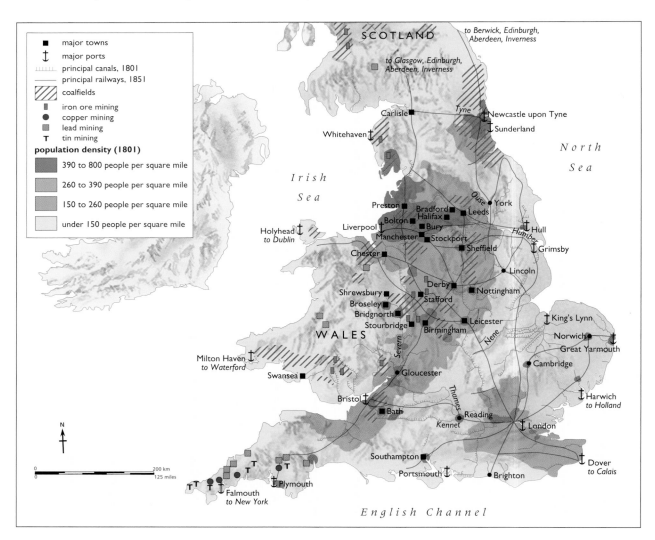

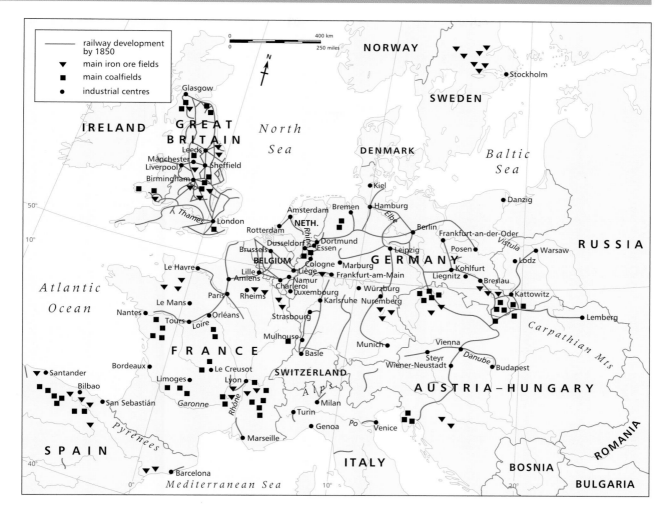

Map key:
- railway development by 1850
- ▼ main iron ore fields
- ■ main coalfields
- • industrial centres

0   400 km
0   250 miles

N

NORWAY

SWEDEN

• Stockholm

IRELAND

GREAT BRITAIN

• Glasgow

North Sea

DENMARK

Baltic Sea

• Kiel
• Danzig

• Leeds
• Manchester
• Liverpool
• Sheffield
• Birmingham

Thames
• London

Amsterdam
Bremen
• Hamburg
Elbe

• Berlin

• Frankfurt-an-der-Oder

RUSSIA

Rotterdam
NETH.
Rhine
Dusseldorf
Dortmund
Essen
Brussels
BELGIUM
Cologne
Liège
Namur
Charleroi
Luxembourg

Leipzig
Posen
Vistula
• Warsaw
• Lódz
Kohlfurt
Liegnitz
Breslau
Kattowitz

GERMANY

Marburg
Frankfurt-am-Main
Karlsruhe
Würzburg
Nuremberg

Atlantic Ocean

• Le Havre
Lille
Amiens
Paris
Rheims
Strasbourg
Mulhouse

• Le Mans
Nantes
Tours
Loire
Orléans

Munich
Basle

Vienna
Steyr
Wiener-Neustadt
Danube
Budapest

Lemberg
Carpathian Mts

FRANCE

Bordeaux
Limoges
Le Creusot
Lyon
Garonne
Rhône

SWITZERLAND

Alps
• Milan
• Turin
Po
Venice
Genoa

AUSTRIA–HUNGARY

• Santander
Bilbao
San Sebastián
Pyrenees

Marseille

ITALY

BOSNIA

ROMANIA

SPAIN

Mediterranean Sea
• Barcelona

BULGARIA

---

tury had ushered in a new society in which manufactured goods, imported foodstuffs, cotton cloth, ease of transportation, and continued progress were taken for granted. To celebrate the new age, the British prepared the first world's fair, the Great Exhibition, which would open in 1851 in the immense and specially constructed iron and glass Crystal Palace. Meanwhile every city in Europe, the Americas, and beyond was looking to the new industrial era to bring its citizens prosperity and an array of creature comforts. Each city aspired to become the nexus of a transportation system composed of canals, railroads, and improved roadways.

Indeed the density of the railroad network was one clue to the development of an industrial society in a coun-

Map 77 The Industrial Revolution in Europe to 1850. This map can be viewed in two ways. The first is to see it as a series of national railroad networks. Another way is to look at the rail system as a whole, without respect to international boundaries. The emerging rail structure in Germany seems to encourage unification while the one in Italy does not seem to be guided by national ambitions.

try. The date 1850 is early in the story of industrial cities, but note Britain was already criss-crossed with railways. France, in contrast, was just beginning to put together a rail network while the process had hardly begun in Spain, Italy, Russia, and Scandinavia. The iron ore and coal fields found throughout the continent, however, promised that the railroad network would soon be extended to include every area marked by a symbol.

The United States in the Nineteenth Century

THE RISE of the United States of America is one of the major themes of world history in the nineteenth century. From its roots as the world's first nation to gain independence from a European seaborne empire, it became a powerful state with an overseas empire in its own right. The story includes tales of expansion across the continent (see map 73, p. 93) and in the oceans (see map 83, p. 108). But it also narrates the tensions between different regions within the nation that climaxed in a civil war, the root cause of which was the presence of slavery in the American South and Southwest.

If slavery was the major factor pulling the nation apart in the early nineteenth century, the development of transportation and communication facilities worked to bind it together. Even the desolate plains in the interior of North America were pulled into a national economy by the railroads, which took cattle one or two thousand miles to markets, especially in cities east of the Mississippi.

These cities needed increased food supplies to feed large numbers of immigrants who were continuing in the nineteenth century patterns of migration established in previous centuries. The newcomers came to new cities, transformed by the industrial revolution into great concentrations of millions of people. New York, which became the nation's largest city, went from a population of less than 100,000 in 1800 to about 3.5 million in 1900.

Map 78 The United States of America, 1850–1865. By 1850 railroads had assumed two major functions in the American economy. The first was to move the products of farms, mills, mines, and industries to markets in cities for processing or transshipment. The second was to connect distant cities to facilitate the exchange of goods and encourage passenger travel between them.

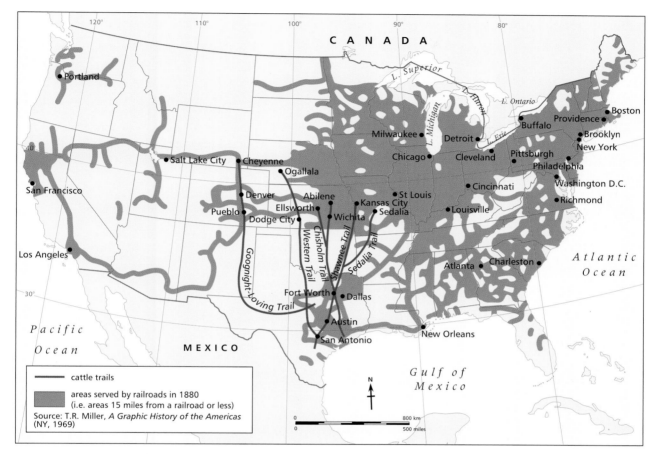

Map 79 The United States of America, 1865–1880. This map
shows how patterns of railroad development inaugurated before the
Civil War continued in its aftermath. Any location within 15 miles of
a railroad was placed within the orbit of the iron horse because this
was a convenient half-day journey by team and wagon to haul
goods to the railroad, leaving the other half-day for the return.
The positions of the cattle trails illustrate how the railroads also
influenced economic development many miles from their tracks
or railheads.

Many immigrants to the United States settled in
rural areas as well as in cities, populating new states
with the encouragement of the liberal land policy of the
federal government. By 1900 almost all of the land nat-
urally suitable for agriculture had been exploited. Some
marginal land was already being abandoned, especially
in the Atlantic coast states. New concerns were being
voiced about the need for large-scale irrigation projects
in the dry western reaches of the continent.

Thus maps showing the development of overland
trails and routes for cattle drives suggest major themes
such as national expansion, commercial integration, population growth, industrialism, immigration, migration,
and the emergence of a national market economy. On the
other hand, the history of the United States after the Revolution is also instructive when viewed in the light of
its experience as the first new nation. Economic development and national integration are dominant themes in
this perspective as well, but so are localism, sectionalism,
and relations with neighboring states.

It took almost a century after 1776 for the United
States to achieve a state of peace with its neighbors and
domestic stability. Along the way, it fought with Canada
and Mexico before plunging into a terrible Civil War
that sacrificed many of its young men in the quest for
an undisputed polity.

The Qing Dynasty in China: Rise and Decline, 1618–1900

RUSSIAN EMPIRE

KAZAKHSTAN

Tien Shan

L.Balkhash

Altai

L.Baikal

OUTER MONGOLIA

Gobi

MARITIME
PROVINCES
to Russia 1858

Aihun

Amur

Harbin

MANCHURIA

Changchun

FENGTIAN

Vladivostok

Shenyang

Niuzhuang

KOREA

TURKESTAN

to Russia 1854

ILI VALLEY

**XINJIANG
(EASTERN TURKESTAN)**

DZUNGARIA

Turfan Basin

Tarim Basin

Taklimakan

REHE

Kalgan

Beijing Tianjin

CHIHLI

Port Arthur
(Russian 1898)

Weihaiwei
(British 1898)

INNER MONGOLIA

Yellow River (Huang H.)

GANSU

Taiyuan

Qingdao

SHANDONG

JAPAN

TSINGHAI

C H I N A

Kaifeng

SHAANXI **JIANGSU**

HENAN

Zhenjiang Wusong

Pukou Shanghai

Wuhu

Suzhou Ningbo

ZHEJIANG Wenzhou

*East
China
Sea*

TIBET

Himalayas

HUBEI

ANHUI

Yichang

Yangzi

Hankou Jiujiang

SICHUAN

Chongqing

Yuezhou

Santsao

Fuzhou

NEPAL

BHUTAN

ASSAM

JIANGXI

FUJIAN

Xiame

BRITISH INDIA

YUNNAN

GUIZHOU

Kunming

GUANGDONG

Shantou

TAIWAN

Dengyue

Mengzi

GUANGXI

Guangzhou
(Canton)

Kowloon

Hong Kong

BURMA

Simao

Manhou

Nanning

Macao *(British 1842)*
(Portuguese)

Longzhou

Pakhoi Guangzhouwan

*South
China
Sea*

LAOS

FRENCH INDO-CHINA

*Bay of
Bengal*

SIAM

800 km

500 miles

N

Qing (Manchu) Empire in 1850	☀ other 19th-century revolts
→ British attacks during Opium War 1839–42	■ treaty ports
⬭ area of Taiping rebellion 1853–63	
⬭ area of Nian rebellion 1853–68	
⬭ area of Boxer uprising 1900–01	

Russian

Japanese

French

British

German

areas of
influence

Map 80 China in the Nineteenth Century. The expansion of the Manchu (Qing) Empire to include underpopulated regions around China's historic core areas led to a greater concept of China which included Tibet, Sinkiang, Mongolia, and Manchuria. Ethnic Chinese entered into these lands, beyond the Great Wall, making it a relic from a past era, and propelling a Chinese version of westward expansion that continues today.

AFTER UNRAVELLING the various strands of this complex map one is left in awe at the extent of the Qing (Manchu) Empire at its height. The Manchu, a federation of pastoral tribes from Manchuria, were bold enough to attack China in 1618. After wresting some frontier territory away from the Ming Empire, they proclaimed their leader as the Chinese emperor and adopted a government, social order, and cultural life according to traditional Confucian teachings. These early efforts enabled the Qing ruler to take advantage of a state of civil unrest developing in China. Within a few years he ruled all of the former Ming territories and set out on a series of conquests to reach the far-flung borders traced here by the green line.

Even more significant was the explosion of China's population under Qing rule, due in part to new crops from the Americas such as sweet potatoes, peanuts, and maize, as well as the utilization of techniques for intensive cultivation. In the first century of Qing rule, China's population doubled to reach 200 million people by 1750. After another century, it doubled again.

By the early 1700s all of East Asia was either included in the Qing Empire or stood in awe of the power and achievement of Chinese civilization. Peace and an expanding population ushered in a period of prosperity and cultural achievement. From an early date, Qing emperors included Jesuit missionaries among their advisors. In this way Western ideas gained some influence among the Chinese, and vice versa. Voltaire, for example, modelled his ideal philosopher-king after the Qing emperor.

The success of the Qing Empire lay in its ability to manage a variety of different lands and peoples, incorporating new ideas and technologies while at the same time appearing in the traditional guise of Confucian rule. The absorption of Mongol lands into China brought Qing influence deep into Central Asia where it eventually came into contact with Russian interests coming from the opposite direction. A series of treaties divided up the interior of Asia, Russia taking the northern part and extending its empire along China's northern border, across Siberia, and then crossing the North Pacific to Alaska.

Chinese interests looked to warmer climes, using the tribute system and commercial colonies to extend Qing influence throughout maritime East Asia. Thus the Qing court received a steady stream of ambassadors, students, merchants, pilgrims and dignitaries from Korea, Indo-China, Malaya, the East Indies and Burma.

The growing Chinese Empire was documented in maps created in the Western style under the guidance of Jesuit scholars resident at the Qing court. As these Europeans gained influence with the imperial family, a cultural backlash developed. On their part, the Jesuits used the traditional dress of Chinese scholar-officials, learned the language, memorized the Confucian classics, and became important conduits through which East Asian ideas reached Europeans. Jesuit influence in China declined in the 1700s, but at the same time tea, porcelain, and Chinese decorative items joined silk and spices as products desired by Europeans.

The Qing golden age reached its limits as the rapidly growing population pressed against the limited amount of arable land. As plots were divided up into smaller units, they often could not feed a family, brought on debts and eventual loss of land. Wealthy money lenders seemed to benefit from the suffering of small farmers. Peasant rebellions in China began to occur in 1774.

Meanwhile, the Chinese emperors, confident in the superiority of their way of life, resisted change and cut themselves off from outside influences. When European trading empires tried to enter the vast Chinese market, they were rebuffed. Eventually British interests developed a trade in opium by smuggling and bribing officials. War broke out between Britain and China when the emperor's officials tried to suppress the illicit commerce.

The Opium Wars (1840–41) forced China to open more trade ports, which, in turn, stimulated rebellions within China from hungry peasants as well as from Chinese who resented the Western intrusions. A group which the latter founded called the Society of Harmonious Fists rose up against Western missionaries and traders. When this "Boxer" Rebellion (1900–01) was put down by foreign troops, China was almost completely dominated by outside interests.

The Boxer movement marshalled ideas and images from Confucian, Taoist, and Buddhist traditions in China, but in other ways it expressed thoroughly modern national liberation themes. The acts of evil perpetrated by the imperial powers angered the Court in Heaven which would, the Boxers believed, send great sages to instruct the youth of China in right living and to redress the wrongs.

European Imperialism in Africa, 1870–1900

I N THIS DRAMATIC presentation, the cartographer of map 81 has created an invasion map of the world's second largest continent. All of the invaders have come from Europe and all have arrived by sea. Note that the map uses no political boundaries within Africa in order to emphasize the thrust of the invasion indicated by the colored arrows. The key speaks of the "penetration" of the continent, which implies gaining entry by use of overpowering force.

The resistance was provided by nature and by people. Africa's natural characteristics – rapids and waterfalls – restricted ocean-going ships from reaching the interior. The one exception was the lower Nile, which had made Egypt an important part of the Mediterranean world for four millennia.

Another factor restricting European access to Africa was the great extent of the Sahara which placed a forbidding landscape, in some places 1,000 miles (1,600km) wide, between the Mediterranean Sea and the productive lands of Africa's savanna belt. The Nile provided the only convenient avenue across the desert, but a series of cataracts interrupted riverine transportation, making it difficult or impossible above the first cataract.

Finally, the well-developed cultural patterns within Africa supported tightly-knit trading systems which limited outside interests to contact at designated places near the edge of the continent, often on islands just off the coast. As the map shows, some coastal areas had been taken over by European nations in 1880. After 1880, however, European governments began to scramble amongst themselves to carve out colonies in the African interior. Each nation competed with the others to control lands which might supply raw materials for the industrial revolution, to gain peoples who might become markets for manufactured goods, and to color patches on a map which might indicate the extent of national glory.

Map 85 (p. 110) shows how Africa was eventually partitioned into colonies by the European powers in the period from 1880 to 1914. Note that Ethiopia (Abyssinia) held on to its independence, although it was later occupied by Italian troops (1935–1941).

Although Africa's Mediterranean region, Egypt, and the coastal areas of the Red Sea and the Indian Ocean were known to the outside world for thousands of years, it was not until the nineteenth century that European explorers were able to piece together an accurate map of the continent's interior.

Mungo Park led the way in 1795. A young doctor from Scotland, he took over an initiative by the recently established African Association in London and ventured up the Gambia river. Like most Europeans, he soon fell victim to tropical diseases but he struggled on, crossing the low divide and reaching the Niger river at Segou. He determined that the Niger flowed eastward before he was forced to retrace his steps. A second expedition in 1805 brought with it supplies so that the members could construct boats when they reached the Niger, since they planned to then float down the river on a great voyage of discovery. A party of 38 explorers left London, but only 10 were alive by the time the expedition reached the Niger. Park, three other Europeans, and four Africans then set off on rafts and floated downstream for over 1,000 miles (1,600km), passing Timbuktu and Gao before coming to grief in some rapids on the edge of Dahomey. One African survived and managed to bring Park's notes to the coast. When these notes arrived in London, they created a sensation and launched a century of African exploration.

David Livingstone, another Scot, became the most famous African explorer. He was a missionary and soon became obsessed with finding routes by which to reach peoples in the continent's interior. In 1855 he discovered Victoria Falls on the Zambezi river, which he named after his queen. Continued exploration of the great lakes region of East Africa cut Livingstone off from European contacts. Then a brash reporter, Henry Stanley, ventured into the unknown to locate the explorer, following an ancient trade route from Zanzibar to Lake Tanganyika. There he spotted a European and offered his famous greeting, "Dr. Livingstone, I presume."

Map 81 European Imperialism in Africa, 1870–1900. The public fascination with the exploits of such people as Park, Livingstone, and Stanley paralleled the political and economic interests of the imperial powers. Soon there would be a mad scramble to divide up the continent into colonies, the results of which are illustrated on map 85. But the fascination with interior Africa continued, often mixed with an enthusiasm for erecting an imperialistic framework to carry out the "white man's burden" of bringing Christianity and European civilization to the "Dark Continent", as it was called by westerners.

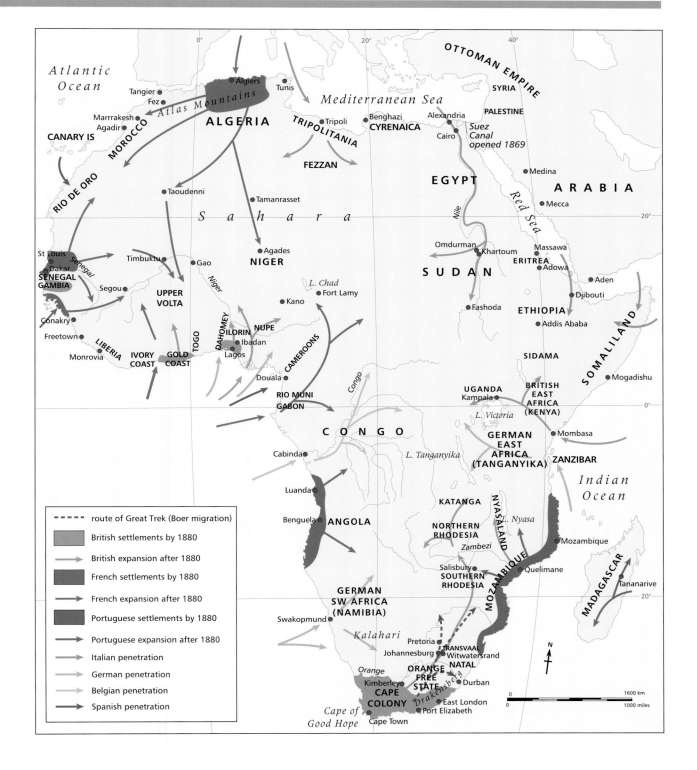

Atlantic Ocean

OTTOMAN EMPIRE

Tangier
Fez
Algiers
Tunis
Mediterranean Sea
SYRIA
PALESTINE

Marrrakesh
Agadir
Atlas Mountains
ALGERIA
TRIPOLITANIA
Tripoli
Benghazi
CYRENAICA
Alexandria
Cairo
Suez Canal opened 1869

CANARY IS
MOROCCO
FEZZAN

RIO DE ORO

Taoudenni
S a h a r a
Tamanrasset
EGYPT
Medina
A R A B I A
Mecca

Nile
Red Sea

St Louis
Senegal
Timbuktu
Gao
Agades
NIGER
Omdurman
Khartoum
Massawa
ERITREA
Adowa
Aden

Dakar
SENEGAL
GAMBIA
Segou
UPPER VOLTA
Niger
Kano
L. Chad
Fort Lamy
SUDAN
Fashoda
ETHIOPIA
Addis Ababa
Djibouti

Conakry
Freetown
LIBERIA
Monrovia
IVORY COAST
GOLD COAST
TOGO
DAHOMEY
ILORIN
Ibadan
Lagos
NUPE
Douala
CAMEROONS
RIO MUNI
GABON
Congo
SIDAMA
SOMALILAND
Mogadishu

UGANDA
Kampala
BRITISH EAST AFRICA (KENYA)
Mombasa

C O N G O
L. Victoria
GERMAN EAST AFRICA (TANGANYIKA)
ZANZIBAR
Indian Ocean

Cabinda
L. Tanganyika

Luanda
KATANGA
NORTHERN RHODESIA
NYASALAND
L. Nyasa
Mozambique

Benguela
ANGOLA
Zambezi
MOZAMBIQUE
Quelimane
Salisbury
SOUTHERN RHODESIA
MADAGASCAR
Tananarive

GERMAN SW AFRICA (NAMIBIA)
Swakopmund
Kalahari
Pretoria
Johannesburg
Witwatersrand
TRANSVAAL
NATAL
Orange
ORANGE FREE STATE
Kimberley
CAPE COLONY
Drakensberg
Durban
East London
Port Elizabeth
Cape of Good Hope
Cape Town

N

- - - - route of Great Trek (Boer migration)
British settlements by 1880
British expansion after 1880
French settlements by 1880
French expansion after 1880
Portuguese settlements by 1880
Portuguese expansion after 1880
Italian penetration
German penetration
Belgian penetration
Spanish penetration

0   1600 km
0   1000 miles

The Expansion of Japan, 1872–1910

JAPAN'S INSULAR situation created a unique history. The emergence of a single language and an integrated political structure at an early date created a strong sense of national identity on the islands even in times of turmoil, internal strife, and dislocation. One dynasty of emperors, although varying in power from period to period, had headed the Japanese state since the seventh century of the Common Era.

Although Japan often looked on China as a cultural leader, it resisted invasions on several occasions and never became a Chinese province. It turned back the Mongols and when Europeans started arriving in force, the government closed Japan to outside influences. Westerners called it the "Hermit Kingdom." After 1641 only one European ship (a Dutch vessel) was permitted to trade with Japan each year, although the Chinese were allowed to develop a regular system of commerce, but only under severe restrictions.

In the early nineteenth century the shogun, a hereditary military dictator who was subservient to the emperor in theory but ruled Japan in fact, showed signs of revising the policy of isolationism. By 1850 the whaling industry of the United States and other nations brought foreigners into Japanese waters. These contacts led the American government to send an expedition to Edo Bay (Tokyo) to open up Japan to American commerce.

In 1853 Commodore Matthew C. Perry arrived with a letter from the US president requesting a commercial treaty. He returned the following year and secured the opening of two ports to a regulated trade. Agreements with other European nations followed. Soon the outsiders moved to destroy Japan's coastal defenses and take control of its commerce. It looked like Japan would be carved up into various "spheres of influence" by the Western powers.

But internal struggles over the next decade severely weakened the shogunate, the so-called feudal system on which it was built, and the policy of isolationism. Finally in 1867 the new shogun resigned, and a vigorous young emperor who was open to new ways took over direct rule of the nation. The Meiji restoration, as it was called, marked the beginning of modern Japan.

Edo, the former seat of the shogun, was renamed Tokyo ("Eastern Capital") and the regional warlords soon turned over their estates to the emperor. It was a new Japan and the new leaders pushed to bring the nation up to date as soon as possible. They modernized agricultural practices and encouraged this sector of the economy. The government then sponsored the building of railroads, telegraph lines, mines, factories, and mills. The old feudal estates were turned into centers to spread the new industrial way of life, many of them becoming new towns outfitted with streetcars and modern buildings.

When Tokyo became the capital in 1868 it had a population of over one million inhabitants, making it one of the largest cities in the world. The center of the city was the old great castle of the shogun, with a chaotic pattern of residential areas, temples, markets, and gardens surrounding it in every direction. With the Meiji program of modernization, Tokyo became the hub of the national railway network. By 1890 the city had a twelve-story skyscraper with an elevator imported from the United States. Large, new department stores were very popular with the inhabitants. Some of the wares were imported, but new factories soon supplied stores with local products too.

The housing stock of Tokyo was the last element of the city to assume a modern character. The trend was set by a row of brick houses in Western styles erected along the Ginza for the leaders of Japan's industrial revolution.

Even so, by 1895, only one in eight Japanese people lived in a city. But the number expanded rapidly so that four decades later almost half of the people were urbanites. International trade opened new horizons to the Japanese and the rapid industrialization of the economy pointed to the need for raw materials and new markets. Japanese forces started to fashion an empire in East Asia, asserting control over nearby islands and territories.

Expansion meant fighting China, which traditionally had controlled these areas, and then Russia, which had extended its empire across Siberia to the Pacific Ocean and the Sea of Japan. Victories in 1895 and 1905 gave the Japanese a taste for more adventures. In 1910 they annexed Korea and turned their attention to Manchuria.

Map 82 The Expansion of Japan, 1872–1910. In the early 1870s Japan established a national system of education and founded a modern navy. Both help to explain what is shown in this map: how the "Hermit Kingdom" still living in a feudal situation in the 1850s could modernize and industrialize in a generation. Wars with China (1894–5) and then Russia (1904–5) made Japan a world power. The new navy was employed in Japan's early expansion, taking the Ryuku islands, including Okinawa, in 1872 and the Kurile Islands in 1875. Both Korea and Formosa were renamed when annexed by Japan.

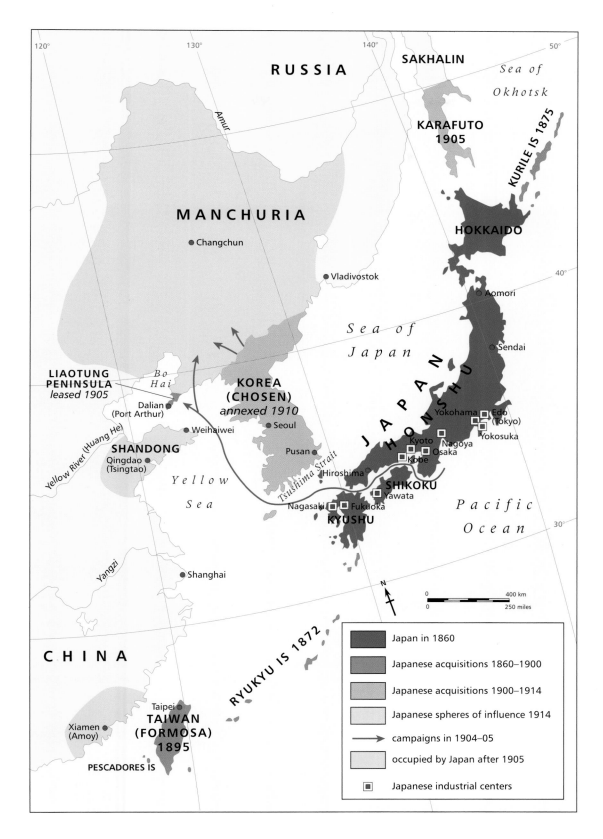

| | 120° | 130° | 140° | 50° |

RUSSIA

SAKHALIN

Sea of Okhotsk

KARAFUTO 1905

Amur

KURILE IS 1875

MANCHURIA

● Changchun

HOKKAIDO

● Vladivostok

40°

○ Aomori

Sea of Japan

○ Sendai

LIAOTUNG PENINSULA *leased 1905*

Bo Hai

KOREA (CHOSEN) *annexed 1910*

Dalian ● (Port Arthur)

● Seoul

J A P A N

H O N S H U

Yokohama □ ● ○ Edo (Tokyo)

● Weihaiwei

Pusan ○

Kyoto □ Nagoya Yokosuka

SHANDONG

Osaka

Qingdao ● (Tsingtao)

Yellow River (Huang He)

Yellow Sea

Kobe □

Tsushima Strait

Hiroshima ●

SHIKOKU

Pacific Ocean

Yawata □

30°

Nagasaki □ □ Fukuoka

KYUSHU

Yangzi

● Shanghai

N

| 0 | 400 km |
| 0 | 250 miles |

RYUKYU IS 1872

CHINA

Taipei ●

Xiamen ● (Amoy)

TAIWAN (FORMOSA) 1895

PESCADORES IS

■	Japan in 1860	
■	Japanese acquisitions 1860–1900	
■	Japanese acquisitions 1900–1914	
■	Japanese spheres of influence 1914	
→	campaigns in 1904–05	
■	occupied by Japan after 1905	
⊡	Japanese industrial centers	

The Twentieth
Century

THE PRIMARY source maps that illustrate the introductions to each section of this atlas have been chosen to represent mapmaking from different parts of the world. The first one was probably created in Babylon in Mesopotamia. Ptolemy's map, our second example, was conceived in Egypt but the version shown in this atlas (see p. 46) was drawn centuries later in Italy. Then, the Chinese image of the eastern hemisphere presented a European-type map in an Asian style. Africa, Asia, and Europe have all been represented, and so now we turn to the New World for a global perspective in the twentieth century. But even this has roots in the Old World.

ONE MAN'S WORLD VIEW
Hendrik Willem Van Loon was born in 1882 in Holland in a town which lies 12 feet below sea level. As a child he drew maps and as an adolescent started to compile an encyclopedia of world history. Later in life he became a cele-

brated American man of letters and his *Geography* was a bestseller when published in 1932. It was exceeded in influence and popularity only by his earlier account of the *Story of Mankind* (1921).

The dust jacket of Van Loon's *Geography*, when removed and turned inside out, contained the map of the world shown opposite. It was drawn by the author and used, in parts, to illustrate the text. The legend indicates that Van Loon used the projection of "his good neighbor," Gerhard Mercator, to present a familiar image, but he personalized the shapes and decorated the surface according to his own insights. The earth was brought together into a single design by the cartographer's artistic strokes, even if Japan and New Zealand needed to be squeezed in at the right-hand margin.

MERCATOR'S LEGACY

Mercator, who published his great map of the world in 1569, had carefully worked out the mathematics for a new projection which would stretch the map as it proceeded poleward so that directions on the sheet would remain constant, thus always presenting lands in their true shape. To achieve this great advantage for navigators, the cartographer had to distort the size of the lands and seas with each increase in latitude. Mercator was not so concerned about how the projection would look, but he wanted it to be an accurate portrayal that would also aid navigation.

The 1569 map was to be an object of study for individuals wanting to know about the world. Therefore Mercator included long notes about a variety of geographical topics and some discussion of how the world was seen by people in times past. Like Ptolemy of ancient times, Mercator provided a frame into which new discoveries could be placed. It took a long time for his world to be accepted by sailors but cartographers immediately appreciated his industry in compiling such a large map and used his data, albeit on different projections, for their own world maps. Almost every world map printed in the next four decades used information from this map.

Gradually Mercator's projection also became the standard not only for navigation and scientific purposes, but also for popular maps, school books, and even geographical games. It remains our classic image of the world, readily obtained at a neighborhood store and often displayed behind desks in offices of authority.

CENTURY OF CHANGE

It is not difficult to find examples throughout history of individuals like Mercator who thought they lived in a time of unprecedented change. It is therefore not surprising to find scholars referring to the twentieth century as one of constant change, a period of flux when civilization always seems to be transforming itself. What is worthy of note, however, is how almost everyone seems to agree with this assessment.

The advent of weapons of mass destruction certainly gives this interpretation much validity as does the realization that the earth as an ecological system is being degraded each day. Then there is the population explosion which doubled the number of the world's people in the first half of the twentieth century, doubled it again in a few decades and is threatening to double it once more as the new century begins.

In the midst of rapid change, however, the historian's angle of vision reminds us to look for continuity as well as change. The forces moving any contemporary society are always difficult to understand. A world which has witnessed two world wars, economic collapse, the breakup of global empires, the threat of nuclear bombs, the distorting fears of the Cold War, the sweeping refashioning of life by technology, the explosion of the population, and a complete reorientation in patterns of thought may well conclude that it lives in a perpetual revolution. Yet it must also address the basic facts of human nature – a constant that dates back to our earliest records – and the well defined heritage that tells us who we are.

History's bridge between past and present constantly reminds students to balance their thinking, to consider continuity in the midst of change and visa versa. As world history calls for them to define questions in global terms and use the ends of the earth to frame their studies, it also reminds them of their identity in communities of kinship and neighborhood, in ethnic traditions and religious persuasions, in regional identification and national citizenship.

The purpose of Van Loon's map, indicated in the text, was to help viewers see themselves as "fellow-passengers on the same planet, all of us equally responsible for the happiness and well-being of the world in which we happen to live."

Europe and Its Empires in 1914

MAPS WHICH tell the story of world history in the nineteenth and the early twentieth centuries take on a Eurocentric character. It is no accident that the prime meridian, the current starting point for measuring longitude, runs through England, France, and Spain. Thus to survey European affairs in 1914, on the eve of World War I, two maps focused on Europe are really needed. One map should show conditions in Europe itself and a second one should record the extent of its empires.

After the age of American independence (1776–1838; see map 75, p. 95), however, it is no longer absolutely necessary to include the Western Hemisphere in the purview.

Canada, it is true, was aligned with Great Britain, and European nations still retained a variety of small colonies in the Caribbean, but European imperial holdings in 1914 were centered in Africa and Asia.

On map 83 the nations of Europe which possessed overseas empires are assigned a particular color. The same color is then used to indicate areas they controlled as colonies

Map 83 European Empires in 1914. The British Empire, because of its far-flung nature, was especially dependant on control of essential sea lanes. It had key naval bases at Gibraltar, Malta, Cyprus, the Suez Canal, the entrance to the Red Sea, the head of the Gulf of Aden, and on the Strait of Malacca between Malaya and Sumatra.

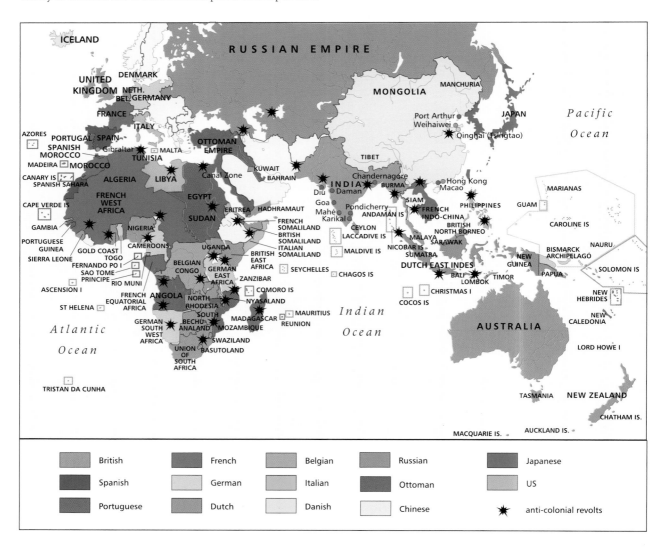

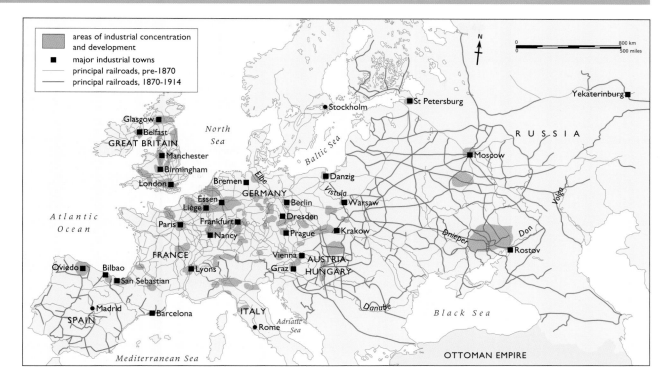

Map 84 Industrialized Europe in 1914. Between 1870 and 1914 railroads seemed to link the various nations together into a continental system. This map makes it difficult to see the national boundaries and certainly does not readily show the fault lines which would soon divide the continent into two warring alliances. The map does, however, suggest which nations entered the industrial era at a later date by the age of the various national railroad systems.

or protectorates. For example, France is colored blue on the map and then the color is repeated in the wide expanses of French West Africa, French Equatorial Africa, Madagascar, and French Indo-China. A close scrutiny of the map will show that France also controlled a variety of islands from the Comoro Islands and Reunion in the Indian Ocean to New Caledonia in the South Pacific.

A comparison between this map and map 74 (p. 94) which portrays European imperialism from 1815 to 1870 shows some significant changes. The Spanish Empire, for example, was substantially reduced by 1914 to the Spanish Sahara and a few islands along Africa's west coast. Also, two rivals to European domination appear on the twentieth-century map: the United States and Japan. The United States, as a result of the Spanish-American War

in 1898, took over Spain's former colonies in the Philippine Islands and on Guam.

In 1868 Japan, after the restoration of the authority of the Meiji Emperor, sought knowledge from all over the world in an effort to become a first-class power. Rapid industrialization and widespread reforms soon followed. As Japan entered the competition for world markets and raw materials, its interests clashed with those of China and Russia. After two wars with these empires, the Japanese controlled Korea, Formosa, and Sakhalin (see map 82, p. 104).

Three long established empires on this map faced severe problems in 1914. China still extended its authority over a wide area, but suffered from commercial inroads made by European powers as well as the loss of territories to Russia and Japan. The Ottoman Empire was often referred to as "the sick man of Europe," struggling to control a variety of subject peoples in the Near East. Austria-Hungary in Europe was also seeking ways to manage the discontent of minority populations, an episode of which would soon ignite World War I and lead to a revision of this map (see maps 88 and 89, pp. 114–15).

Africa in 1914

THE EUROPEAN discovery of the heart of Africa (see map 81, p. 103) proceeded from east to west, starting from ancient cities on the Indian Ocean commercial route, proceeding over the highlands and the rift valleys with their great lakes, and then tracing the Congo river from its sources to the Atlantic. In 1877 Henry Morton Stanley arrived at the mouth of the Congo after a three-year expedition. European nations were ready to follow up their discoveries with forces to occupy the continent and financial investments to construct roads, railways, and cities. In return, they expected a return on their investment.

Before 1875 European leaders saw little advantage in acquiring African territories. But France's defeat by Prussia in 1871 seemed to set off a new way of thinking about empire. French interests suggested that gaining colonies abroad might balance some losses at home. Mercantilist ideas returned pointing out that colonial resources and markets might lead to national self-sufficiency. Then governments could set high, protective tariffs that would help new industries develop at home, building up national power.

Meanwhile Germany and later Italy, newly unified nations (see map 72, p. 91), did not have imperial holdings and felt left out. They looked at the world map and concluded that Britain's prosperity, and its leadership in the Industrial Revolution (see map 76, p. 96), were consequences of its far-flung empire (see maps 67 and 68, pp. 86–7). They demanded their share. The dedication of missionary efforts and the quest for knowledge thus blended with nationalism, economic gain, and military expansion in a race for colonies.

Leopold II of Belgium was one of the leaders of the renewed interest in tropical Africa. His own small nation was granted its independence from the Netherlands in 1831 after a liberal and national revolt (see map 71, p. 90). The king took a personal interest in the Congo and a Belgian association employed Stanley to return there in 1880 to advance Christianity and civilization. Pierre Savorgnan de Brazza was already exploring the area for France and soon a race was on between the two European nations for the lion's share of the territory. The newcomers soon erected two capital cities near the mouth of the river: Brazzaville on the right bank and Leopoldville, now Kinshasa, on the left.

In nearby Angola, Portuguese slave castles and the few settlements along the coast had little direct contact with the interior. As the slave trade declined and slavery was outlawed in 1858, Portuguese traders began venturing inland, eventually hoping to develop connections with Portuguese holdings on the Indian Ocean. But these ambitions proved too great for a small nation.

When the great powers addressed the African situation at a conference in Berlin (1884–5) and in a series of subsequent agreements, a wedge of English colonies was recognized in central Africa and Germany was given rights to Togoland and extensive areas in the Cameroons, Southwest, and East Africa. The treaty, signed by 14 European nations, recognized French equatorial lands, extensive holdings in West Africa, and the Madagascar colony. Italy received coastal lands on the horn of Africa and Libya. The Belgian Congo stretched eastward to the Great Rift Valley. Spain was left with only a few scattered holdings, a measure of its diminished status in the European halls of power.

British interests were well represented in tropical West Africa, along the Indian Ocean, and in South and Central Africa. They also controlled Egypt and later added the Sudan after a confrontation with the French.

Both the French and the British tried to group their African colonies in a contiguous arrangement. Most of the French holdings were clustered in West Africa where the tricolor flag flew over imperial outposts stretching from the Mediterranean Sea to the Equator. Nigeria however, the most heavily populated colony in West Africa, was a British possession.

The axis of the British Empire in Africa extended from Cairo to Cape Town, but it weakened in the center of the continent where the Belgian Congo reached across to abut German East Africa. In fact, the limits of power for Britain, France or any other imperial presence in Africa around 1900 had less to do with colored areas on a map than the problems of actually occupying such vast colonies and establishing an effective administration. Transportation and communication facilities, economic development, and winning the loyalty of local peoples would be needed to secure the bands of empire. Pacification of subject peoples, which allowed the partitioning of the continent, depended in no small measure on utilizing existing African institutions for imperial ends.

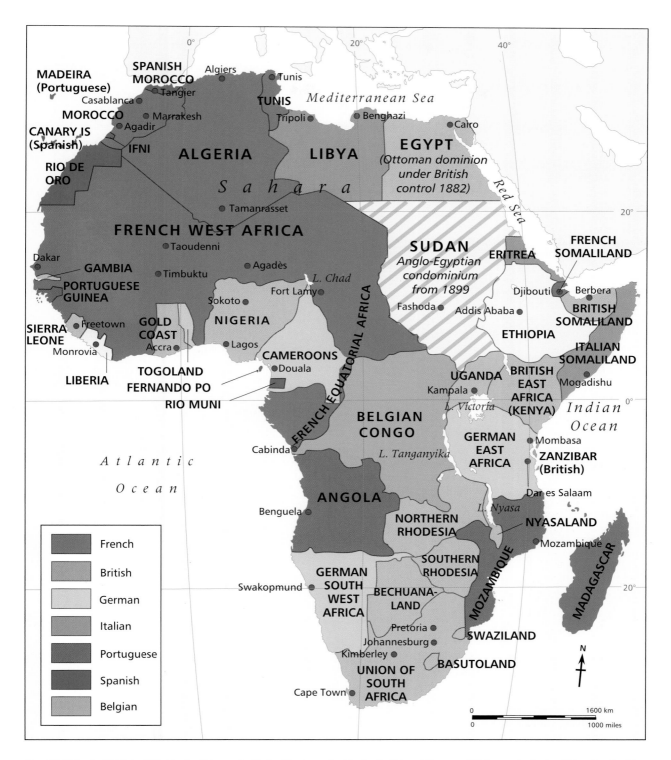

Map 85 Africa in 1914. In 1871, the Englishman Cecil John Rhodes arrived in South Africa at the age of 18 in search of a healthier climate. His investments in the diamond fields paid off handsomely and by 1890 he controlled 90 percent of the world's production of that gemstone. Then he turned to gold mining, politics, economic development, and imperial expansion. His dream of a railroad along a British right-of-way between Cairo and Cape Town almost came within striking distance, as illustrated on this map.

World War I, 1914–1918

IN 1914 the system of international alliances designed to keep the peace failed, bringing on a war that seemed to come by accident rather than by design. At the beginning of the war Central Europe pulled together into one alliance system connecting Germany, Austria-Hungary, and the Ottoman Empire. It presented a seemingly solid front until one recalls the "sick man" status of the Ottoman Empire

Map 86 World War I in Europe. The major battles of World War I in Europe centered in three theaters: the eastern front, where German forces pushed Russian troops back until the Revolution of 1917 took Russia out of the war; the western front, along the armistice line, which was the scene of the mutual butchery highlighted on the inset map; and the important battles that also took place at the head of the Adriatic Sea where Austria-Hungary bordered Italy.

and the fragile circumstances of minority populations on the Balkan Peninsula.

The Balkan Peninsula is also an ideal place to focus on the causes and the results of the Great War. This stretch of land between the Black, the Aegean, and the Adriatic seas was divided in 1914 between Austria-Hungarian provinces in the north, the Ottoman Empire and its ally, Bulgaria, in the south, and a series of former Ottoman territories which looked to the Triple Entente Powers for protection.

The Triple Entente balanced the might of the Central Powers. Its leading states were Britain, France, and Russia. Italy and several other nations also joined these allies.

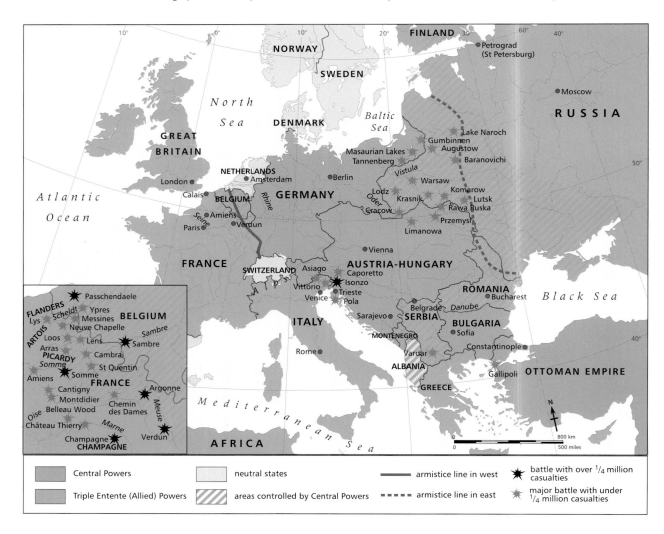

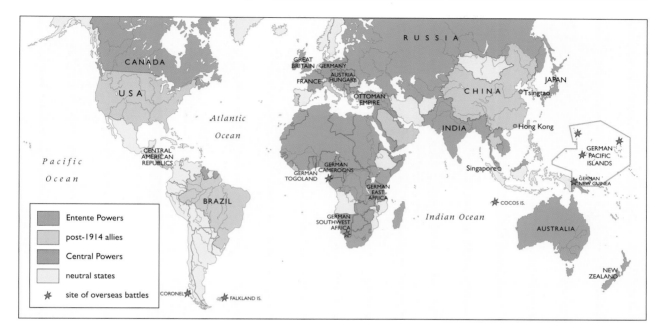

Map 87 A World at War. When the war broke out, there were eight German cruisers stationed around its empire. Count von Spee took three of these ships from China and sailed for South America where two more ships joined the flotilla. In action off the coast of Chile, at Coronel, Spee destroyed a smaller British fleet and then stopped to attack the British colony of the Falkland Islands on his way to Europe. A British fleet in the South Atlantic surprised the Germans, sinking four of their five ships. Another German cruiser from China attacked British merchant ships in the Indian Ocean before it was sunk near Cocos Island.

Switzerland, the Netherlands, Scandinavia, and newly independent Albania remained neutral. In the course of the fighting the Central Powers were able to accomplish three objectives: to regain control of the Balkan Peninsula; to extend east into Russian territory, knocking it out of the war; and to fight French and British troops to a standstill along a bloody line through Belgium and France.

The tide of war started to turn after the United States entered the war and the Russian Revolution complicated the picture in 1917. The armistice lines in 1918 were therefore closer to the original borders of the Central Powers. The peace arrangements, however, would completely change the map, paying little attention to the armistice lines.

Woodrow Wilson, the American president, laid down "Fourteen Points" as the basis for a peace which would follow the Great War. One of these, the "national self-deter-

mination" of peoples, provided an ideological basis for constantly changing political maps ever after.

The Treaty of Versailles (1919) sank many of Wilson's lofty goals by a series of compromises and vindictive arrangements. These also meant that the map of Europe would be in flux for the rest of the century.

Although most of the fighting centered in Europe itself, the conflict had world-wide proportions, as map 87 makes clear. Germany's overseas empire was especially vulnerable. Some Pacific possessions were lost to the British navy in the first year of the war. Britain's African colonists and an international contingent of forces helped take Togoland, the Cameroons, and Southwest Africa from stubborn German defenders by 1917. German East Africa held out but was lost at the Versailles peace table.

The Japanese used the declaration of war in 1914 to send an ultimatum to Germany demanding that it hand over its territorial rights in China. When Germany refused, Japan entered the conflict as an ally and seized German holdings in China and various islands in the Pacific.

The overseas colonies (and former colonies) of Great Britain and France supplied many troops to fight battles in Europe. The Russian and Ottoman armies also drew on many subject peoples to support the war effort. People from all over the globe fought in Europe.

The Aftermath of World War I

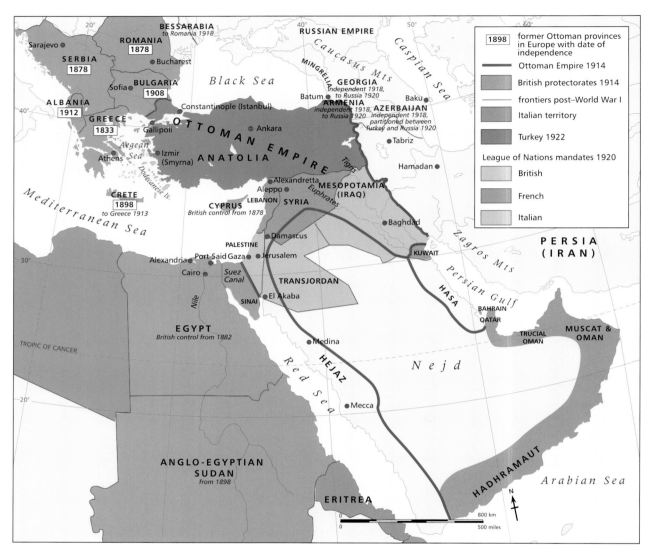

Map 88 The End of the Ottoman Empire. The political changes recorded on this map began in the 1870s when uprisings on the Balkan Peninsula led Russia to declare war on the Ottoman Empire in 1877. Its success brought a measure of freedom to some provinces, but led other nations to fear an upset to the balance of power. The British sent a fleet to the Black Sea and called for a conference. All the changes dated 1878 on the map were a result of this Congress of Berlin.

THE TREATY of Versailles, drawn up in 1919, created a series of new nations (see map 89) but much of this process can also be viewed as the disintegration of the Ottoman Empire. This process took a century or more: the final phase is summarized on map 88. To put those developments in context, compare both of these with maps 54 and 62 (pp. 69 and 79).

The Ottoman Empire lasted a long time and it gradually lost territories to the expanding power of its neighbors, Austria-Hungary and Russia, both of which acted as "guardians" for former subject populations on the Balkan Peninsula. World War I accelerated the process because the Ottomans were on the losing side, but the advance of French and British interests into Egypt and the Near East started long before 1914.

Map 89 summarizes the political results of World War I and shows developments up to the 1930s. Some political changes shown on this map were provided in the treaty arrangements. These appear in dark green. Other changes had underlying causes reaching back to times before the war. Some came as a result of various peoples making their own bid for a nation-state. None of these fledgling nations, colored apple green on the map, lasted long.

A final series of cartographic alterations (colored light green) had to be made after the death of the "sick man" of Europe. The old Ottoman Empire was divided up by the British and French into mandates and protectorates, with Turkey emerging as an independent successor state. At the very end of the process Saudi Arabia was recognized as an independent nation in 1932.

The formation of new nations, of course, came at the expense of old ones. Germany lost territories both on the east to new states and on the west to France. Poland was reconstituted from lands that had been taken away from her earlier by Germany, Russia, and Austria. Old Austria-Hungary probably lost the most, being split into two second-rank nations and its former imperial lands turning into Czechoslovakia and Yugoslavia.

The extension of the French and British Empires into the former Ottoman territory in the Near East was no longer carried out according to the old colonial model. Instead these lands were placed under the protection of a great power until they gained enough strength to take an independent role in world affairs. Other areas were mandated, or placed in the hands of "enlightened" empires to provide a responsible government while they were on the road to eventual national independence. Former German colonies in Africa and the Pacific were also entrusted to one of the Allies by the League of Nations.

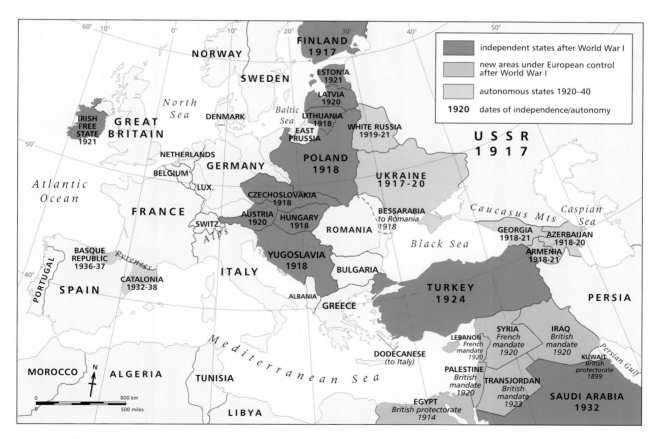

Map 89 Political Changes in Europe and the Near East, 1917–1938. The Polish Corridor gave Poland an outlet to the North Sea but at the same time divided East Prussia from the rest of Germany. Many territories of Czarist Russia tried to set up independent states during the struggles following the communist Revolution in 1917, but these efforts were soon suppressed. A similar movement took place during the Spanish Civil War in the 1930s when General Francisco Franco led a military coup against the Spanish Republic, eventually crushing Catalonia and the Basque Republic with help from the Fascist governments in Germany and Italy.

World War II in Europe, 1939–1945

ALMOST EVERY scholar who has looked for the caus-es of World War II has traced them back to fatal flaws in the peace treaty of 1919. It is therefore natural to consult the map of the Europe that emerged from the Treaty of Versailles when considering the onset and early course of World War II.

The second great war in Europe again involved two blocks of nations pitted against each other: the Axis Pow-ers versus the Allies, comprising France, Great Britain, and eventually the Soviet Union. Germany teamed up with Italy to complete an axis from Berlin to Rome, and this alliance had the unmaking of the Versailles settlement as its first order of business. A series of bold moves car-ried out by the German National Socialist government had started this revision of the treaty even before the outbreak of war. Then, empowered by alliances with Fascist Italy and Soviet Russia, the German military forces conduct-ed *blitzkrieg* ("lightning war") campaigns, not only to recoup the losses inflicted on them in 1919, but also to make a bid for world domination.

German forces took over Denmark in April 1940, then invaded Norway. In May they struck the Netherlands and Belgium. Seemingly unstoppable, the Nazis rolled into France, which fell by the end of June. Marshall Petain agreed to set up a new government, which was friendly to Germany, at Vichy in southern France. Last of all, Germany occupied Yugoslavia and Greece. Italy then entered the war in June, just as the Battle of Britain began between the German Luftwaffe and the Royal Air Force.

Meanwhile Hitler's secret alliance with the Soviet Union permitted the Eurasian power to expand its territories westward, occupying, for a brief time, a large swathe of Eastern Europe from Estonia to Bessarabia (putty colored on the map). Then Hitler stabbed his neighbor in the back, sending German armies eastward toward Moscow and Stalingrad. Once again, as in Napoleon's day, the invaders met their match in a heroic Russian defense of their home-land combined with harsh winter conditions. Note that the line marking the extent of Axis conquests in the east falls just short of Stalingrad. The city was almost entire-ly destroyed, but it remained in Russian hands.

The Axis powers occupied or controlled almost all of continental Europe from the Pyrenees mountains to the Baltic and Black seas. Great Britain held out against sus-tained bombardment from the air in 1940, and when the United States entered the war a year later, following Japan's attack on Pearl Harbor, plans were laid to invade Axis territory. The first Allied successes came in North Africa at the same time that Russian troops were start-ing to push back the invading armies on the eastern front. The Allies then attacked the "soft underbelly" of the Axis Powers in Italy. Finally, in 1944, a huge Allied army landed at Normandy, penetrating Nazi defenses in the west. As it advanced toward Germany this army of lib-eration turned aside a massive counter attack in the Battle of the Bulge. Six months later, the war in Europe was over. This map follows the ebb and flow of power by highlighting conditions in four key years: 1939, 1940, 1941, and 1942.

In 1939 the Nazi Party had been in power for five years in Germany. During this brief period Adolf Hitler murdered his rivals within the party, began persecuting the Jews, seized territory in the Rhineland, supported Fran-co in the Spanish Civil War, united Austria with Germany, and secured parts of Czechoslovakia in the Munich Agree-ment of 1938. He had a "friendly understanding" with Italy and in August, 1939, signed a non-aggression pact with the Soviet Union. Thus the dark green on the map creating an axis along the 14th east meridian must be sup-plemented by keeping in mind Germany's pact with the USSR and a lack of resistance from France and Britain to Axis moves.

The second date on the map, 1940, shows how Joseph Stalin took advantage of the non-aggression pact with Ger-many and gained control of a wide swathe of territory on Russia's western flank.

The Russo-German agreement also explains the third date on the map, mid-1941. As the USSR stood by, the light green areas could be added to Axis control quickly after Germany invaded Poland. By the end of 1940, Nazi successes had brought Hungary, Romania, and Bulgaria into its fold. By June 1, 1941, German and Ital-ian troops overran Yugoslavia and Greece, and took Crete with a parachute invasion.

The fourth date on the map, 1942, shows how far the German armies advanced into the Soviet Union after

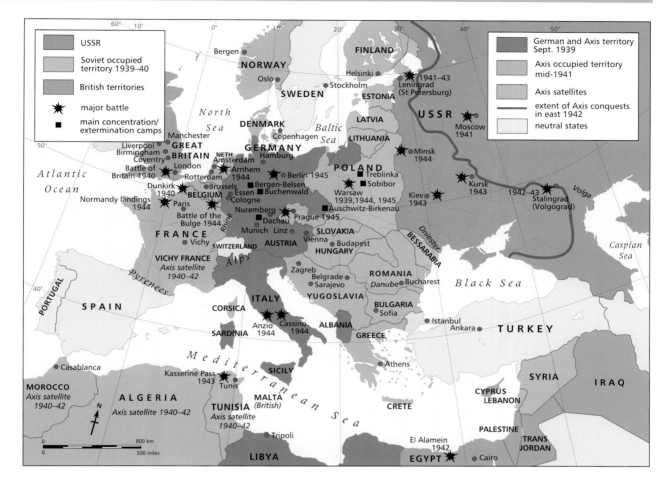

Map 90 World War II in Europe, 1939–1945. One historian has labeled World War II "Germany's Second Bid for European Dominance." In the early days, the Nazi forces met one success after another and by 1942 may be said to have achieved dominance on the continent, at least in its central expanses. It was at the edges, on the British Isles and in the vastness of the Russian landscape that Germany was not able to exert its will. And then there was the context of wider world concerns, evident in September, 1940 when Japan joined Germany and Italy in a pact. This meant that when Japan attacked the United States a year later, Germany was at war with the United States as well. A stalemate such as the one that ended World War I would no longer be possible.

the surprise invasion of June 22, 1941. The move pushed Russia into a mutual aid agreement with Britain. On September 4 the Germans, using Finland as a base of operations, surrounded Leningrad, a siege which would not be lifted until January, 1943. By then the tables had turned on the Eastern front and Soviet forces were pushing the Axis forces backward.

The battles marked on the map, when placed in chronological order, mark the compression of Axis territory as Russian forces advanced westward, Allied armies struck northward from Africa into Italy, and as the Allies moved eastward across France after the Normandy invasion. The last battle, which took place at Berlin on May 1 1945, marked the end of the war in Europe.

World War II in the Pacific, 1941–1945

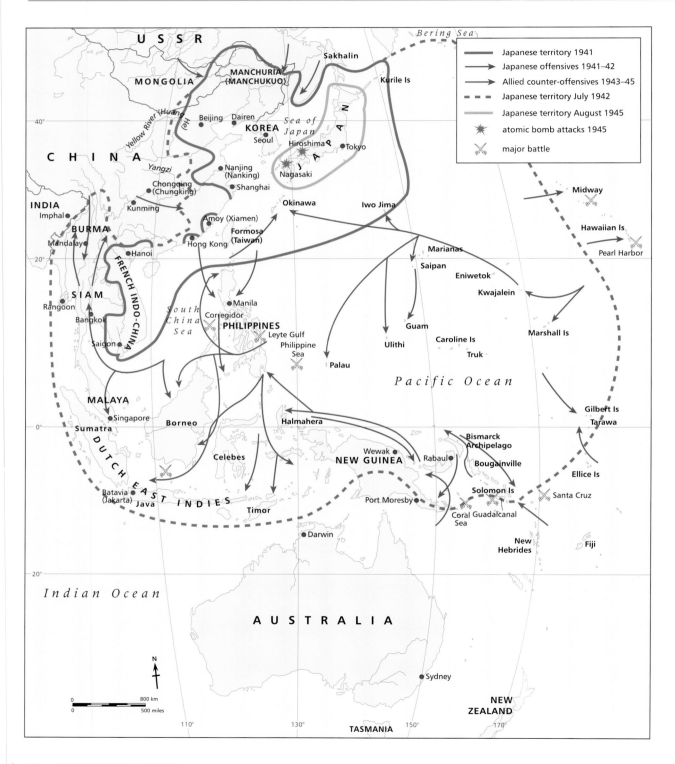

Legend:
- Japanese territory 1941
- Japanese offensives 1941–42
- Allied counter-offensives 1943–45
- Japanese territory July 1942
- Japanese territory August 1945
- atomic bomb attacks 1945
- major battle

USSR

Bering Sea

MONGOLIA

MANCHURIA (MANCHUKUO)

Sakhalin

Kurile Is

Yellow River (Huang He)

Beijing

Dairen

KOREA

Sea of Japan

JAPAN

Midway

CHINA

Seoul

Hiroshima

Tokyo

Hawaiian Is

Yangzi

Nanjing (Nanking)

Nagasaki

Iwo Jima

Pearl Harbor

Chongqing (Chungking)

Shanghai

INDIA

Kunming

Okinawa

Marianas

Imphal

Amoy (Xiamen)

Saipan

Eniwetok

BURMA

Formosa (Taiwan)

Hong Kong

Kwajalein

Mandalay

Hanoi

FRENCH INDO-CHINA

Marshall Is

SIAM

Rangoon

Manila

South China Sea

Corregidor

PHILIPPINES

Guam

Bangkok

Leyte Gulf

Ulithi

Caroline Is

Saigon

Philippine Sea

Truk

Palau

Pacific Ocean

Gilbert Is

MALAYA

Tarawa

Singapore

Borneo

Halmahera

Bismarck Archipelago

Sumatra

DUTCH EAST INDIES

Celebes

Wewak

NEW GUINEA

Rabaul

Bougainville

Ellice Is

Batavia (Jakarta)

Java

Timor

Port Moresby

Solomon Is

Santa Cruz

Coral Sea

Guadalcanal

New Hebrides

Fiji

Darwin

Indian Ocean

AUSTRALIA

N

0   800 km
0   500 miles

Sydney

NEW ZEALAND

110°   130°   150°   170°

TASMANIA

THE BASIS for World War II in the Pacific was Japan's bid for regional domination by taking advantage of the war in Europe. By joining the Axis Powers, Japan could help them when it attacked European and American colonies in the Far East. In return, Germany and Italy would recognize the New Order Japan planned to impose in the Pacific region.

As in Europe, the narrative must begin five years or so before the war started. Japan's success in gaining an empire early in the twentieth century is illustrated on map 82 (p. 104). Economic stress that led to a worldwide depression, in addition to the dislocations in Japan itself caused by rapid industrialization and a growing population, encouraged Japanese leaders to see an expanding empire as a way out of their problems. Expansion also meant massive military expenditures.

In July 1937, as Japan pushed for further concessions from a weakened China, fighting erupted, a full-scale war ensued, and Japanese troops laid waste to the Chinese capital at Nanking as Chiang Kai-shek and the Chinese army fled to the interior. The "rape of Nanking" alarmed the United States and Great Britain who used diplomatic roadblocks to thwart the Japanese ambitions.

Japan, in turn, joined with the Axis powers and laid plans to initiate surprise attacks on the US and British Pacific fleets, to overrun the European and American colonies, and to set up a Greater East Asian Co-Prosperity Sphere. Hitler would keep Allied forces occupied in Europe while Japan rearranged the Pacific.

Map 91 thus begins in 1941 showing the extent of the Japanese Empire when it decided to launch an attack on the US Pacific Fleet at Pearl Harbor. Note that Japan had already expanded its control in northeast China and had occupied French Indo-China after the fall of France in 1940. It had also seized Amoy and Hong Kong.

On December 7, 1941, the surprise attack on Pearl Harbor and the Philippines temporarily disabled the

US fleet and Japanese forces quickly took advantage of the situation, pushing their empire outward to include the Philippines, the East Indies, Malaya, Siam, and Burma. The US base at Corregidor fell in May, 1942 but when Japanese and US fleets met in the Coral Sea during that same month, the ships fought to a draw.

When Japan sent her largest fleet against American ships guarding Midway Island, the westernmost outpost of the Hawaiian chain, the tide turned. Between June 4 and 7, as four Japanese aircraft carriers were lost, her ability to take the offensive in the Pacific sank as well. It is said that modern Japan never lost a major battle before Midway and never won one after that.

But years of hard fighting were ahead of the United States, which shouldered most of the Allied burden of fighting in the Pacific. Island hopping, the Americans called it, as key islands were invaded by the marines after naval forces cleared out support for the Japanese defenders. The naval battles of Leyte Gulf and the Philippine Sea forced Japanese ships to return to home waters and set up a defensive perimeter around their own country.

When the United States took Iwo Jima in March 1945, it raised a flag on an island airstrip 750 miles (1,206km) from Japan, within striking distance. Then Okinawa fell to the United States in April, and the defeat of the Axis Powers in Europe left Japan alone to face the onslaught of the greatest air offensive of the war. The new atomic bombs dropped on Hiroshima and Nagasaki ended the war, but they also opened a new age of fear. Japan's leaders decided to surrender, and World War II was over.

Not only was the war over, but so was the militarists' dream that Japan could prosper through military conquest. With limited resources, the Japanese clearly saw that peace and commercial development offered better avenues to prosperity. But first a devastated land needed to be rebuilt. Air raids had destroyed about half of the Japanese homes by the summer of 1945.

Perhaps drawing on the experience of rebuilding after frequent natural disasters such as earthquakes and typhoons, and also reaching into deep reserves of national character, Japan accepted defeat and set about reconstructing a nation. US occupation policies speeded up the process so that in 1951 a peace treaty recognized Japan as an independent nation.

Map 91 World War II in the Pacific, 1941–1945. The last months of the war in the Pacific were often clouded by maneuvering among the allies and among local interests for advantageous positions at the end of the war. Japan still had large armies in China when Russian forces entered the Pacific war in August 1945, attacking Manchuria. Chinese opposition forces at the same time necessitated a Japanese army of occupation of almost a million soldiers. When the Japanese in China surrendered, it was not clear who would eventually take their place.

After World War II: Political Changes in East Asia and Europe

T HE END of World War II in Europe and in East Asia may be assigned very specific dates, but the political changes that were ushered in took years to materialize. Indeed some of those adjustments were waiting in the wings, so to speak, while the actors of the world con-

Map 92 East Asia, 1933–1945. In the Long March, a 6000 mile (9600 km) strategic retreat, the Communist Army shrunk from 80,000 to only 20,000 soldiers, and half of the survivors were new recruits picked up on the way. The commitment of the survivors to the cause became the cement which held the Communist leadership together for the next half century.

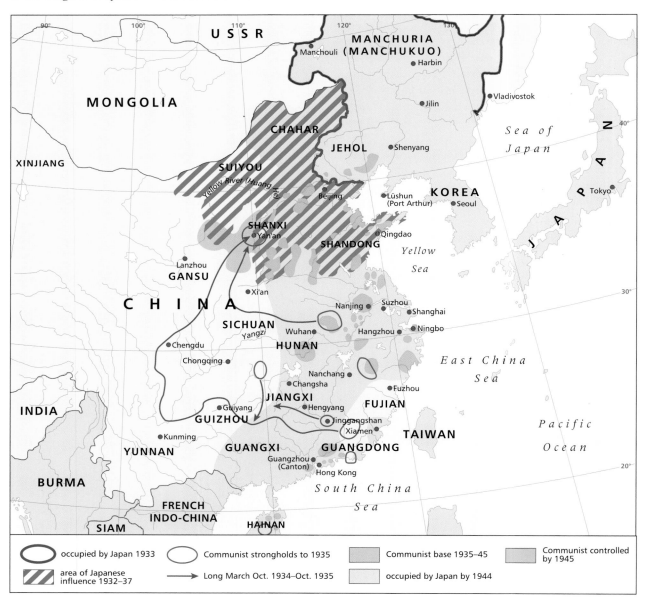

◯ occupied by Japan 1933	◯ Communist strongholds to 1935	▨ Communist base 1935–45	Communist controlled by 1945
▨ area of Japanese influence 1932–37	→ Long March Oct. 1934–Oct. 1935	occupied by Japan by 1944	

flict did their parts. After the fighting was over, they could advance to center stage. Such was the situation in China.

Thus map 92 illustrates two developments: the expansion of Japanese influence from 1933 until 1945, when the entire empire was lost in the World War, and the internal struggle between the two major Chinese factions, the Nationalists and the Communists. This second narrative, the revolutionary struggle, goes back to the founding of the Communist Party in 1921 and reached its climax in 1949 when the defeated Nationalists fled to Taiwan and Mao Zedong proclaimed the People's Republic of China.

When the Chinese Empire, dating back several thousand years, ended in 1912, Dr. Sun Yat-Sen was recognized as the leader of a national renewal that would subdue the regional warlords and start building China into a modern, industrial nation. But Sun Yat-Sen, who died in 1925, was never able to really assume control of China. Meanwhile, Japan took advantage of Chinese disunity to expand its influence (see map 82, p. 104).

Meanwhile, the situation in Europe between 1945 and 1950 saw the division of the continent into two armed camps. Map 93 needs to use only two colors, a yellow-orange to designate the Free World, which combined forces in the North Atlantic Treaty Organization (NATO), and several shades of green to mark the expansion of Communism to those states which eventually signed the Warsaw Pact. The six nations which remained neutral are not colored.

Note how the Soviet Union incorporated the three Baltic states as well as a strip of land along its western border as its troops pushed back the Nazi invaders. These are territories that the Soviets briefly occupied in 1939 to 1940 under the terms of a secret agreement with Hitler. They are shaded medium green on the map.

Germany, after its defeat in 1945, was divided into occupation zones by the Allies. These gradually developed into two separate states: East Germany within the Soviet Bloc and West Germany which was admitted to NATO.

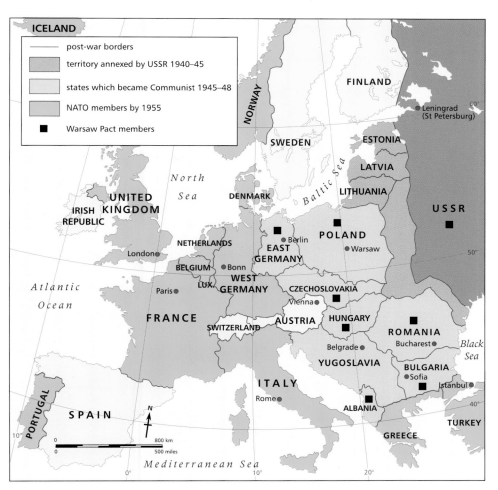

Map 93 Post-War Europe, 1945–1955. Winston Churchill, the British wartime leader, told an American audience that an Iron Curtain had descended over Europe, separating the Free Nations from the Communist World. This map shows that division. At the time, in 1946, the divide ran through Austria which was also split up into occupation zones. In 1956, however, a rare agreement between the Cold War adversaries permitted Austria to be unified as an independent nation on the condition that it would remain neutral.

Asia Since 1945

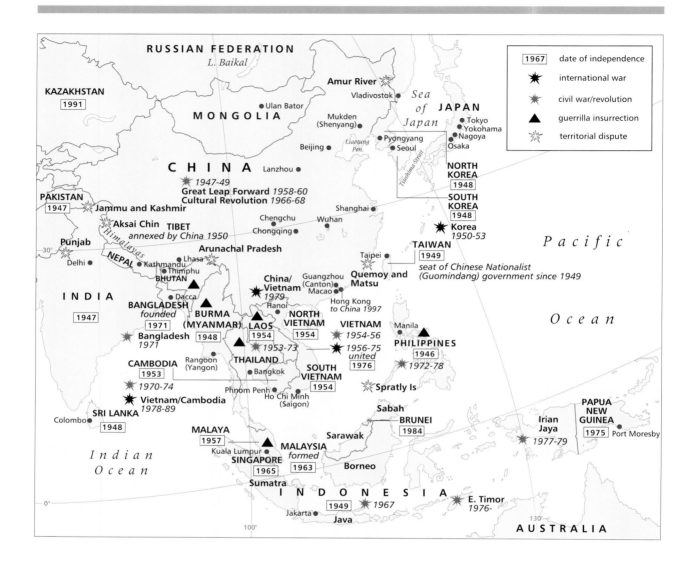

RUSSIAN FEDERATION
L. Baikal

KAZAKHSTAN
1991

MONGOLIA

Ulan Bator

Amur River

Vladivostok

Mukden
(Shenyang)

Sea of Japan

JAPAN

Tokyo
Yokohama
Nagoya
Osaka

Liaotung Pen.

Pyongyang
Seoul

Beijing

CHINA   Lanzhou

1947-49
Great Leap Forward 1958-60
Cultural Revolution 1966-68

PAKISTAN
1947

Jammu and Kashmir

Aksai Chin   TIBET
annexed by China 1950

Chengchu
Chongqing

Wuhan

Shanghai

Tsushima Strait

NORTH
KOREA
1948

SOUTH
KOREA
1948

Korea
1950-53

TAIWAN
1949

Pacific

Punjab
Delhi

Himalayas

NEPAL
Kathmandu

Arunachal Pradesh

Lhasa
Thimphu
BHUTAN

Taipei

seat of Chinese Nationalist
(Guomindang) government since 1949

Ocean

INDIA

Dacca

BANGLADESH
founded
1971

BURMA
(MYANMAR)
1948

China/
Vietnam
1979

Guangzhou
(Canton)
Macao

Hanoi

Quemoy and
Matsu

Hong Kong
to China 1997

LAOS
1954

NORTH
VIETNAM
1954

VIETNAM
1954-56

Manila

Bangladesh
1971

1953-73

CAMBODIA
1953

Rangoon
(Yangon)

THAILAND

Bangkok

SOUTH
VIETNAM
1954

1956-75
united
1976

PHILIPPINES
1946

1972-78

1970-74

Phnom Penh

Ho Chi Minh
(Saigon)

Spratly Is

Vietnam/Cambodia
1978-89

SRI LANKA
1948

Colombo

MALAYA
1957

Kuala Lumpur

SINGAPORE
1965

Sabah

SARAWAK

BRUNEI
1984

Irian
Jaya
1977-79

PAPUA
NEW
GUINEA
1975

Port Moresby

MALAYSIA
formed
1963

Borneo

*Indian
Ocean*

Sumatra

INDONESIA

Jakarta

1949

Java

1967

E. Timor
1976-

AUSTRALIA

Legend:
- 1967 — date of independence
- international war
- civil war/revolution
- guerrilla insurrection
- territorial dispute

M APS 94 AND 95 convey different general messages, but they are part of the same narrative: the development of East, South, and Southeast Asia since 1945. Map 94, which continues the developments shown in map 92 (see p. 120), presents an active scene, full of dynamic symbols noting the achievement of political independence, civil conflicts, insurrections, international wars, and on-going territorial disputes. Although the map records boundaries between nation states, and names each one, it uses only one color, suggesting the common experiences of the region.

Map 94 Asia Since 1945. In 1949 Mao Zedong and the Communists proclaimed the People's Republic of China and suppressed opposition parties, chasing the Republican forces to Taiwan. By 1956 the Chinese had split with the Soviet Union and would soon embark on the "Great Leap Forward." This program divided rural China into communes and tried to disperse industry into small local enterprises scattered throughout the towns and villages. It proved to be an economic disaster. The Great Proletarian Cultural Revolution (1966–8), purged intellectual leaders and teachers suspected of backsliding in an attempt to reignite the dedication of revolutionary elements. Anarchy almost brought China to a standstill. But in the last quarter of the twentieth century China made steady gains in economic development.

Map 95 South Asia Since 1945. This map takes as its basis the march across India organized by Mohandas K. Gandhi in 1930 to protest a tax on salt imposed by the British overlords. Gandhi's message of nonviolent resistance, his appeal to moral truth, and his recurring theme of personal liberation through the struggle for human rights, all fell on fertile ground and flourished after 1945. His attack on colonialism connects with this map, but his simultaneous assault on the roots of discrimination and oppression is a battle that was still being waged at the beginning of the new millennium.

Map 95, on the other hand, takes full advantage of bold coloring to emphasize how South Asia was divided into a set of separate political entities after 1947. It does not employ dramatic symbols, although the area had its share of violence, dislocation, and abrupt change. Instead, it shows how the area was first partitioned into the large nation of India and its northern neighbor Pakistan in 1947. Then, a ring of smaller entities surrounded these two well-populated states: Ceylon, which became Sri Lanka, Burma, Nepal, Bhutan, and Afghanistan. East Pakistan broke away to become an independent country, Bangladesh, in 1971. Meanwhile Tibet and several neighboring territories were annexed by China.

Note that Bangladesh is marked with a civil war/revolution symbol on map 94 and that both maps point to continuing disputes over territory in Jammu and Kashmir.

A partition line established by the United Nations in 1949 divided control of this disputed area between India and Pakistan, but neither nation has accepted the division as a permanent boundary. Fighting broke out along this line once again in 1999, the same year that witnessed a bloody separation of East Timor from Indonesia.

The major international wars recorded on map 94 both involved the United States as a major protagonist. The Korean Conflict (1950–53), ended in a truce which drew an armistice line across the peninsula close to the original parallel which divided Korea into two occupation zones set at the end of World War II. The war in Viet Nam was more complex, reaching back to a civil war or revolution in the 1950s and finally ending with the withdrawal of US troops in 1975 and the union of North and South Vietnam the following year.

Southwest Asia and Its Environs Since World War II

The maps on these pages show the emergence of the modern day world in the lands encircled by the Mediterranean, Black, Caspian, Arabian, and Red seas. The region is often called the Near or Middle East, betraying a Eurocentric bias. The Persian Gulf and

Map 96 Israel and Its Neighbors, 1947 to the Present. The state of Israel was created in 1947 with the support of the Western powers. Until the 1990s there was a clash of arms every decade over Israel's borders and its very right to exist. Then Egypt in 1978 and Jordan in 1996 recognized Israel, leading to a growing accommodation between the Jewish state and its neighbors.

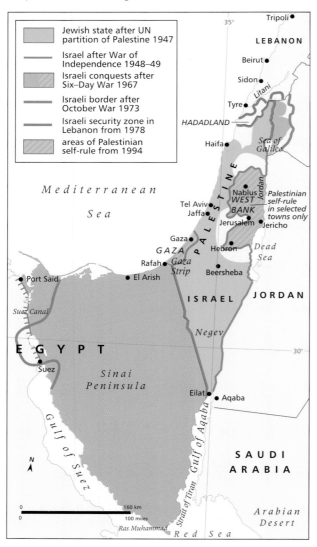

Mesopotamia divide the encircled lands into two segments with Iran dominating the eastern reaches. No nation dominates the other part, although Saudi Arabia would achieve great wealth from its petroleum resources in the last half of the twentieth century. Turkey and Egypt remain the region's most populous nations. Turkey would enjoy special status as a member of NATO and a bridgehead to Europe. Egypt was similarly placed to serve as a connecting link to the rest of Africa.

World War I hastened the dissolution of the Ottoman Empire which for centuries dominated the western segment of the region (see maps 62 and 88, pp. 79 and 114). T.E. Lawrence ("of Arabia"), a British soldier and archaeologist, joined the Arab revolt against the Turks during the 1914–1918 war. Afterwards, in his writings and legend, he tried to present things from the subaltern point of view. In 1919 the area was divided between Britain and France into mandates from the League of Nations. The British occupied Baghdad in 1919 and then proclaimed the former king of Syria as the king of Iraq after the people voted in his favor. Under King Faisel Iraq evolved into a constitutional monarchy allied with Great Britain.

Not until the end of World War II did any other nation in the region gain its independence from the mandate system. Various local rivals contested Arabia until Ibn Saud gained control of the territory and international recognition between 1919 and 1932. Independence came to the other states on the Arabian Peninsula much later, in the 1960s and 1970s.

Meanwhile, in Palestine, the British had promised to facilitate the establishment of "a national home for the Jewish people" without prejudicing "the civil and religious rights of existing non-Jewish communities." Between 1937 and 1947 various plans were advanced to divide the Holy Land into Jewish and Palestinian states, but all were rejected by one party or another. Then, in November, 1947, the United Nations approved a partition plan which the Jews accepted. The Arabs rejected it because it gave the Jews, who made up about one-third of the population, half of the land. On May 14, 1948, Israel was proclaimed as a state by the Jewish inhabitants. Arab armies invaded the new nation the next day. Six months later the Israeli war for independence ended. Israel expanded its borders even further, although neither the Palestinians nor the Arab nations recognized it as a nation.

Map 97 Southwest Asia Since World War II. Four major themes inform this map. The first is the decolonization movement, which led to the recognition of many new nation states in the twentieth century. The second is the extensive petroleum resources located in favored places, especially around the Persian Gulf. The third involved disputes over politics with religious subtexts, led by the long struggle over Israel but also including a bitter, 8-year contest between Iraq and Iran. The fourth theme is the intervention of outside powers in the area, especially the United States which was concerned about the free flow of oil into the world's commercial channels.

In 1967 Israel launched a pre-emptive strike against Egypt and its Arab allies, expanding its territory. In 1973 Egypt and Syria surprised Israel in another war. A series of agreements followed which led to Israeli withdrawal from the Sinai Peninsula. But it was not until 1993 that the Palestine Liberation Organization signed a peace agreement with Israel and a process began to shift control of the West Bank and the Gaza strip to the Palestinians.

The Decolonization of Africa

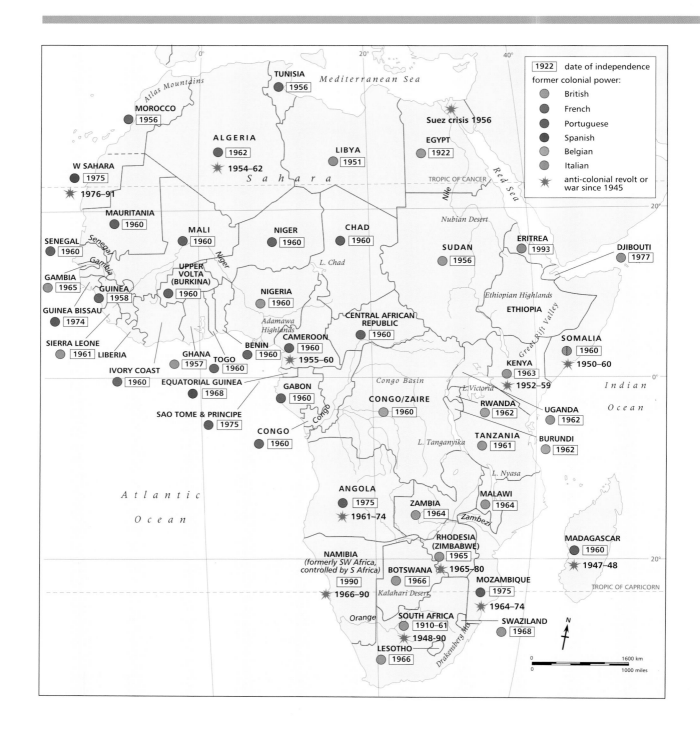

1922 date of independence
former colonial power:
- British
- French
- Portuguese
- Spanish
- Belgian
- Italian
- ✴ anti-colonial revolt or war since 1945

TUNISIA 1956

Atlas Mountains

MOROCCO 1956

ALGERIA 1962
✴ 1954–62

W SAHARA 1975
✴ 1976–91

Mediterranean Sea

LIBYA 1951

Suez crisis 1956

EGYPT 1922

TROPIC OF CANCER

Red Sea

Nile

Sahara

MAURITANIA 1960

SENEGAL 1960

Senegal

Gambia

GAMBIA 1965

GUINEA 1958

GUINEA BISSAU 1974

SIERRA LEONE 1961 LIBERIA

IVORY COAST 1960

MALI 1960

Niger

UPPER VOLTA (BURKINA) 1960

GHANA 1957 TOGO 1960

EQUATORIAL GUINEA 1968

SAO TOME & PRINCIPE 1975

NIGER 1960

NIGERIA 1960

Adamawa Highlands

BENIN 1960

TOGO 1960

CAMEROON 1960
✴ 1955–60

GABON 1960

CONGO 1960

Congo

CHAD 1960

L. Chad

CENTRAL AFRICAN REPUBLIC 1960

Nubian Desert

SUDAN 1956

Ethiopian Highlands

ETHIOPIA

Great Rift Valley

ERITREA 1993

DJIBOUTI 1977

SOMALIA 1960
✴ 1950–60

KENYA 1963
✴ 1952–59

CONGO/ZAIRE 1960

L. Victoria

RWANDA 1962

UGANDA 1962

TANZANIA 1961

BURUNDI 1962

L. Tanganyika

Indian Ocean

Congo Basin

Atlantic Ocean

ANGOLA 1975
✴ 1961–74

ZAMBIA 1964

L. Nyasa

MALAWI 1964

Zambezi

RHODESIA (ZIMBABWE) 1965
✴ 1965–80

NAMIBIA (formerly SW Africa, controlled by S Africa) 1990
✴ 1966–90

Kalahari Desert

BOTSWANA 1966

MOZAMBIQUE 1975
✴ 1964–74

Orange

SOUTH AFRICA 1910–61
✴ 1948–90

LESOTHO 1966

SWAZILAND 1968

Drakensberg Mts

MADAGASCAR 1960
✴ 1947–48

TROPIC OF CAPRICORN

N

0 — 1600 km
0 — 1000 miles

Map 98 The Decolonization of Africa. Independence often came to African nations without providing the appropriate boundary lines which would gather all of the related peoples into one nation. As a result, border conflicts often followed independence. But Eritrea and Ethiopia waged a bitter war in 1998 and 1999 for another reason. Ethiopia largely gave its blessing when Eritrea split off in 1993 and the two neighbors continued to trade extensively with each other. Then an economic dispute over a new Eritrean currency led to a war over an ill-defined border region. Thousands of soldiers died contesting a largely uninhabited region with little value to either side.

THE DECADES that followed World War II witnessed the transformation of the political map of Africa as former colonies gained their independence and became new nations. This was not a simple process. It took a different form in each country and often produced contrasting results. Freedom came at various times and under diverse circumstances.

The map shown opposite summarizes the achievement of African independence by providing four kinds of data for each nation: the former colonial power is indicated by the color code, the date of independence is noted in the appropriate box, the current (as of 2000) name of the country is provided by the label, and a special symbol indicates where an anti-colonial movement was forced into violent revolt.

Independence in the Maghreb came from France, Spain, and Italy between 1951 and 1975. The Maghreb includes all of North Africa west of Egypt up to the mouth of the Senegal River. The name means "the west" in Arabic, although at an earlier date this region was called the Barbary Coast after the Berber-speaking people who dominated the area before the Arabic conquest (see maps 38 and 40, pp. 52 and 53) The area east of Morocco was included in the Ottoman Empire at one time, but the Western European nations gradually replaced the Turks as overlords. Note that the struggle for Algerian independence lasted eight years, and the conflict in the former Spanish Sahara continued even longer.

Egypt, which gained independence from Britain in 1922, really took several more decades to throw off the last vestiges of outside control. One point pressed by the British in 1924 was the withdrawal of Egyptian troops from the Sudan. Even before World War II, however, Egypt regained some influence in the Sudan. After the war it tried to assume leadership in the Maghreb and in 1958 united with Syria to form the short-lived United Arab Republic. Thus Egypt attempted to reach out and influence affairs in all directions.

The horn of Africa included Ethiopia, long an independent Christian nation which was conquered by Italy in 1936. Liberated by the British five years later, it resumed its independent status, but it lost its coastal province when Eritrea gained its freedom from Ethiopia in 1993. Djibouti, the former French Somaliland, did not get its independence until 17 years after British and Italian Somali colonies gained their freedom as a united nation. This new nation of Somalia then wanted to annex parts of Ethiopia and Kenya with Somali populations, a source of potential conflict in the years ahead.

West Africa is generally considered to include all of the tropical nations west of the Sudan, between the Senegal and Congo rivers. The extensive French empire in this region came to an abrupt end in 1960 when a dozen of its former colonies (including the island of Madagascar) chose independence but accepted an association with the French Community. Only Guinea, two years earlier, selected full independence without any association with its former colonizer.

The British colonies in West, East, and South Africa, also became independent between 1956 and 1968, usually maintaining membership in the Commonwealth of Nations. Belgium and Portugal, two small European countries, controlled extensive lands in central and south Africa. The Belgian colonies received their freedom without a major colonial revolt between 1960 and 1962, but the Portuguese imperial holdings of Angola and Mozambique both endured long conflicts before independence was acknowledged in 1975.

Namibia, formerly German Southwest Africa, was in 1990 one of the last areas to become independent, having first been assigned to South Africa as a mandate by the League of Nations.

Economic Development in Africa

ACCORDING to the visions of the decolonization movement, political stability and economic development were to proceed hand in hand once independence was achieved. As the African economies matured, they would shed their colonial character and the resulting benefits would result in improved standards of living. A better way of life would then reinforce loyalties to the new nations. But this scenario often broke down due to the difficulties of creating viable political structures.

Instead, the new nations of Africa often encountered internal struggles between ethnic groups, clashes in border areas where ill-defined boundaries failed to mark effective frontiers, and a willingness by contending parties to use mass violence for political ends. A continuing dependence on foreign capital often kept investments at the service of outside interests rather than oriented to national development. Moreover, decisions about how to allocate resources internally many times were made according to the interests of individual leaders, parochial parties, or favored localities instead of the good of the whole. In short, the grand visions of independence day speeches which struck such positive notes on map 98 (see p. 127), often gave way to strife, suffering, and the discouraging categories illustrated on map 99.

The soft pink tones cannot hide the fact that in most of the continent the gross national product (GNP) in 1995 divided by the total population indicated that each individual benefited from less than US$1000 in the market economy. It is true that subsistence agriculture, traditionally a major factor in the African economy, did not register in these statistics. But given the increasingly urban character of Africa's population, and the glimpse of the good life promised by an industrial economy that everyone had seen in advertising and on television, the GNP per capita in 1995 was simply unacceptable and would lead to mass deprivation if not outright starvation.

When looking for patterns on the map, note that the very low GNP per capita is characteristic of all of Africa between the tropics, with only a few exceptions. All of the nations north of the Tropic of Cancer, that is Egypt and the Maghreb, have a higher GNP per capita. The only nation below the Tropic of Cancer with a figure above

$3000, bringing it close to worldwide averages for industrial economies, is South Africa.

A key indicator on the map, which also employs a pink symbol, indicates a current amount of internal investment sufficient enough to push the development of the economy beyond the rate at which its productive machinery is wearing out. In other words, the nations with "substantial inward investment" are those which can slowly improve their economy on the basis of internal resources. Only six nations fit that description in 1995 and only two of these, Nigeria and Kenya, were on a track to pull themselves up out of the lowest GNP classification on their own. Outside investment therefore was an absolute necessity for Africa's economic development in 1995 and throughout the post-independence era.

The key on the map shows the main exports of the various nations in 1995: an impressive variety of products. Some nations have five major exports, but many have only one or two, subjecting their economies to the price fluctuations of single markets. Upon reflection, however, it also becomes clear that an economic map focused on exports emphasizes the continuing colonial status of the continent.

Two other symbols used on the map are keys to the development of African economies: the centers of industry and hydro-electric plants are fairly well distributed across the continent, except in desert areas. Most of these centers, especially in North and West Africa, are port cities with ready access to international trade. They represent substantial markets as well as sources of production. The major hydro-electricity plants also tend to be located near the coast because Africa's plateau-like topography places steep gradients near the mouths of its rivers.

Map 99 The African Economy, 1995. In 1995 Eritrea was one of the brightest spots on this map. Its economy was growing by 7 percent each year as foreign investment poured into the newly independent nation. Fishing, tourism, and commerce all flourished and the Eritreans developed a reputation as an industrious, well-organized work force. Much of the new nation's commercial activity was a result of serving as a port for Ethiopian exports. When a bitter war broke out in 1998, things rapidly changed as Eritrea diverted resources to support the fight against its former trading partner.

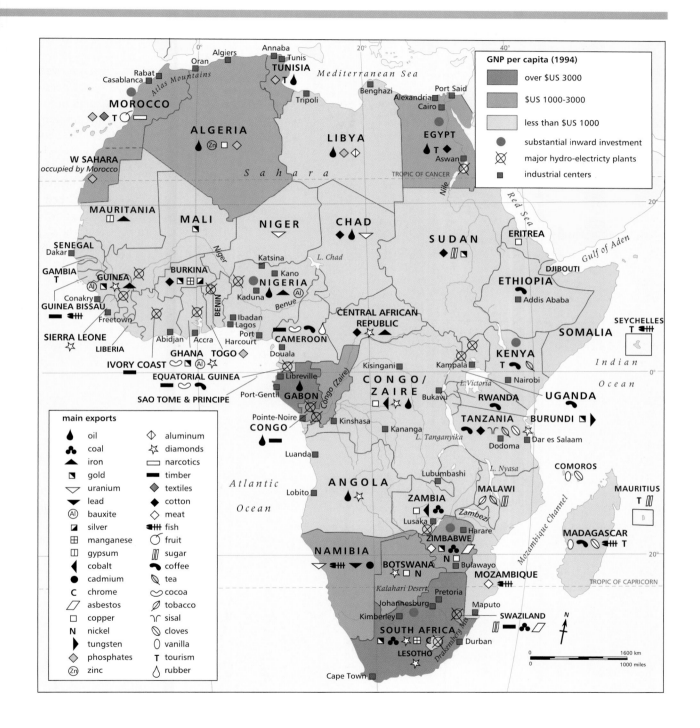

Latin American Politics in the Twentieth Century

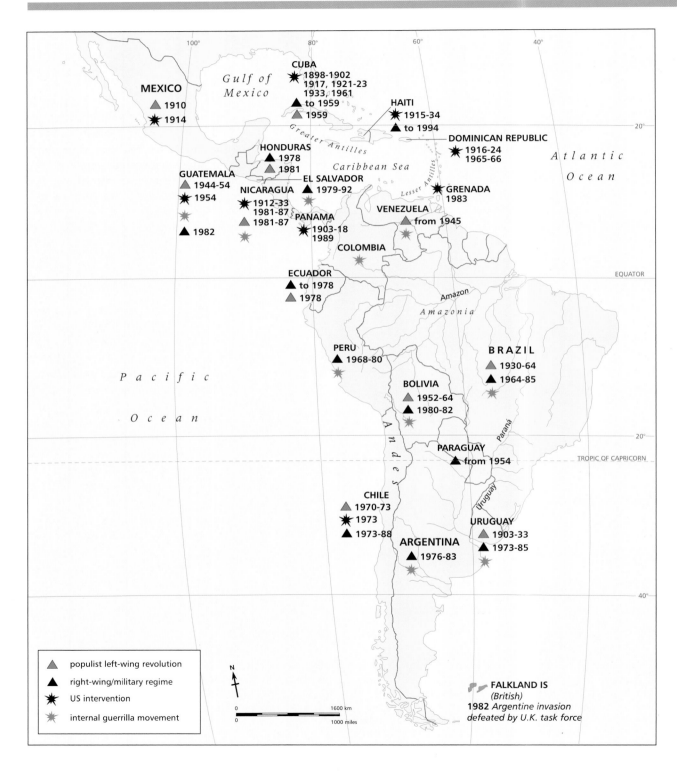

MEXICO
▲ 1910
✳ 1914

CUBA
✳ 1898-1902
1917, 1921-23
1933, 1961
▲ to 1959
▲ 1959

HAITI
✳ 1915-34
▲ to 1994

DOMINICAN REPUBLIC
✳ 1916-24
1965-66

HONDURAS
▲ 1978
▲ 1981

EL SALVADOR
▲ 1979-92

GUATEMALA
▲ 1944-54
✳ 1954
✳
▲ 1982

NICARAGUA
✳ 1912-33
1981-87
▲ 1981-87

PANAMA
✳ 1903-18
1989

GRENADA
✳ 1983

VENEZUELA
▲ from 1945

COLOMBIA

ECUADOR
▲ to 1978
▲ 1978

PERU
▲ 1968-80

BRAZIL
▲ 1930-64
▲ 1964-85

BOLIVIA
▲ 1952-64
▲ 1980-82

PARAGUAY
▲ from 1954

CHILE
▲ 1970-73
✳ 1973
▲ 1973-88

URUGUAY
▲ 1903-33
▲ 1973-85

ARGENTINA
▲ 1976-83

Gulf of Mexico

Greater Antilles

Caribbean Sea

Lesser Antilles

Atlantic Ocean

EQUATOR

Amazon

Amazonia

Paraná

Andes

Uruguay

Pacific Ocean

20°

20°

TROPIC OF CAPRICORN

40°

Legend
▲ populist left-wing revolution
▲ right-wing/military regime
✳ US intervention
✳ internal guerrilla movement

N

0   1600 km
0   1000 miles

FALKLAND IS
(British)
1982 Argentine invasion
defeated by U.K. task force

ONE KEY to understanding Latin American political developments in the twentieth century is to note the stark division of most nations into two classes of people. A wealthy upper class, small in numbers, but controlling most of the wealth and the institutions in the society, will often go to any length to maintain the status quo and keep their privileged position. The second class, the poor, accounts for the vast majority of people in the society. Life for these people is a constant struggle to maintain their livelihood and to grasp some aspects of the better life that they can see the wealthier classes enjoying. The middle classes, between these two extremes, have traditionally been quite small. The expansion of their ranks in recent times offers hope for the future.

The rigid and unbalanced class structure in Latin America is one of the major differences between its experience and that of the United States and Canada. The geography of the two American continents also differs. The lands in South America are more tropical and more mountainous, with proportionally fewer acres of good farming lands in the temperate climatic zones. Latin America also has a less advantageous position on a world map. It is closer by far to the Old World, but it faces Africa rather than Europe. Thus its trading connections to the former mother countries were generally more distant, especially in the days before air travel.

The terrain of Latin America, characterized by a long spine of high mountains and vast basins containing dense rainforests, split the land up into a series of regions. Political leaders in the struggle for independence attempted to transcend a regional focus, but their efforts at creating larger national states were not entirely successful. Colombia, in the vision of Simón Bolivar, would have included Venezuela, Ecuador, and Peru. It survived as the only nation in South America to stretch across the continent, but it soon fractured into distinct nations and then, in the twentieth century, it lost the province of Panama as well. As the map indicates, the secession of the isthmus

was aided and abetted by the United States which intervened to control the building of the Panama Canal.

Direct US intervention was common in the Caribbean region. In South America the United States relied more on the indirect methods of dollar diplomacy and the support of right-wing military regimes to exert control of hemispheric affairs. Thus Latin American politics in the twentieth century must be illuminated by the active presence of the United States in addition to the geographic regionalism and unbalanced class structure. As map 101 (p. 133) will suggest, colonial and underdeveloped economies also played major roles in political affairs.

Map 100 features four types of political events and records the dates during which these occurred for each nation. Not a single nation escaped political violence. The populist left-wing revolutions were supported by the masses of impoverished people, both rural peasants and urban poor. They were leftist in orientation because they embraced radical change as a way to improve conditions.

A right-wing military regime usually took the opposite approach, trusting in the army to control the land, with the government led by a general with dictatorial powers. The wealthy classes often supported these rightist regimes because they maintained the status quo. US military intervention was often provoked by the collapse of a right-wing government or by the threat of deep-seated changes by left-wing forces. Internal guerrilla movements were rooted in both regional and ideological differences plus the tendency of military regimes to operate outside the rule of law, forcing their opponents into underground activities.

As the twentieth century drew to its close there were hopeful signs that the traditional pattern of politics in Latin America was changing. The spread of education, the expansion of the middle class, fuller participation in world affairs, and a focus on internal economic development based on free markets all seemed to work together to stabilize, in some measure, Latin American political life, especially in the ABC nations (Argentina, Brazil and Chile).

A major issue in these nations, especially Brazil, centers on how best to make use of natural resources. Brazil possesses most of the huge Amazon basin. How to take advantage of this region for the benefit of the nation as a whole, balancing native peoples' rights, social needs, economic development, and ecological concerns would be a test for any political process.

Map 100 Latin American Politics in the Twentieth Century. This map calls attention to the populist revolutions which pushed for fundamental changes in the society's distribution of resources. These left-wing political movements were usually contested by the right wing which often turned to a military dictator to maintain the existing order by force. Oppression then spawned additional support for the guerrilla movements, while the threat of disturbance often triggered intervention by the United States to protect its interests.

Economic Development in Latin America

I T HAS OFTEN been noted that the colonial legacy pressed heavily on the subsequent events of Latin American nations. Independence came in the early nineteenth century, but colonial patterns continued. In colonial times the king embodied legitimate political authority. Independence meant that the king was discarded, but the new government needed to establish its legitimacy. A lack of political experience and the exclusion of the common people from the political process made the transition to democratic republics difficult. Moreover, certain aspects of the former monarchical government, like strong central powers, authoritarian attitudes, and a dependence on a small class of aristocratic leaders, continued to drive Latin American politics. This led to a clash between new democratic aspirations and a colonial mentality which encouraged an authoritarian state. The resulting political instability retarded development in the first half of the twentieth century and kept the economy in a colonial model as well.

To place this map in its proper context, the reader must note that Latin America as a whole experienced a measure of economic development in the last half of the twentieth century. It would be well to compare this map with the corresponding economic picture of Africa (see map 99, p. 129). Both present the situation in 1994–1995 and both suggest the colonial dimension of the respective economies by featuring the major exports. But there are some telling differences between the two maps.

The first thing to note is the color code on the two maps relating to the per capita gross national product. Although US dollars are used as the scale in both instances, the cut-off point for the lowest category in Latin America is twice the amount of Africa's: $2000 versus $1000. Even with this higher cut off for the least developed economies, a much smaller portion of Latin America falls into this impoverished category.

The second color category, designating the mid-level economies in Latin America, uses a narrower range of income than the African presentation: a spread of only $1,000 compared to the larger amount used for the old world continent. This was done by the cartographer so that the national economies could be conveniently divided into three categories on each map. Note that only South Africa and Gabon were in the same class as Argentina, Brazil, Chile, and Mexico in the New World. Actually, Argentina's economy was by far the most productive on these two continents, with a per capita GNP of about $8000 in 1995. The comparable figure for the United States, by the way, was over $25,000, roughly the same as Western Europe as a whole. Luxembourg, the most industrial of all the nations, registered a figure of almost $40,000 in this statistic.

Thus comparing the Latin American and the African maps suggests that the former continent had a much more developed industrial economy as a whole. Latin America thus had a handful of nations in the upper tier of development. The percentage of nations with substantial inward investment was also much greater in the New World. The industrial centers have a similar geographic distribution on both maps, however, with a definite leaning toward coastal locations.

Comparing the major exports on both maps, one finds that the list for Latin America is not as lengthy, containing fewer minerals but with similar agricultural products. Tourism appears on both lists but is especially prominent in the West Indies. Financial services is a category unique to Latin America, occupying a prominent role in several Caribbean nations and in Uruguay.

It would also be instructive to consider how this map of the Latin American economy in 1995 connects with map 100 (see p. 130) on Latin American politics in the twentieth century. Perhaps the connection between economic development and political freedom can be considered as a possible connecting link. Generally speaking democracies hesitate to make war on each other, budgeting their resources for other expenditures such as social welfare. The economist Amartya Sen even went so far as to conclude that "no famine has ever taken place in the history of the world in a functioning democracy." Whether the nation is rich or poor, democracies hold their leaders accountable to find ways of alleviating food shortages. Thus the development of functioning democracies might be the key to the improvement of living conditions in developing economies.

Map 101 The Latin American Economy, 1995. When the Foreign Minister of Brazil, Luiz Felipe Lamprela, addressed the General Assembly of the United Nations in September, 1999, he pointed with pride to the "new international image" that Latin America had fashioned. "The return to democracy" he reported, "had a decisive role …in fostering respect for human rights." Much remained to be done, he concluded, but economic development "made it possible to provide mutual assistance." (Speech reported in the *New York Times*, September 21, 1999).

Tijuana
Ciudad Juarez
100°
80°
60°
40°
20°
Rio Grande
Gulf of Mexico
Monterrey
MEXICO
T
Aguascalientes
Guadalajara
Mexico City
Puebla
Veracruz
JAMAICA
T
Havana
CUBA
N T
Mérida
BAHAMAS
T
HAITI
DOMINICAN REPUBLIC
N T
PUERTO RICO
Greater Antilles
ANTIGUA AND BARBUDA T
ST KITTS AND NEVIS
T
DOMINICA
ST LUCIA T
BARBADOS T
ST VINCENT AND GRENADINES
GRENADA
T
TRINIDAD AND TOBAGO
T
BELIZE
HONDURAS
GUATEMALA
Guatemala City
EL SALVADOR
Caribbean Sea
Lesser Antilles
Managua
NICARAGUA
Barranquilla
Maracaibo
Caracas
COSTA RICA
Panama City
Orinoco
Ciudad Guayana
GUYANA
Georgetown
Paramaribo
SURINAME
FRENCH GUIANA
Atlantic Ocean
PANAMA
COLOMBIA
Medellín
Bogotá
Cali
Guiana Highlands
VENEZUELA
EQUATOR
Quito
ECUADOR
Guayaquil
Manaus
Belém
Amazon
Amazon Basin
Iquitos
Fortaleza
Pacific Ocean
Chiclayo
PERU
Chimbote
BRAZIL
Recife
Maceio
Lima
Cusco
Salvador
Mato Grosso
Brazilian Highlands
BOLIVIA
Brasilia
Arequipa
La Paz
Arica
Pantanal
Paraná
Iquique
Andes
PARAGUAY
Belo Horizonte
Rio de Janeiro
Antofagasta
São Paulo
TROPIC OF CAPRICORN
Gran Chaco
Uruguay
CHILE
Porto Alegre
Córdoba
Rio Grande
Rosario
URUGUAY
Valparaíso
Santiago
Montevideo
ARGENTINA
Buenos Aires
Pampas
Concepción
Neuquén
Patagonia
FALKLAND IS (British)
N
Punta Arenas
0 1600 km
0 1000 miles
GNP per capita (1995)
over $US 3000
$US 2000-3000
less than $US 2000
substantial inward investment
industrial centers
main exports
oil
coal
iron
bauxite
gold
silver
zinc
nickel
lead
copper
tin
emeralds
diamonds
fertilizers
timber
cotton
beef
wool
wheat
fruit
tobacco
narcotics
coffee
sugar
bananas
nutmeg
soya
rice
fish/shellfish
tourism
financial services

The Cold War and the End of the Soviet Union, 1945–1995

THE UNION of Soviet Socialist Republics was born during the Russian Revolution, which was itself intertwined with World War I. Only after a protracted struggle were the Communists able to gain control of the former Russian Empire. Various ethnic groups were given their own republics and these states joined together under Russian leadership to form the USSR. In theory a confederation, the Soviet Union soon functioned as a police state headed by a dictator.

World War II, known in Russia as the Great Patriotic War, provided a severe test, but the USSR emerged from the ordeal as one of the world's two superpowers, aggres-

sively pursuing its interests in Eastern Europe, the Far East, and Central Asia. In addition, the expansive Communist ideology gave the Soviets a rationale for involvement in every part of the globe. Many aspects of the independence movements in Africa, the populist revolutions in Latin America, the anti-colonial strivings in Asia, and even social-

Map 102 The Cold War, 1955. China, as a Communist nation, had some affinity with the Soviet Union in 1955, but it also shared a long border with its neighbor which was often a source of friction between them. Note how the USSR maintained a cluster of ICBM (intercontinental ballistic missile) bases near its Pacific coast to exert influence in that part of the world.

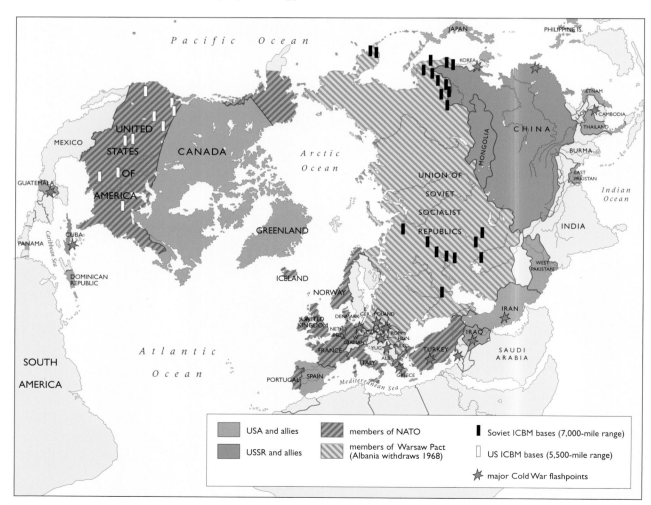

ist leanings in Western democracies were colored, in many contemporary minds, by the threat of Russian expansion and its potential world domination.

The Cold War between 1945 and 1989 centered around efforts by the United States and its Free World allies to contain the Soviet threat. By the late 1980s however the Soviet Union started to fall apart because of its own internal weaknesses. The various non-Russian Soviet Republics began pursuing their own interests as independent states and by 1991 the USSR had ceased to function. In its place the Russian Federation remained the dominant power with lands stretching across Eurasia.

Map 103 The Breakup of the Soviet Union and Changes in Eastern Europe. The last chapter of the Cold War story began in Poland where workers pushed a crumbling Communist Party to agree to multiparty elections in 1989. Mikhail Gorbachev, the Soviet leader, recognized the need for change when he came to power in 1985. Instead of sending military forces to prop up Communist governments in Eastern Europe, the Soviet Union let free elections proceed in Poland. Soon Russia's satellites regained their independence, adopting democratic governments and favoring market-based economic systems. Then, in 1991 the Soviet Union itself followed suit, with its various republics becoming independent states.

Map 102 uses a polar projection to show how the two superpowers faced each other across the frozen Arctic Ocean during the Cold War. Great circle routes over the North Pole often provided the most direct paths for the intercontinental ballistic missiles of one superpower to reach targets in the other.

The tensions of a bi-polar world pulled many nations into the orbit of one superpower or the other. Those nations that tried to remain outside of the North Atlantic Treaty Organization (the Free World) or the Warsaw Pact (the Communist World) were called non-aligned states. Many of the new nations in Africa and Asia took this route, hoping to form a "Third World" in which they could pursue economic development free from the burdens imposed by membership in one of the rival blocs.

The year 1955 was a key year in the Cold War because it marked the official signing of the Warsaw Pact and the admission of West Germany into NATO. Also, on a hopeful note, the leaders of France, the Soviet Union, the United Kingdom, and the United States met in the first "summit conference" to discuss issues and try to find ways to reduce the stresses pulling the world apart.

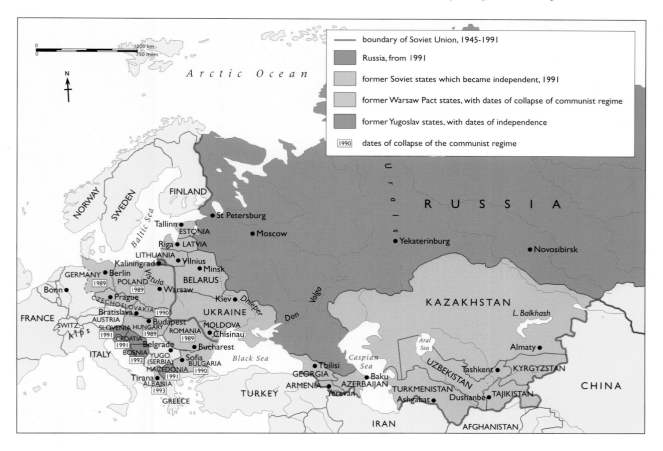

The United States in the 1990s

THE UNITED STATES at the end of the twentieth century was the world's sole surviving superpower. For world history, this state of affairs probably meant more because America was the hub of a global economy and the cultural model for modernization than it did in terms of a traditional political empire with the ability to dictate its will in distant places. Thus, instead of viewing the United States in a global context, map 104 focuses on its internal workings, how it is tied together by the inter-

Map 104 The United States of America in the 1990s. All of the highways in the interstate system were designed for speeds of 55 to 70 miles per hour. Even in mountainous areas, grades were evened out and tunnels dug so that traffic would flow at an even pace across the nation. It was possible to mark off the time of a journey on a map, 60 miles equaling an hour's drive. Distance was not conquered, but made regular and predictable. Thus people began to look at maps in new ways, as measures of time.

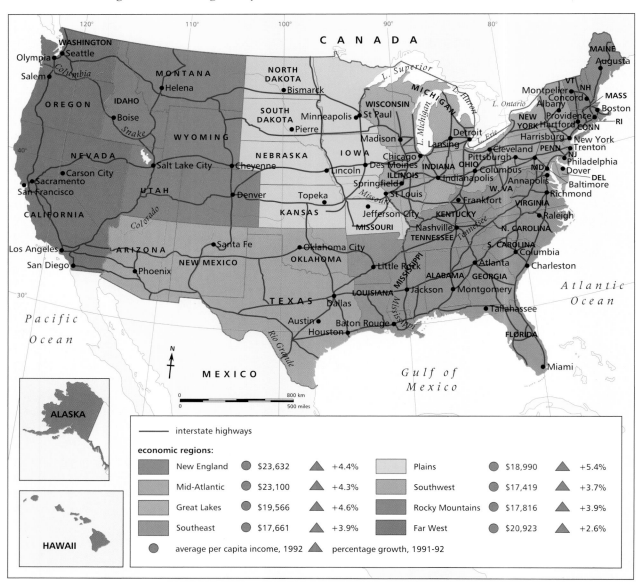

economic regions:	average per capita income, 1992	percentage growth, 1991-92
New England	$23,632	+4.4%
Mid-Atlantic	$23,100	+4.3%
Great Lakes	$19,566	+4.6%
Southeast	$17,661	+3.9%
Plains	$18,990	+5.4%
Southwest	$17,419	+3.7%
Rocky Mountains	$17,816	+3.9%
Far West	$20,923	+2.6%

interstate highways

state highway system and how it remains divided into sections with different levels of economic prosperity and rates of development.

It is often difficult to divide a large, integrated nation into meaningful sections, and the straight lines (state boundaries) used on this map suggest that the regional setup used here is largely one of convenience. It was employed by the US Department of Labor to compare statistics of per-capita incomes in 1992 and the percentage of gain in these figures from the preceding year. Thus New England, the most highly educated region of the United States, was also the leader in per-capita income in 1992. Wage earners in the Mid-Atlantic States were not far behind and both of these regions posted healthy gains over the preceding twelve months.

The Plains and Great Lakes states showed slightly more robust rates of growth, but lagged behind in total average incomes. The Far West, however, which included Alaska and Hawaii, posted a relatively high per-capita income but with a much lower rate of growth. This points to the steep decline in defense spending accompanying the end of the Cold War. The closing of military bases and a slow-down in defense contracts, among other factors, hit California's economy with particular force in the early part of the decade.

The Southwest, which contained the former states of the Confederacy (see map 78, p. 98), recorded relatively low incomes but average rates of growth. Although one could point to examples of a lag in economic development with roots reaching back to the days of slavery, the major topic in a discussion of the economy in this region in the 1990s would focus on the rise of the Sun Belt, the accompanying expansion of urban populations, and the migrations of people, both retired workers and vacationers, seeking a mild climate. In an economy giving more emphasis to services than the production of goods, the Sun Belt had attractive advantages.

The Eisenhower Interstate Highway System, named after the president who secured federal funding for the network of roads, was a major factor in tying the nation together in the 1990s. Modeled after pioneering superhighways built in Germany and Italy before World War II, the concrete network which crisscrossed the continent was a response to both the triumph of an automobile culture among its people and the need to rapidly deploy troops and materials in the Cold War. The legislation establishing the network in 1956 referred to the "interstate and defense highways."

While the exact location of the new roads was left up to state and local decisions and the standards of highway construction were set by an association of state highway officials, the federal government paid for most of the construction and maintenance costs from a National Highway Trust Fund supported by a tax on gasoline.

By 1990 the system was virtually completed. By then, most Americans lived in the suburbs, moving out of the cities to gain living space and to be closer to new shopping centers that sprang up at key points along the interstate highways. Businesses also moved out to the ring highways that circled the old cities, creating new types of urban development which a commentator named "edge cities" in 1991. One prerequisite for an edge city was convenient access to a major airport where connections could be made to reach any commercial center in the world in a day's time.

As Americans moved to the suburbs in the second half of the twentieth century, creating a new type of landscape, they also began to realize that some things were being lost in the process. The dependence on the automobile, the abandonment of city centers, the neglect of public transportation, the lack of variety in the housing stock, the inability to walk to activities, and a sense that they were missing out on the stimulation found downtown all supported a movement towards a "New Urbanism" in the late 1990s.

Suburbs began to be concerned about their own downtown areas. Their new housing developments favoured multi-story residences. Front porches began appearing on suburban homes, which were clustered close together. The new suburbs took on an urban appearance at the same time that the old city neighborhoods tore down buildings to accommodate automobiles. Suburbanization even reached the central business districts where open space and places for automobiles took on a new importance.

Thus the good life in the United States at the turn of the millennium came to be defined in more urban terms. Yet people wanted more space and government policies continued to favor new construction on open land over the remodeling of older structures to meet current needs. As a major cultural leader these trends in the United States assumed a broader importance as the new media broadcast American tastes throughout the globe.

Women of the World in the 1990s

M APS ARE used for many purposes and one of their most important functions in contemporary society is to help readers understand the present state of the world. Any survey of current conditions in a place would benefit by considering maps which show the spatial distribution of the subjects of interest. With the modern recognition of the fundamental importance of gender in the functioning of human societies, it is no accident that a map of global conditions at the end of twentieth century should focus on the status of women.

This map addresses several important issues. The first, the female deficit – a concept developed by the economist Amartya Sen – measures the extent to which women, who would normally be present in a society at a certain number, are missing. When a census is taken, sex is one of the basic categories counted. The expectation is that the number of males and females would be in balance. Given certain biological factors and the nature of statistical averages, when the number of females falls below the number of males by a ratio of 97 to 100, some intervention into the natural order of things should be suspected.

Disproportionate feeding and health care, for example, might explain why there are more males than females in a particular country, causing a female deficit. Other factors, such as the risks of childbearing or selective infanticide and feticide, also may result in a higher death rate for women, increasing the female deficit. Other cultural or biological factors may, of course produce a female surplus and a male deficit. Warfare, for example, is almost always a major factor in reducing the percentage of males in a society.

Map 105 divides the nations of the world into four categories plus a classification for "no data available" situations. There are nations with a surplus of women and others where the shortage of women is within the statistically insignificant range. But note the number of states where the female deficit is between 3 percent and 10 percent as well as the most serious cases, where the difference is above 10 percent.

The quantitative data, however, say nothing about the quality of life, the second important issue. If education is the key to a better life, the widespread illiteracy of women in Africa, the Middle East, and South Asia is a cause for major concern. The symbol of the open book on the map indicates those nations where more than half of the

least discriminating states
(number of women = 97% the number of men)

states with a surplus of women

states with a deficit of up to 10%

states with a deficit of over 10%

states with no data available

countries in which more than 20% of women say they have experienced domestic violence

countries in which more than 51% of adult women are illiterate

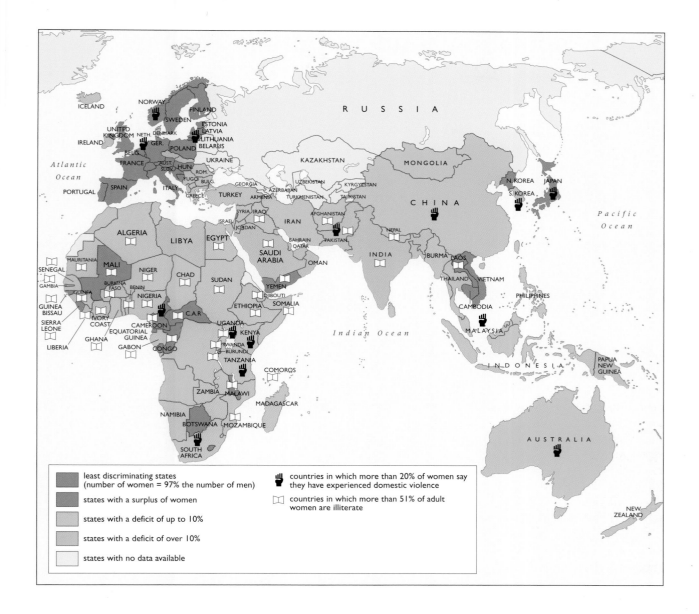

Map 105 Women of the World in the 1990s. It is estimated that in China, where the female population deficit is about 5 percent, there are about 22 million missing women. The total of all female deficits in the world probably reaches well above 100 million women. This is balanced by the characteristic surplus of women in many nations with modern, industrial economies. This male deficit is often explained, in part, by the different employment of men and women in the workforce.

adult women cannot read or write. Perhaps a closed book would have been a more appropriate indicator.

The third set of data on the map presents the results of surveys taken in the 1990s to determine the extent of domestic violence in which women were the victims. Those nations in which more than 20 percent of the women reported that they had experienced domestic violence are indicated with an open hand symbol. Not all of the nations of the world were included in these surveys but the presence of modernized, industrialized nations such as the United States, Canada, Norway, Japan, and Australia in this rank is both depressing and a call to action.

World Population at the End of the Twentieth Century

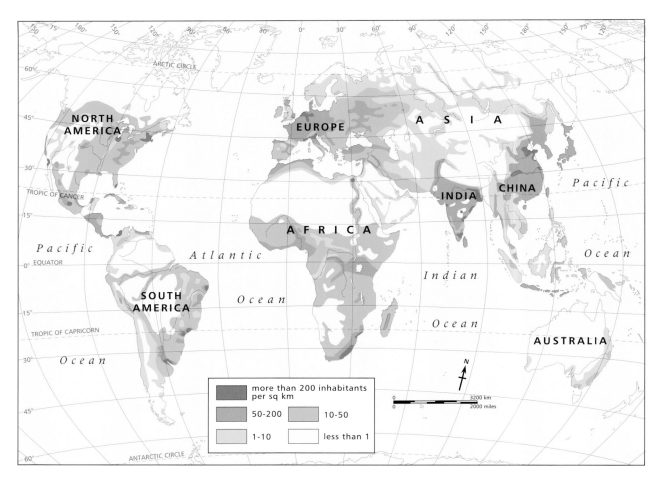

The two cartographic images on these pages present similar data in different ways. Thus they invite comparison. The cartogram (map 107) is really a chart indicating the relative size of the populations of the leading nations. Map 106 takes a different approach, showing how people are clustered on the earth's surface. It accomplishes this objective by dividing the world's population density (people per square kilometer) into five categories and marking these areas with a color code.

The reddish color indicates that more than 200 inhabitants per square kilometer or about 500 people per square mile live in a given area. These are heavily urbanized regions, often surrounded by intensive agriculture. The cartographer has excluded many individual cities from this category in order to emphasize the general density of the population over a wider region than just the metropolitan area.

Map 106 World Population Distribution, 2000. A line of sparse settlement extends across Siberia along the route of the railroad. Further south in Central Asia, one can use the lines of sparse population extending into the desert to indicate the route of the old silk road. The Nile and the Amazon corridors are more clearly marked by a heavier population along their banks.

The blush pink color indicates regions of 50 to 200 inhabitants per square kilometer (about 125 to 500 per square mile). Note how extensive these heavily populated areas are in China, India, Japan, Korea, the East Indies, Europe, East Central Africa, and Nigeria. These areas shade off to the caramel color indicating agricultural areas supporting between 10 to 50 inhabitants per square kilometer (25 to 125 per square mile). The light sand color (1 to 25 per square mile) often shows grazing lands, or forest product areas.

Map 107 should be viewed as a graph as well as a map. Cartograms use a two-dimensional unit of measure to present the relative size of various examples of a single item. Instead of arranging this data in the shape of a pie or of a bar graph, the two-dimensional units, because they are geographically based, can be arranged in a way to resemble a map. The divergence of the cartogram from a standard map helps it to make its major points.

This chart presenting the population of the countries of the world in 1990 emphasizes the great number of people in Asia and Europe compared to the Americas and Australia. At the same time the chart uses a color key to indicate the rate of population increase or decrease in the year 1993. The deeper the tone, the greater the increase. This aspect adds a dynamic quality to the illustration, signaling future trends as well as present realities.

Map 107 Cartogram of World Population, 1993. Experts estimated that the six-billionth person was born in 1999. They also pointed out that the the population reached over a billion for the first time about 1800, climbing to two billion in 1930. The three billion mark was hit about 1960, followed by four billion in 1975 and five billion in 1987.

The cartogram, unlike a normal map, sizes countries by population rather than according to actual geographical size. This becomes obvious when the cartogram is compared to a normal map.

If all the blocks that make up this cartogram were to be reassembled in a regular chart, it would show that Asia contains more than half of the world's population. Note that Europe and Africa also have a greater portion of the world's people than they have of its living space.

At some point in 1999, probably about the middle of October, the number of human beings on Earth crossed the six billion mark. Over a third of these people live in just two countries, China and India. Both of these Asian nations realized that the well-being of their people in the future required constraints on population growth. Official policies in China slowed the rate of growth and even recorded a slight decline in population. India, less able to control its growth because of its more democratic tradition, is expected to continue to increase its population. If these trends continue, India will replace China as the world's most populous nation in the near future.

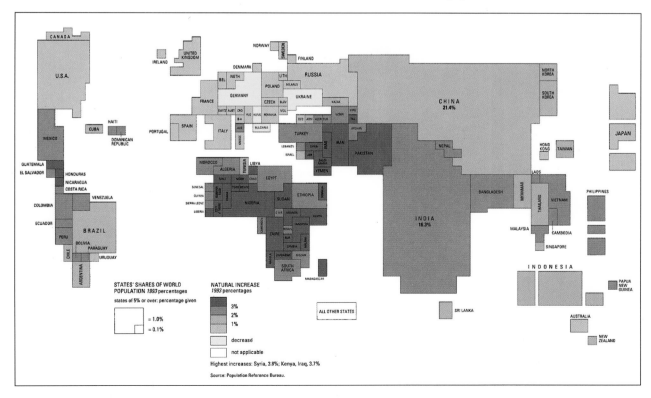

Index

This index includes major places, events and peoples covered by the text and maps. It does not include every name shown on the maps. Page numbers in italics refer to maps, captions and illustrations.